The Concept of Work Ability

P.I.E. Peter Lang

Bruxelles · Bern · Berlin · Frankfurt am Main · New York · Oxford · Wien

Lennart NORDENFELT

The Concept of Work Ability

The book has received financial support from The Swedish
Council for Working Life and Social Research

© P.I.E. PETER LANG s.a.
Éditions scientifiques internationales
Brussels, 2008
1 avenue Maurice, B-1050 Brussels, Belgium
info@peterlang.com; www.peterlang.com

ISBN 978-90-5201-450-0
D/2008/5678/53

Library of Congress Cataloging-in-Publication Data
Nordenfelt, Lennart, 1945- The concept of work ability /
Lennart Nordenfelt.   p. ; cm. ISBN 978-90-5201-450-0
1. Work capacity evaluation. 2. Disability evaluation. 3. Vocational evaluation.
I. Title. [DNLM: 1. Employment—legislation & jurisprudence. 2. Work Capacity
Evaluation. 3. Disabled Persons—legislation & jurisprudence. 4. Occupational
Medicine—methods. 5. Professional Competence. W 925 N829c 2008]
    RC963.4.N67 2008   616.07'5—dc22   2008037884

CIP also available from the British Library, GB.
Bibliographic information published by "Die Deutsche Bibliothek". "Die Deutsche
Bibliothek" lists this publication in the "Deutsche National-bibliografie": detailed
bibliographic data is available on the Internet at <http://dnb.ddb.de>.

Contents

Preface

This book is the result of two converging interests of mine: one is my life-long interest in the analysis and explication of the notion of rational action; the other is my interest in the theory of health. The first interest has led me, among other things, to attempt to give a complex characterization of the notion of ability, i.e. of what it means to be able to perform an action. The other interest has prompted me to characterize and distinguish between medical concepts such as health, illness, disease, injury and defect.

These interests have converged and supported each other in many ways. The concept of ability has become central in my analysis of health. My studies of the notions of disease, injury and defect have contributed to insights with regard to the causes of a person's reduced ability to act. The latter is of particular interest when the issue, as in this book, is work ability. In the medical insurance context, which is a fundamental context – although not the only one – in this book, a person's reduced ability to do his or her work should be attributable to a medical condition. Most definitions of such disability entail that the incapacity should have resulted from a condition such as disease, impairment or injury.

In the project that has resulted in this book I have combined my earlier analyses and added substantial new ones, where the object of study has been ability in relation to a profession or work in general. The context with regard to disciplines has then become broadened to include results from subjects such as education, psychology and sociology, in addition to philosophy and occupational medicine.

Because of my previous research in action theory and the theory of health I have been able to use some arguments, and even a few complete passages, from works of mine that have been published earlier. With regard to action theory this holds for parts of Chapter 8. The main source for many of the distinctions there is my book: *Action, Ability and Health: Essays in the Philosophy of Action and Welfare* (Dordrecht: Kluwer, 2000). My reasoning on the distinctions between competence and ability were first presented in "On ability, opportunity, and competence: An inquiry into people's possibility for action". In: G. Holmström-Hintikka and R. Tuomela (1997): *Contemporary Action Theory*, vol. 1: Individual action, Synthese Library, vol. 266, pp. 145-158. I re-use parts of this material with kind permission of Springer Science and Business

11

Media. With regard to the analysis of health presented in Part III, Chapter 17, the main source is my *Health, Science and Ordinary Language* (Amsterdam: Rodopi, 2001) published by Rodopi, Amsterdam. Elements of Chapter 10 and 11 are further developed in Nordenfelt L., "Ability, Competence and Qualification: Fundamental Concepts in the Philosophy of Disability". In: D. Christopher Ralston and Justin Ho (eds.) *Philosophical Reflections on Disability* (Dordrecht: Springer, forthcoming).

In this project I have received advice and support from Dr. Per-Anders Tengland, Malmö University College, who has himself written a valuable pilot study on work ability. Dr. Hans-Magnus Solli, Oslo University, has offered substantial comments especially on Part III of the book. Professor Peter Westerholm, Uppsala University, Dr. Mikael Thyberg, Linköping University, and Dr. Wout de Boer, The Netherlands Organization for Applied Scientific Research, Amsterdam, have contributed with further helpful comments on parts of the manuscript for this book. I also wish to thank Professor Kerstin Ekberg, Linköping University, for her continuous encouragement of my project on work ability.

I have been able to use most of the academic year of 2006-2007 to complete this manuscript. I had the privilege of spending this year as a Fellow at the Swedish Collegium for Advanced Study in the Social Sciences (SCAS) at Uppsala, Sweden. I wish to extend my thanks to the Board of the Collegium, its Principal, Professor Björn Wittrock, as well as its Vice Principal, Professor Barbro Klein, for providing me with this new opportunity for systematic research. I also wish to thank my colleagues at the Institute for commenting so constructively on my seminar presentations. As on several previous occasions Mr. Malcolm Forbes has given me substantial help in putting my English into publishable condition.

Linköping, May 2008

Lennart Nordenfelt

Introduction

This project is prompted by one of the greatest social problems in Sweden and in many other Western countries. A large part of the population are every day absent from their work and on sickness leave because they have a reduced ability (or claim that they have a reduced ability) to do their work because of some disease or disorder. This is, first, a great existential problem for the individuals who are affected. But it is also an economic problem for the people themselves and for society. In 2003 on average 14% of the Swedish population were absent because of sickness. The cost for sickness compensation that year amounted to no less than 12 billion euros. To this should be added the enormous cost for health care and the economic losses due to the reduced production at the workplaces.[1]

This crucial social fact calls for various kinds of research and this in various disciplines. In this project I concentrate on the issue of work ability. I ask: what are the conceptual problems involved in assessing a person's work ability and what are the empirical problems?

The Swedish National Insurance Act (originally from 1962 but many changes and additions have been made later) states in one of its central paragraphs that economic compensation will be given to a sick-listed person if, and only if, his or her work ability is reduced by disease or injury by at least 25%. The Norwegian National Insurance Act (1997) states in a similar way that a person who cannot perform more than one half of his or her work duties because of some medical disability is entitled to economic compensation. These statements are loaded with presuppositions. They require that we should be able to measure a person's work ability in degrees. Moreover we should be able to determine whether a reduced ability is caused by a disease or an injury and not by some other phenomenon.

My own research method is the one of conceptual analysis. I ask questions such as: What do we mean by work ability and what *should* we mean? Is the statement that a person *A* has work ability to the degree of 30% an unequivocal statement? Can such a statement be taken seriously in a decision about a person's sick leave and thereby about his or her economic compensation? There are many issues to analyze here. A

---

[1] See Gustafsson and Lundberg, 2005.

first requirement obviously is to relate A's ability to a particular set of goals and to a particular occupation. But is this sufficient?

The social insurance context is however not the only social context where the notion of work ability plays a crucial role. There are at least *three* other major contexts that are all related to the labour market. The first is the context of training for a vocation or a profession, which presupposes an analysis of what a person pursuing the vocation or profession must be able to do. This has been the focus of many studies in educational science. The second context is constituted by the situation where a job-seeker is evaluated with regard to his or her competencies. The third context is the one of job evaluation, when an individual or a whole profession is evaluated for the purpose of setting adequate wages for the individual or the profession as a whole. In all these contexts more aspects of work ability are actualized than in the situation of administering sickness benefits. In particular it is here not only a question of what is minimally required of a person for him or her to do the job. There is also a question of excellence. One can ask: How much better is this person than other persons in his or her field?

In this book I will make a systematic analysis of the notion of work ability with a very broad approach encompassing the different pragmatic requirements. I think there is a need to make a logical investigation into the notion of work ability from different angles. It will then perhaps become apparent that the instruments devised for the various purposes may have neglected some crucial elements which are entailed in the concept of ability or in some adjacent concepts.

Thus my theoretical platform lies within general action-theory. On the basis of an action-theoretic analysis of ability I will study the stratification of the notion of work ability. This includes a survey of the various kinds of condition for work ability, some of which are called in the literature *qualifications* for work. I will first briefly outline the structure of my analysis.

In the first part of the book I present and briefly analyse some methods and instruments designed in the various contexts for characterizing and assessing work ability. I start with the medico-legal context, where instruments are constructed for the purpose of deciding about sickness benefits and also for the purpose of rehabilitation for work. This survey of contemporary classifications of work ability is supplemented by a presentation of two American taxonomies not particularly designed for the medico-legal purpose: the Handbook of Human Abilities and the American Dictionary of Occupational Titles (DOT). In the subsequent chapters I attempt to summarize some developments in the area of learning for work. This includes a description of how the vertical model of education, focusing on formal and abstract learning in traditional

14

subjects, has gradually been transformed into a more horizontal model, where learning within or at least close to a workplace has come to the fore. It is emphasized that learning in a context, for instance in the context of a workplace, is an interactive relationship where the student gives and takes and where the changing context is as crucial as the traditional knowledge input.

With regard to the context of recruitment and employment the concept of *employability* has gained popularity. The chapter *Employability: qualifications necessary for employment* presents some of the developments in this area. The concept is used in a number of senses, which are described in the chapter. One of the most useful definitions of employability is given by the Confederation of British Industry:

> Employability is the possession by an individual of the qualities and competencies required to meet the changing needs of employers and customers and thereby help to realize his or her aspirations and potential in work.[2]

In one chapter I pay particular attention to the context of job evaluation where the purpose is to find criteria for setting adequate wages and establishing reasonable working conditions for people in a certain occupation. Instruments have been proposed for this purpose. I present one Swedish model, the so-called HAC model of qualifications, and illustrate it with a few examples.

These presentations are supplemented by an analysis of a renowned sociological study of work content by Anselm Strauss and his associates.[3] In this work the authors make a detailed investigation into the nature of medical work and trace a multitude of aspects of this work, some of which are hardly ever taken into account in traditional descriptions of occupations or professions. The authors present and scrutinize many of the consequences of the simple fact that much work, including medical, is performed *both on and together with acting people.* This entails that work such as comfort work and sentimental work must be emphasized.

Part II gives the theoretical foundation for my analysis of work ability. This analysis is based on my previous work on ability in a health-theoretic context.[4] A crucial element in the analysis of human ability is to get an understanding of and list all the various conditions for performing actions. A substantial section is devoted to this topic, where the notions of practical possibility, ability and opportunity are introduced. It

---

2   Confederation of British Industry (CBI), 1999.

3   Strauss *et al.*, 1985.

4   Nordenfelt, 1995 and 2000.

is noted that every assessment of ability must be made against a certain background, a set of circumstances. When these circumstances are not explicitly mentioned they must be presupposed implicitly. The presupposed circumstances are either considered to be *standard* in the culture in question or they are considered to be *reasonable* in the relevant context.

The chapter *From ability to work ability* constitutes the central analysis of this book. I summarize the main results of the analysis in the form of a set of basic categories of competencies and other abilities involved in work ability. These categories are the following: technical competence, general competence and personal competence, the latter including empathy and ethical competence in general. The chapter also emphasizes the role of *interaction* in most occupations. Interaction entails a number of factors, some of which are positive, for instance colleagues can help each other or replace each other in various situations; but some of which are negative, for instance colleagues may confront or even impede each other in the work context.

Part III of the book is devoted to the issue of work ability and its relation to medical conditions. I discuss first some basic facts about the international and, in particular, the Norwegian and the Swedish legal arena. What do the laws say about such work ability as can entitle to sickness or disability compensation from the state? In the subsequent section I turn to a substantial analysis of the notion of disease and try to answer the question whether there is a viable notion of disease that can answer the demands of objectivity often raised by the insurance offices. This discussion draws heavily on my own previous analyses of health and illness in the books.[5] The aim of this discussion, which runs deeper than is usual in the context of insurance medicine, is to demonstrate in some detail that there is no easy theoretical answer to the question of the nature of disease and illness. Therefore, for the medico-legal purposes we must find pragmatic ways out in terms of consensus decisions. In a final chapter I will outline some guidelines for this endeavour.

---

[5] Nordenfelt, 1995 and 2000.

PART 1

WORK AND WORK ABILITY
IN CONTEMPORARY LITERATURE

CHAPTER 1

The International Classification of Functioning, Disability and Health (ICF)

The Starting Point: The ICIDH

The World Health Organization (WHO) issues every decade a new version of the International Classification of Diseases, Injuries and Related Conditions (ICD). The most recent edition, the Tenth Revision, dates from 1992. The purpose of this classification is to provide a taxonomy and nomenclature for the whole range of diseases and injuries. In the present version there are 17 classes of diseases and injuries. In addition to this there is a special heading for external causes of injury and poisoning. This international classification, along with its elaborate numerical index system (to a four-digit level), is extensively used in the health care systems of all countries. It plays a particularly crucial role in medical statistics, for instance in statistics of death.

The ICD fails, however, to reflect the full range of problems that lead people to seek medical help. It covers well what medical science considers to be diseases or causes of diseases, but it stops short of the consequences of diseases, such as disabilities or handicaps. The latter are precisely such factors as intrude upon everyday life and as are directly observed by the bearer.

By the 1970s many physicians and other health professionals thus felt a great need for a strict vocabulary and a classification of the health consequences of diseases and injuries. In order to fulfil this need the WHO issued in 1980 a tentative proposal for such a classification, namely the International Classification of Impairments, Disabilities and Handicaps (ICIDH). This classification was to be used for a variety of purposes. First, it was a statistical tool in the collection and recording of data, for instance in population studies. Second, it was a research tool, to measure outcomes such as quality of life. Third, it was a clinical tool in needs assessment and matching treatments with specific conditions. Fourth, it also served as a social policy tool in social security planning and in policy design.

The key concepts to be defined and subclassified in this system are: impairment, disability and handicap. These three kinds of phenomena were viewed as the typical consequences of diseases – and those which are of particular interest for the medical personnel. In the standard case they form a certain causal sequence depicted in the ICIDH in the following way:

Disease → Impairment → Disability → Handicap.

A disease causes one or more impairments. An impairment causes in its turn one or more disabilities, and a disability causes one or more handicaps.

For an understanding of these relations some definitions of the key concepts are required. The ICIDH provides explicit definitions for the consequence-concepts (impairment, disability and handicap). The notion of disease is not explicitly defined but there is an informal characterization of the elements contained in the disease process:

A chain of causal circumstance, the "etiology", gives rise to changes in the structure or functioning of the body, the "pathology". Pathological changes may or may not make themselves evident; when they do they are described as "manifestations", which, in medical parlance, are usually distinguished as "symptoms and signs".[1]

The formal definitions of the consequence concepts are the following:

- Impairment: "In the context of health experience, an impairment is any loss or abnormality of physiological psychological or anatomical structure or function."[2]
- Disability: "In the context of health experience, a disability is any restriction or lack (resulting from an impairment) of ability to perform an activity in the manner or within the range considered normal for a human being".[3]
- Handicap: "In the context of health experience, a handicap is a disadvantage for a given individual, resulting from an impairment or a disability, that limits or prevents the fulfilment of a role that is normal (depending on age, sex, and social and cultural factors) for the individual."[4]

It is emphasized in the manual that there is a standard causal relation from impairment via disability to handicap. However, this need not be the case. Handicap may result from impairment without the mediation of a state of disability. A disfigurement, for instance, may cause a break in

---

[1] ICIDH, 1980, p. 25.
[2] *Ibid.*, p. 47.
[3] *Ibid.*, p. 143.
[4] *Ibid.*

social relationships and may thus constitute a real disadvantage without the existence of a particular disability. Moreover, there can be disruptions at every stage. One can be impaired without being disabled, and one can be disabled without being handicapped. Some influence in the reverse direction is also possible. The experience of certain handicaps can engender depression and thereby illness.

In sum, the ICIDH constituted a major step forward in the conceptualization of medical conditions and became a useful tool for medical personnel, not least in the field of rehabilitation. However, there are both theoretical and practical problems surrounding this manual. From a theoretical point of view there were problems in distinguishing between the main categories. The distinction between disease and impairment is unclear since pathological states and impairments are described in almost identical ways in the manual. The distinction between impairments and disabilities is blurred when it comes to the mental "impairments" acknowledged in the ICIDH. Most of the so-called mental impairments, when carefully analysed, turn out to be some kind of disabilities. Consider the following salient examples. *Agnosia, apraxia* and *acalculia* are all listed as impairments in the ICIDH. However, they are all defined in terms of disabilities; *agnosia*: disturbed ability to recognize objects; *apraxia*: disturbed ability to perform learned purposeful movements; *acalculia*: disturbed ability to count and operate with numbers. Finally, it is difficult to maintain a distinction between disabilities and handicaps on the criterion of social values. In practice, many of the items in the nosology of disabilities turn out to be value-laden.[5] Although the ICIDH in a way introduced the societal perspective it did not do so in a full-blown way. Handicaps are acknowledged as socially constructed disadvantages but the genesis of handicaps is still looked upon in a unidimensional way:

> Disadvantage accrues as a result of [the individual] being unable to conform to the norms of his universe. Handicap is thus a social phenomenon, representing the social and environmental consequences for the individual stemming from the presence of impairments and disabilities.[6]

If handicaps are almost always seen as stemming from impairments and disabilities then one seems not to be able to record or measure the affect of a disadvantageous environment on people's lives. "The user can record changes in a person's level of ability, but would have no way

---

[5]   For a detailed analysis, see Nordenfelt, 1997.

[6]   ICIDH, 1980, p. 29.

of knowing whether that was the result of changes to the person or changes to the social and physical environment."[7]

The ICIDH was put to a number of practical tests in many areas and lots of suggestions were made with regard to its improvement. During the late 1990s the WHO was prepared to make a major revision of the manual. This resulted first in ICIDH 2 (1999) and finally in the International Classification of Disability, Functioning and Health (ICF) (2001).

The ICF

According to its own description, the ICF encompasses all aspects of human health and some health-related components of well-being. It excludes circumstances that are not health-related, for example such as are brought about by socio-economic factors, race, gender and religion. ICF, as contrasted with the earlier classification (ICIDH), deals with both functioning as the positive category and disability as the negative category. Thus ICF is applicable to all people.

The manual organizes its information in two major parts. The first part deals with and classifies functioning and disability and their subcategories. The second part provides lists of environmental factors and personal factors that can apply to people having some disability.

The major subcategories of functioning are body functions and body structures, activities and participation. The major subcategories of disability are impairment (related to body function or body structure), activity limitations and participation restrictions. The subcategories are defined as follows. Body functions are primarily the physiological functions of body systems. It is notable, though, that this subcategory also includes mental functions. Body structures are anatomical parts of the body such as organs, limbs and their components. Impairments are problems in body function or structure constituting significant deviation or loss. Activity is the execution of a task or action by an individual. Activity limitations are difficulties an individual may have with regard to executing activities. Participation is involvement in a life situation. Participation restrictions are problems an individual may experience with regard to involvement in life situations.

All these subcategories encompass several specific items, regarding specific anatomical parts, bodily functions, activities and participations. All these items are numbered and meticulously classified, analogously

---

[7]   Bickenbach *et al.*, 1999.

to the classification of specific diseases in the International Classification of Diseases and Related Health Conditions (ICD).[8]

The ICF codes are only complete with the presence of a qualifier which denotes the magnitude of the level of health.[9] The two qualifiers for the Activities and Participation component are the *performance* qualifier and the *capacity* qualifier. The performance qualifier describes what an individual does in his or her current environment. The current environment brings in a societal context. Thus performance as described here can be understood as involvement in a life situation. The capacity qualifier describes an individual's ability to execute a task or an action. The capacity is measured in a uniform or standard environment, and thus reflects the environmentally adjusted ability of the individual.

Both capacity and performance are measured according to the following scale:

0	No difficulty
1	Mild difficulty
2	Moderate difficulty
3	Severe difficulty
4.	Complete difficulty

As a result of this structure ICF provides a multi-perspective approach to the classification of functioning and disability as an interactive and evolutionary process. If the full health perspective is to be described all components in this schema are useful.[10] For example, a person may have impairments without having ability limitations (for instance, a disfigurement in leprosy may have no effect on a person's ability). A person may have performance problems and ability limitations without evident impairment (for instance, reduced performance in daily activities associated with many different diseases). Moreover, a person may have performance problems without either impairment or ability limitation (for instance, an HIV-positive individual, or an ex-patient recovered from mental illness, facing stigmatization in interpersonal relations or at work). Moreover, a person may have restricted participation in some area of life exclusively because of external circumstances. The individual may be poor and cannot afford school or housing. He or she may be prohibited by law from entering a school or a workplace.

It has to be emphasized, however, that ICF remains a health classification. This means that, although acknowledged, those disadvantages

---

[8] ICD, 1992.
[9] ICF, pp. 121-122.
[10] *Ibid.*, p. 27.

that are exclusively caused by external conditions are not taken into account in the application of ICF. The restrictions of disablement which are focused on are such as are in some way related to an impairment or a limitation of an activity.

CHAPTER 2

Some Methods for Assessing Work and Work Ability in the Medico-Legal Context

There have been several contemporary attempts to construct instruments for the assessment of work ability in the medico-legal context. Most of them are designed for estimating work ability in the context of determining sickness benefits or, in a few cases, for the purpose of rehabilitative work. The constructors mainly have their professional background in occupational medicine or in paramedical disciplines such as occupational therapy. I will here (and in Appendix 1) present the main tenets of some such instruments. Most of the examples are from Scandinavia.

The ambitions and the more specific purposes vary. Some instruments are highly pragmatic and designed to be directly useful in routine assessments by the family doctor. This holds in particular for the Finnish Work Ability Index. Other instruments are more detailed and comprehensive and are primarily geared to assessments by a specialist. This is the case with the Dutch Functional Capacity list. The Swedish instrument DOA is even more detailed and presupposes a lengthy dialogue between a rehabilitator and a patient.[1]

I restrict myself here to describing a few examples of instruments but I will give a detailed account of the following instruments in Appendix 1: The Personal Capability Instrument (Department for Work and Pensions, UK), Assessment of Work Performance (AWP, Linköping, Sweden) and Dialogue About Ability Related to Work (DOA, Jönköping, Sweden.)

The WAI Index[2]

The WAI Index is a tool to be used in occupational health care and it expresses how well the employee can manage his or her work. It is a method for assessing the work ability in the context of health checks or

---

[1] Linddahl et al., 2003.

[2] Tuomi et al., 1994 and 1998.

investigations of the workplaces. The Index consists of a set of questions concerning the physical and mental demands put on the employee as well as the health status and resources of the employee. The employee fills in the form but the answers may be supplemented at the clinic. The work ability is assessed on a scale of points between 7 and 49. 7-27 points is considered to be a bad work ability (the work ability should be restored), 28-36 points is considered to be a moderate work ability (the work ability should be improved), 37-43 points is considered to be a good work ability (the work ability should be strengthened), 44-49 points is considered to be an excellent work ability (the work ability should be maintained). The Index is also intended to predict work ability in the future.

The main areas of the Index are the following:

• The present work ability compared to when it was best during the person's life-time
• The work ability in relation to the demands of the work
• The number of diseases diagnosed by a doctor
• The impact of the diseases during the last year
• Days of absence from work during the last year
• Self-assessment of how health will permit work within the next two years
• Mental resources.

It may be noted here that the instrument uses broad categories and does not include detailed questions. It is the employee that introduces the details. The instrument is also strictly disease-oriented. Two of the items directly refer to diseases. The Index is original in that it involves a question about expectations for the future.[3]

This brief and concise instrument should be contrasted and supplemented with some more recent developments at the Finnish Institute of Occupational Health. Ilmarinen introduces a very broad concept of work ability where he emphasizes that individual work ability is a process of human resources in relation to work.

Human resources can be described by (1) health and functional capacities (physical, mental, social), (2) education and competence, (3) values and attitudes, and (4) motivation. When this comprehensive set of individual factors is related to (5) work demands (physical and mental), (6) work community and management, and (7) work environment, the outcome can be called the

---

[3] For an application of this instrument in Sweden, see Torgén, 2006. For a reliability test of the same instrument, see de Swartz *et al.* 2002.

individual work ability. The work ability concept is a dynamic process that changes greatly for several reasons throughout an individual's work life.[4]

Ilmarinen here introduces a number of concepts to be dealt with in great detail in subsequent chapters of this book. In my own analysis I will however make a sharp distinction between the individual's inner resources (the ability) and his or her external conditions (the opportunity). There are, as I will argue, strong theoretical reasons for differentiating between the two categories. I will also distinguish between abilities and other internal qualities (sometimes called qualifications) of a person. To these qualities belong virtues, attitudes and motivations.

The Norwegian Scheme for the Assessment of Function

The Norwegian Scheme for the Assessment of Function is based on the WHO's Classification of Functioning, Disability and Health (ICF), which was presented in Chapter 1. A working group attached to *Rikstrygdeverket* tried to assess what activities (out of the 120 in the ICF) are relevant to working life. The scheme was tested on roughly 800 persons in April 2001. The purpose of the scheme is to provide a subjective assessment of working capacity.[5]

The basic question in the scheme is: Have you for health reasons had difficulty in performing the following activities during the last week?

Walk/stand (stand, walk less than 1 km, walk more than 1 km on a flat surface, on a varying surface, walk up or down stairs, do daily shopping, put on shoes and stockings)

Hold/pick up (pick a coin, hold and steer a wheel, drive a car, prepare food, write, perform daily tasks, take part in leisure activities, dress and undress)

Lift/carry (lift an empty bag from the floor, carry bags from a shop, carry a small bag on one's shoulder or back, stretch out one's arms, do ordinary cleaning, wash clothes)

Sit (sit on a kitchen chair, travel in a car as a passenger, use public transport)

Master (be attentive and concentrated, work in a group, lead others in their activities, manage one's responsibilities in ordinary life, master the strains of ordinary life, stand criticism, control one's aggression)

---

[4]   Ilmarinen, 2001b, p. 548.

[5]   Brage *et al.*, 2004.

Cooperation and communication (remember, apprehend oral information, apprehend written information, converse, participate in conversation with several persons, use a telephone)

Perception (watch TV, listen to the radio)

General work ability.

It can be noted that this instrument is quite focused on physical activities. A few items, in particular in the Master category, involve more holistic capacities such as taking responsibility and mastering the strains of ordinary life.

The Functional Capacity List

From the year 2000 on the Dutch disability legislation is explicitly based on the WHO's conceptualization of chronic consequences of disease or disorder. This conceptualization is now formulated in the International Classification of Functioning, Disability and Health (ICF).[6] A special list of functional capacities has been formulated on the basis of ICF. This list plays a crucial role in the assessment of an individual's work ability in the social insurance context.

In the Netherlands a system of job-matching is used to determine if the functional capacities as determined by the doctor, imply a capacity to earn. In order to do so jobs and functional capacities are described in comparable terms and the doctors are asked to pronounce their judgement not only in the form of an ordinary diagnosis but also in terms of functional capacities and to indicate if the claimant is capable, partially capable or incapable of performing these functions. There are 56 functional descriptions, clustered into 6 categories. On closer inspection one will see that they are only partially functional capacities. They consist partly of potentialities for handling the environment or descriptions of body structures and functions.[7]

Major categories:

- Personal functioning
- Social functioning
- Adaptation to physical environment
- Dynamic actions
- Static posture
- Working hours.

---

[6] For a full presentation of ICF, see above in Chapter 1.

[7] For a summary of this nomenclature and its background, see de Boer *et al.*, 2006.

28

Personal functioning (focusing of attention, dividing of attention, remembering, insight into one's own abilities, acting efficiently, acting independently, speed of action, other incapacities, specific restrictions of work-environmental factors)

Social functioning (seeing, hearing, speaking, writing, reading, dealing with other people's emotional problems, expressing own feelings, dealing with conflicts, cooperation, transportation, other restrictions, specific restrictions of work, e.g. unsatisfactory contact with clients and colleagues)

Adaptation to physical environment (heat, cold, draught, contact with skin, protection devices, dust, smoke, gas, damp, noise, vibration, other specific restrictions, for instance allergy)

Dynamic action (left or right dominant, localization of restrictions, use of hand and finger, sense of touch, handling keyboard, working with keyboard and mouse, screw with hand and arm, reaching out, frequent reaching out, bending over, frequent bending over, turning trunk, pushing or pulling, lifting or carrying, handling objects, moving the head, walking, climbing stairs, climbing a ladder, kneeling and crawling, other restrictions, specific conditions of work)

Static posture (sitting, standing, being active while kneeling or squatting, being active while bowing or turning, being active above the head, fixing the head in a specific position, changes of posture, other restrictions, specific conditions)

Working hours (periods in 14 hours, hours per day, hours per week, other restrictions with regard to working hours).

The classification here is somewhat unusual. Most of the physical capacities are collected under the heading of "dynamic action". As in most similar systems the physical capacities dominate. However, it could be noted that the social functioning category includes items for dealing with other people's emotional problems. Among specific restrictions for work is also mentioned unsatisfactory contact with clients and colleagues. The instrument, in contradistinction to most others, also contains a category dealing with adaptations to the environment. However, like the Norwegian instrument, it lacks a motivation category. There is nothing about what the subject wants or expects to achieve given his or her present state of health. For a presentation of the implementation of the Dutch instrument see Chapter 16.[8]

---

[8] See Westerholm *et al.*, 2008, for the medical use of instruments for assessing work ability.

CHAPTER 3

Current Classifications of Work and Work Ability

Outside the specific medico-legal context there exist some interesting attempts to make comprehensive analyses and classifications of people's ability to work. Some of these have the primary purpose of helping authorities and organizations place people in the right occupation. I will here describe two large-scale American attempts.

The Handbook of Human Abilities

There is a whole sub-discipline of psychology that is devoted to performance research. One of the leading representatives of this line of research is the American psychologist E.A. Fleishman who has summarized several results of these endeavours. Fleishman and his colleagues have been particularly interested in constructing valid and reliable taxonomies in the area. They want to discern "robust" ability entities that can be measured empirically, be tested and provide a basis for training and rehabilitation. The general purpose can also be described as defining the fewest independent ability categories describing performance in the widest variety of tasks. Thus factor analysis of clustering is used to define this minimal number of relevant ability categories. For example, Fleishman claims to have demonstrated in this way that the ability of Multi-limb coordination is common to tasks involving two hands, or hands and feet, in operating various pieces of equipment. However, this ability does not extend to tasks in which the body is in motion, as in certain athletic activities. Another example is Reactor time, which is an ability that represents the speed with which the individual can provide a single motor response to a single stimulus when it appears. This ability is, Fleishman claims, independent of the mode of presentation and also of the type of motor response required. Fleishman and his colleagues have been particularly successful in identifying specific abilities in the domain of psychomotor functions.[1]

---

[1] Fleishman and Quaintance, 1984, pp. 162-167.

Fleishman and his research team have extended their ambitions to the area of work ability. In what is called the *Handbook of Human Abilities*[2] they have brought together a comprehensive taxonomy, including definitions and measurements of the abilities empirically constructed. The Handbook is an attempt to break down abilities for work into small units, logically separated and which can be tested separately. Fleishman provides a substantive list of contemporary test batteries for each ability unit. The connection to the work context is consistently maintained. The author gives examples of occupations and tasks for which each kind of ability is relevant. The Handbook is intended for personnel psychologists, human resource professionals, counsellors and educational specialists.

The resulting list of abilities draws from the cognitive, psychomotor, and physical domains. Later sensory/perceptual abilities, including vision and audition, have been added. Altogether 52 kinds of abilities have been included. I will here list all the cognitive abilities and then give examples from the three other main categories.

- Oral comprehension
- Written comprehension
- Oral expression
- Written expression
- Fluency of ideas
- Originality
- Memorization
- Problem sensitivity
- Mathematical reasoning
- Number facility
- Deductive reasoning
- Inductive reasoning
- Information ordering
- Category flexibility
- Speed of closure (the ability to quickly make sense of information)
- Flexibility of closure (the ability to identify a known pattern)
- Spatial orientation
- Visualization

---

[2]   Fleishman, 1995.

32

- Perceptual speed
- Selective attention (the ability to concentrate on a task over a period of time)
- Time sharing (the ability to shift back and forth efficiently between activities).

Among the psychomotor abilities one can find: control precision, rate control, reaction time and various forms of dexterity. The physical abilities include static strength, dynamic strength and gross body coordination. (No clear distinction is made between the two categories of psychomotor abilities and physical abilities.) The sensory/perceptual abilities include various kinds of vision and hearing but also speech recognition and speech clarity. The two latter abilities seem to come quite close to oral comprehension and oral expression in the category of cognitive abilities. The relationships are not explained.

The amount of experiment and analysis involved in this psychological approach to ability research is impressive. It is certainly of great general interest to know what the leading psychological schools consider to be the minimal list of abilities for "the widest variety of tasks". The fact that there are test batteries and training programmes designed for the abilities as specified in the Handbook is also of great interest to rehabilitators in medicine. However, in spite of its ambitions and degree of detail, the usefulness of the Handbook for the purpose of my own project is quite limited. Partly because of the restrictions that Fleishman and his colleagues have laid on themselves, the Handbook covers only a limited area of human abilities. It does not help us if we wish to get a general overview of the abilities and competencies necessary for work. The Handbook contains only abilities on a very basic person- or even body-centred level. All communicative, social, strategic and empathic abilities are left out.

It is also notable that the environment is completely left out as a factor relevant to people's possibilities of working. Thus, this experimental approach to abilities and skills has been highly criticized by psychological schools such as one known as "situated learning".[3] They claim that skills in practice are so domain-specific and so tied to situational features that the experimental abstraction from the context destroys important elements of what is to be measured.

---

[3] Rogoff and Lave, 1984.

The Dictionary of Occupational Titles (DOT)

The Dictionary of Occupational Titles (DOT) is produced by the Division of Occupational Analysis of the US Employment Service in Washington. DOT is a reference manual, intended mainly to assist Employment Service interviewers in placing workers in jobs. It also provides other users with a broad range of information on the content and characteristics of occupations.[4]

DOT was the result of a decision by the Congress during the economic recession in the 1930s when a national employment service was established to assist workers in finding employment. An occupational research programme was conducted. In 1939 this programme produced the first edition of the Dictionary of Occupational Titles. Subsequent editions have appeared in 1949, 1965, 1977 and 1991. The Dictionary is now continuously being revised and exists in a digital version, as the Enhanced Dictionary of Occupational Titles, eDOT. (See Appendix 2 for details.)

Each edition was intended to provide a catalogue of occupational titles existing in the US economy at the time. It is thus an extremely comprehensive and much used dictionary. It is simultaneously a dictionary providing definitions of occupations, a classification system and a source of data on occupational characteristics. The fourth edition of DOT contains 28,801 titles of which 12,099 (42 per cent) are base titles. Base titles are the titles most frequently used to identify a particular occupation.

The DOT titles are defined according to a highly structured format. Each definition begins with a statement that is intended to summarize the occupation in terms of (1) worker actions, (2) machines, tools, equipment and or work aids used by workers in performing their jobs, (3) the purpose of the worker actions (i.e. what gets done on the job) and (4) materials, products, subject matter and/or services that a worker produces on the job. The lead statement is followed by one or more task element statements, which describe the specific tasks a worker performs to accomplish the overall purpose of the job.[5]

I will here give two examples of definitions of occupations: teacher, secondary school, and supervisor dairy farm.

Teacher, secondary school: Teaches one or more subjects to students in public or private secondary schools: Instructs students, using various methods, such as lecture and demonstration, and uses audiovisual aids and other

---

[4]   Miller *et al.*, 1980, p. 18.

[5]   *Ibid.*, p. 26.

materials to supplement presentations. Prepares course objectives and out-
lines for course of study following curriculum guidelines or requirements of
state and school. Assigns lessons and corrects homework. Administers tests
to evaluate pupil progress, records results, and issues reports to inform parents of progress. Keeps attendance records. Maintains discipline in classroom. Meets with parents to discuss student progress and problems. Partici-
pates in faculty and professional meetings, educational conferences, and
teacher training workshops. Performs related duties such as sponsoring one
or more activities or student organizations, assisting pupils in selecting
course of study, and counseling students in adjustment and academic problems. May be identified according to subject matter taught. May be required
to hold certification from state.

Supervisor, dairy farm: Supervises and coordinates activities of workers engaged in milking, breeding and caring for cows, and performs lay-
veterinarian duties on dairy farm: Assigns workers to tasks, such as feeding
and milking cows, cleaning cattle, barns, and equipment, and assisting with
breeding and health care. Inspects barns and milking parlor for cleanliness
and maintenance and informs workers of actions required to insure compli-
ance with established standards. Studies feed and milk production records to
determine feed formula required to produce maximum milk yield and noti-
fies workers of diet changes. Studies genetic and health records to develop
schedules for activities such as breeding, dehorning, and sale of calves. Observes cows during estrus and artificially inseminates cows to produce desired offspring. Examines cows for evidence of illness, injuries, and calving,
treats illnesses and injuries, delivers calves, and engages veterinarian to care
for serious injuries and illnesses.[6]

After the publication of the fourth edition of DOT in 1977 a special
committee on Occupational Classification and Analysis was established
by the National Research Council's Assembly of Behavioral and Social
Sciences. The task of the committee was to critically review DOT. They
published a comprehensive report, A.R. Miller, D.J Treiman, P.S. Cain,
P.A. Roos: *Work, Jobs, and Occupations: A Critical Review of the
Dictionary of Occupational Titles.*

The reviewers summarize the major ways in which the DOT can be
used in the following ways:

First, the DOT provides a classification structure for organizing information
about job openings in self search job banks located in local Employment
Service offices. Second, the dictionary aspect and, to a more limited extent,
the classification structure are used by placement interviewers and employment counselors in Employment Service offices as aids in matching job applicants with job openings [...] In addition to its direct use as a placement

---

[6]   www.occupationalinfo.org/onet/31308.html.

and counseling tool the DOT serves as a data source for the preparation of a series of career brochures, and the classification structure serves to organize the data for the monthly publication of labor market information by the national office for use in local Employment Service offices.[7]

The reviewers observe that DOT is also used outside the governmental service. A wide variety of organizations have used it for several purposes. Among the various purposes are career and vocational counselling, rehabilitation counselling, personnel management, employment placement and library reference.

The DOT has furthermore attracted the attention of social scientists. The DOT code is often used to describe the socioeconomic distribution of people (in psychological studies) and to match experimental groups with control groups with respect to occupational category and skill level. The worker traits and worker functions have been used in describing the distribution of job characteristics across various sectors of the labour market and in studying changes in the composition of the labour force. Economists have used the worker trait and worker function scales when they have studied the determinants of wage structure, and psychologists use this information in studying the relationship between occupational characteristics and psychological functioning.

Moreover, the DOT can be used for the determination of disability and eligibility for disability benefits. The determination of disability, and hence the eligibility for benefits according to the Social Security Act, depends on establishing that disabilities are debilitating in the sense that they prevent a person from being employed in the same or "similar" work as he or she has performed in the past.

The Social Security Act's definition of disability mandates that a person's ability to perform alternative work, his or her "residual functional capacity", be evaluated before disability benefits can be awarded [...] The underlying principle employed in the evaluation process is that if the disability is not incapacitating – because the physical, mental, and skill levels of the disabled individual are sufficient to meet the [demands] of his or her previous employment – disability benefits are not allowed. If the individual cannot perform his or her past occupation, a determination is made as to whether there exist other jobs in the national economy that the disabled person could perform (i.e. work similar to the previous employment but perhaps requiring a lesser amount of exertion) [...] The worker function (Data, People, and Things) scales [...] are used as rough measures of the skill level of an occupation.[8]

---

[7]   Miller *et al.*, 1980, p. 5.

[8]   *Ibid.*, pp. 68-69.

The DOT project is impressive in its enormous scale and pretensions. It certainly covers a lot of detail in the analysis of job structures and thereby the preconditions for work ability. The emphasis is, however, still on technical abilities. Persons as objects are recognized in some detail. But here people are looked upon as objects that require great technical skills on the part of the worker. The ethical aspects and the empathic aspects so much analysed by Strauss *et al.* and described below in Chapter 7 are notoriously neglected.[9]

The report of the committee mentioned above gives quite a favourable general review of the DOT project, although they have observed a number of weaknesses, not least that the list of occupations is unbalanced both in coverage and analysis. Production process occupations are more finely differentiated than are other occupations, such as clerical, sales and service occupations. The committee notes however that there is no simple way of resolving this problem since there exist no clear ways of determining the boundaries of occupations.

> What constitutes an "occupation" – and how much heterogeneity in the content of a set of jobs justifies a single occupational title – is a difficult question. Historically, the DOT has tended to define occupations by their titles rather than by their content. Jobs with similar titles have been grouped unless the evidence strongly indicated that they differed in content, and occupations with different titles have been defined as being different, regardless of similarity in content.[10]

In spite of the weaknesses, however, the committee finds that the DOT classification with its definitions remains the most comprehensive set of occupational characterizations that exist and is a highly valuable knowledge resource for work-related authorities and organizations.

---

[9] For details of the construction of job description, see Appendix 2.

[10] Miller *et al.*, 1980, p. 194.

CHAPTER 4

Analyses of Competence and Skill
in the Context of Professional Education

The British Experiment with Basic Skills

During the 1970s and 80s there was an interesting educational evolution in Britain towards identifying and training what were called basic skills. The Prime Minister James Callaghan made in 1976 a celebrated speech at Ruskin College, Oxford, where he mapped out a solution to the British economic crisis in general and to the problem of unemployment in particular. He said that schooling must equip children for a "lively constructive place in society and also fit them for a job". This speech indicated that a new era of educational policy had started in Britain.[1]

Already a few years earlier The Manpower Services Commission (MSC) had been created by the Employment and Training Act 1973 and it lasted until its transformation into the Training Commission in 1988. The commission had a short history which was rich in controversy and intrigue. However, it came to represent a new vision of society and the economy. Its leading personnel emphasized the importance of vocational education and training for future economic success. People should be trained for the market and not, as was the earlier slogan, be educated for life.

The MSC set itself three important tasks: (a) to abolish the dichotomy between education and training that had emerged during the 19th century; (b) to elevate the importance of vocational education and training; (c) to redefine the contribution of education to productivity and national development. At the institutional level the MSC attempted a complete revolution of Britain's education and training system. The idea was that vocational training should be incorporated in all education, including the ordinary schools.

In this endeavour the concept of skill became crucial. The vocational training should focus on giving the students a set of basic skills necessary or suitable for a number of jobs. The idea was not to train people in

---

[1]   See Payne, 1999.

the traditional way for one specific vocation such as carpenter, tailor or shoemaker. Instead the students should become basically and generally skilled. They should be trained for the market as a whole. The crux was then to find these basic skills, i.e. skills that are transferable from one vocation to another.

The British Further Education Unit (FEU) set itself to define the notion of basic skill and to list such skills for the new educational programme. In several documents, among others *Basic Skills* FEU proposed a vision of a common or core skills curriculum for prevocational students.[2] It advanced 12 central aims for a skills-based curriculum. Among these were: the ability to develop satisfactory personal relationships with others; the capacity to approach various kinds of problems methodically and effectively; sufficient political and economic literacy to understand the social environment and participate in it; the development of everyday coping skills; and a flexibility of attitude and willingness to learn sufficient to cope with future changes in technology and career.

The FEU noted that advancing such a broad list of aims to prepare students for accomplishing actual tasks on the market is essential. Moreover, employers explicitly ask for broad competencies. They do not just ask for conventional school knowledge but also for particular attitudes and values.

Basic Skills

The document Basic Skills analyses some of the then current research related to skills. It identifies a large number of generic skills common to many jobs, but also emphasizes that employers require from young people certain attitudes as well as conventional skills. The document thus argues that knowledge, experience and attitudes as well as conventional skills should comprise the basic skills to be developed in vocational education. It is insisted that all subject teachers should be teachers of basic skills.

Having a skill, it is said, does not necessarily imply being prepared or able to use it, or knowing all the occasions on which its use is applicable or possible. Skills may have attitudes or values associated with them.

The psychological use of the term skill is that skilled performance requires perception, knowledge, judgements and understanding and at the same time

---

[2]   FEU, 1982.

all skills involve some kind of coordinated, overt activity by hands, of speech etc.[3]

The enterprise of FEU had the following aims: to bring about

- an informed perspective as to the role and status of a young person in an adult society and the world of work
- a basis from which the young person can make an informed and realistic decision with respect to his or her immediate future
- a continuing development of physical and manipulative skills, in both vocational and leisure contexts, and an appreciation of those skills in others
- an ability to develop satisfactory relationships with others
- a basis on which the young person acquires a set of moral values applicable to issues in contemporary society
- a level of achievement in literacy and numeracy appropriate to ability and adequate to meet the basic demands of contemporary society
- competence in a variety of study skills likely to be demanded of the young person
- a capacity to approach various kinds of problems methodically and effectively, and to plan and evaluate courses of action
- sufficient political and economic literacy to understand the social environment and participate in it
- an appreciation of the physical and technological environments, and the relationship between these and the needs of man in general and working life in particular
- a development of the everyday coping skills necessary to promote self-sufficiency in the young people
- a flexibility of attitude and willingness to learn sufficient to cope with future changes in technology and career.[4]

These aims required not only the ability to perform a concrete occupational task but also proficiency in language (reading, writing, speaking and listening); dealing with numbers (calculation, measurement, graphs and tables); manipulative dexterity and coordination; problem solving; everyday coping; interpersonal relationships; computer literacy and learning.

---

[3]   FEU, 1982, p. 1.

[4]   *Ibid.*, p. 1.

According to the FEU the acquisition of a core of skills means a level of ability, achievement and understanding in essential areas of knowledge and skill which will increase a young person's chance of achieving success in adult working life. It is central to much of the skills research, the FEU claims, that the job-specific vocational preparation alone is no longer appropriate. Technological change is likely to alter the structure of many jobs, therefore vocational preparation should provide young people with a range of skills that are useful across vocational areas. And as many individuals move from one job to another their non-specific skills will improve their adaptability. The expression *generic skills* is introduced to describe such skills.[5]

The document exemplifies how various skills can be matched to specific jobs, for instance to the jobs of motor vehicle servicing and commercial work. The former requires in *reading*: job cards, workshop manuals, visual display, micro records; *writing*: reporting faults; *speaking*: asking for guidance, asking for parts; *listening*: receiving instructions. The latter requires in *reading*: letter memoranda; *writing*: various types of business communication; *speaking*: telephone, reception work; *listening*: oral messages and receiving instructions. These are the language skills. In addition number skills for the professions are exemplified.[6]

The programme should be interdisciplinary in nature, avoiding subject learning and the confines of the classroom, and an endeavour should be made to incorporate in the programme some first-hand contact with the world through work experience; the teaching should be carried out as a team operation.[7]

Moreover, there was an emphasis on teaching for transfer:

> The students should first whenever they develop a particular capacity in a given context identify other contexts in which the capacity could be useful, be given practice at applying relevant aspects of previous learning to a new situation, identify any other activities at which they are likely to be successful on the evidence of this learning.[8]

---

[5]   FEU, 1982, p. 3.
[6]   *Ibid.*, p. 5.
[7]   *Ibid.*, p. 7.
[8]   *Ibid.*, p. 8.

Towards a Critique of the Basic Skills Project

Many educators have advanced criticism against the Basic Skills project. Ainley and some colleagues[9] note that the notion of skill in the
FEU programme has been transformed to cover such different kinds of
competencies that one cannot at all compare the procedures of teaching
them. Moreover, many of the listed skills cannot be divorced from their
contexts. Personal and transferable skills are neither personal, transferable nor skills; they are social and generic competencies.

> To present attitudes and habits detached from their cultural context as tech-
> nical abilities that can be acquired piecemeal in performance not only di-
> vorces them from the cultural context that gave them their original meaning
> but represents them as equally accessible to all students whatever their
> class-cultural background, gender or race. It ignores the fact that middle-
> class students already possess many of these competencies as a result of
> their previous education and family socialization.[10]

In *Skills and Vocationalism: The Easy Answer* Holt and others have
made a number of similar observations. I quote from Holt:

> The vocational solution to a complex and many-sided problem is not only
> wrong-headed, it is deeply dangerous. For it allows us to sidestep important
> questions about both education and training and about British industry. It is
> not just the fact that no connection has even been demonstrated between a
> particular form of curriculum and economic success; it is the error of shuf-
> fling off responsibility for our industrial weakness on to schools, when a
> moment's thought indicates that the root causes lie elsewhere.[11]

Among the roots of the problem Holt cites the following: the failure
of the politicians to develop a ministry for industrial and economic
planning; the conservative approach of banks in failing to offer long-
term loans; the social divisiveness of British society; and a "philistine
disregard" for the arts and the nature of design.

In the same volume Richard Smith writes an interesting article
"Teaching on Stilts: A Critique of Classroom Skills". He focuses in
particular on the profession of teacher and discusses skills in relation to
teaching. He asks: do we really want to have teachers who possess a
number of specific teaching skills and nothing more? Can one separate
skills from the person's general personality? He says:

> It is so obvious that personality and character are crucially important in
> teachers that the point would not be worth making were it not that too much

---

[9]   Ainley, 1990 and 1994; Ainley *et al.*, 1990.

[10]   Ainley, 1994, p. 80.

[11]   Holt, 1987, p. 1.

emphasis on skills is effectively a denial of it. We want teachers who are receptive, flexible, patient, willing to take risks, supportive of each other. These are qualities of persons, not skills to be brought into play when you enter the staffroom or classroom.[12]

Smith suggests that *virtues* rather than skills should be at the heart of our conception of a good teacher. Understanding, wisdom as well as courage and unselfishness are some of the virtues that we wish to see in teachers and members of other professions, according to Smith.

It is notable that the FEU itself in Basic Skills refers to an interview study of employers regarding what they value in young people to be employed in their businesses. The authors mention the following properties: versatility, initiative, pride in job, good personal relations, listen to instructions, wide viewpoint, seek work when slack, quality conscious, good time-keepers, ask questions, methodical and neat, report faults, remedy the problem. Many of these properties have to do with personality and virtue. They are hardly skills at all in the ordinary understanding of the word and they cannot easily be learnt in traditional training programmes.

On the other hand the FEU did not want to be traditional. It did not focus on skills in a traditional understanding. Therefore Ainley, Holt and Smith are not altogether fair to the FEU educators. Some of the aims of the FEU include understanding (in: understanding of society) flexibility (in: flexibility of attitude and willingness to learn) as well as the development of satisfactory relationships with others. The FEU did not talk about specific abilities but about more generic competencies. Perhaps the authors should have chosen the general term "competence" instead of "skill". The latter has more mundane connotations. "Competence" is perhaps broad enough to cover some of the virtues mentioned by Smith and the FEU itself.

But the critics certainly have a point when they say that one can hardly develop virtues in governmental schemes of education, however unconventional they are. A person develops virtues basically at home in the early days of his or her upbringing. On the other hand it does no harm, of course, if the vocational courses remind the students of the importance of basic virtues in working life. Some of the students may not have realized this and the vocational training might, if not develop, at least bring out some of the hidden properties of the student.

---

[12]   Smith, 1987, p. 50.

CHAPTER 5

Contemporary Approaches
to the Analysis of Learning
for Work Competence

Introduction

The British experiment with basic skills is only one of many developments in the area of learning for work. A rich literature has grown up in this area and a number of models for learning have appeared. Guile and Griffiths[1] present an illuminating summary of this development. They can demonstrate how the traditional "vertical" model of education, focusing on formal and abstract learning in traditional subjects, has gradually been transformed into a more "horizontal" model where learning within or at least close to a work place has come to the fore. Guile and Griffiths note how traditionally formal learning has taken precedence over other types of learning. Curricula in most schools have been organized through the dissemination of discipline-based knowledge. This was still largely the case in the FEU experiment in spite of its explicit claims to the contrary.

The work context has been largely forgotten in the traditional education. In former days the context was treated as a fairly stable environment that could be settled once and for all. Now it is becoming increasingly evident that the context, including the workplaces, is continuously changeable and is continuously influenced by the subjects themselves. Already John Dewey, the American pragmatist philosopher, in his classical works emphasized the changeable context of learning.

> Traditional education did not have to face this problem [the problem of a changing environment]; it could systematically dodge this responsibility. The school environment of desks, blackboards, a small school yard, was supposed to suffice. There was no demand that the teacher should become intimately acquainted with the conditions of the local community, physical, historical, economic, occupational, etc., in order to utilize them as educational resources.[2]

---

[1]   Guile and Griffiths, 2001.

[2]   Dewey, 1998 [1938], p. 36.

Thus, learning in a context involves an interactive relationship where the student gives and takes and where the changing context is as crucial as the traditional knowledge input in the learning process. In educational theory the term *situated learning*[3] has been launched to express this general idea.

Guile and Griffiths summarize their main points as follows:

> The prime purpose of work experience, from this perspective, would be to help students adjust themselves more successfully to the changing context of work through the opportunity to participate in different communities of practice. The idea of 'attunement' recognises that the development of any individual is affected by the task or activities which he or she is asked to undertake in a specific context and that the context, in turn, is also affected by their development.[4]

Guile and Griffiths themselves propose what they call a *connective* model for learning. This model involves incorporating ideas both from vertical and horizontal learning. The crucial element however is to take account of the influence of the context and in particular the organization of work on the student. This entails an emphasis on training the flexibility of the student and his or her ability to cross boundaries between contexts and workplaces. The students should also be encouraged to do creative work, to understand how their knowledge can be used for a multiple of purposes. This is similar to what the renowned Brazilian educationist Freire has proposed.[5]

Engeström as a promoter of *activity theory*, makes the elements of learning even more integrated:

> For activity theory contexts are neither containers nor situationally created experiential spaces. Contexts are activity systems. An activity system integrates the subject, the object and the instruments (material tools as well as signs and symbols) into a unified whole. An activity system incorporates both the object-oriented productive aspect and the person-oriented communicative aspect of the human conduct.[6]

The general project for Engeström and the activity theorists is to analyze and interpret data that record and describe human behaviour and discourse. Three principles guide this project. First, the unit of analysis is never a separate action of an individual. Instead the unit is a collective activity system such as the one contained in a hospital or a school.

---

[3]   Lave & Wenger, 1991.

[4]   Guile and Griffiths, 2001, p. 125.

[5]   Freire, 2005.

[6]   Engeström, 1993, p. 67.

Second, the activity system should be understood historically. Third, one should trace the inner contradictions of the activity system in order to understand disruptions, but also positive innovations and changes in the system as well as changes in the individuals themselves. Central concepts in activity theory are, apart from subject, object and tool, the concept of division of labour, including the vertical division of power and status, and the concepts of rules and convention. In particular the rules and conventions constitute the cement of the activity system. They define the system and hold it together. See my own analysis in Chapter 8.[7]

On Defining Competence in the Educational Context

Ellström[8] finds that the concepts of competence and qualification are often poorly defined in the literature and makes some conceptual proposals.[9] He makes a primary distinction between competence and qualification in the following way. "Competence is considered to be an attribute of the employee, that is, as a kind of human capital or human resource that can be translated into productivity".[10] Qualification, on the other hand, is defined as the skill requirements of a certain class of work tasks involved in a job. More specifically, Ellström says, the term "competence" is used to refer to the potential capacity of an individual (or a collective) to handle successfully (according to certain formal or informal criteria, set by oneself or by somebody else) certain situations or complete a certain task or job. This capacity may be defined in terms of:

- Perceptual motor skills (e.g. dexterity)
- Cognitive factors (different kinds of knowledge and intellectual skills)
- Affective factors (e.g. attitudes, values and motivation)
- Personality traits (e.g. self-confidence)
- Social skills (e.g. communicative and co-operative skills).[11]

Ellström characterizes the notion of *qualification* more fully as the competence that is objectively required given the character of the tasks of the profession in question and/or what is formally or informally

---

[7]   For further developments of activity theory in relation to cognitive functioning, see Rogoff and Lave, 1984.

[8]   Ellström, 1997.

[9]   Ellström here partly follows Tuomisto, 1986, and Masuch, 1974.

[10]   Ellström, 1997, p. 48.

[11]   *Ibid.*, p. 48.

required by the employer. The term qualification is therefore always related to a particular job. (See later in Chapter 11 that we need an even more inclusive notion of qualification. The point of view of the employer is crucial since it raises the question of loyalty and conformity as ingredients in a person's qualifications.)

Ellström proposes the following taxonomy for qualifications:

- Qualifications related to the task
  - Psychomotor qualifications
  - Cognitive qualifications
  - Knowledge (acquaintance, practical knowledge, theoretical knowledge, metacognitive knowledge)

    Intellectual skills (routine skills, rule-based skills, knowledge-based skills)

    Metacognitive skills (ability to plan and reflect over one's own thinking)
- Social qualifications (leadership and communication)
- Ideological and normative qualifications
  - Affective (attitudes, evaluations, motivation)
  - Personal (diligence, care, quickness and reliability)
- Qualification of development (ability to identify needs, to initiate and perform a development in a firm regarding quality, productivity and environment)[12]
- Qualification as competence in relation to job requirements is divided into:
  - The official demand for competence, for instance as a basis for the setting of wages
  - The competence actually required by the job.[13]

Ellström notes that the official demands for competence are affected by the demand for and supply of qualified people on the market. The officially prescribed competence requirements are often quite different from the actually required competencies. One of the reasons for this is that it is a demanding task to make a reasoned judgment of the actual needs.

It has been observed by other authors recently that the formally requested qualifications for a job can nowadays greatly supersede the

---

[12] Ellström, 1992.
[13] Ellström, 1997, pp. 49-51.

competencies actually utilized or needed to perform the tasks in the job. This has partly to do with the present level of education in Western countries. People tend to be grossly overqualified for their jobs and the formal requirements for jobs have consequently been raised. According to one study among Swedish professionals as many as 30% of the population consider themselves to be overqualified for their job.[14]

Ellström introduces a further notion of competence, namely competence-in use. By this he means the dynamic kind of competence that is a consequence of the competence initially brought to a job and the characteristics of the job. Both factors of the individual and factors related to the job may facilitate or limit the extent to which in respect the individual uses his or her actual competencies.[15]

It seems as if the notion of competence-in-use is conflating two things that should be kept separate. One is (and this I will consider more in Chapter 10 below) that the actual work done is a function of initial competence and work environment. The work is either facilitated or impeded. It is another matter that, as a result of the work process in a specific environment, the competence is also developing. After some time at a work place the worker's competence has also been changed, not necessarily in a positive direction.

---

[14] Svensson, 2002.
[15] Ellström, 1997, p. 51.

CHAPTER 6

Employability and Job Evaluation

Employability: Qualifications Necessary for Employment

The notion of employability has appeared in the scientific literature during the last 20 years. Indeed, it is central to the European Employment Strategy which was defined in the Presidency Conclusions at the European Council Meeting on Employment (Luxembourg, 20-21 November 1997). It constitutes one of the four lines of policy to be followed by the Member States with regard to employment, the others being: developing entrepreneurship, encouraging adaptability in businesses and their employees, and strengthening the policies for equal opportunities. With regard to employability the Member States should ensure that

> every unemployed young person is offered a new start before reaching six months of unemployment, in the form of training, retraining, work practice, a job or other employability measure;

> unemployed adults are also offered a fresh start before reaching twelve months of unemployment by one of the aforementioned means or, more generally, by accompanying individual vocational guidance;

> the number of persons benefiting from active measures to improve their employability will be increased. In order to increase the numbers of unemployed who are offered training or any similar measure, it will in particular fix a target, in the light of the starting situation, of gradually achieving the average of the three most successful Member States, and at least 20%.[1]

It may be noted that the chapter on improving employability is the only one in the Guidelines from the European Commission[2] that contains quantitative targets to be reached by the Member States.

The main rationale of the employability approach is easy to trace. There is no longer secure employment for the European workforce. There is a continual need for adaptation of work, working conditions and competencies in the enterprises. The workers must be given the

---

[1] Gazier, 1999, p. 11.

[2] Guidelines from the European Commission, 1998.

51

opportunity to follow and adapt to these changes. The instruction from the European Commission is thus that the European governments shall pursue and support employability security. Hence the concept of employability has developed into a cornerstone of labour market policies and employment strategies.

The notion of employability is clearly related to that of work ability but it is different from it in the following relevant respects. Employability covers much more than individual ability. It includes various conditions that a person must meet on the labour market *other than possessing certain competencies.* Moreover, the notion is normally not tied to a specific job but to the labour market as a whole.

Gazier who has made a significant analysis of the notion of employability, traces an evolution of the concept from the early 20th century until the present. The earliest definition of the concept (in the UK and the USA) was a dichotomic one. People were considered as either employable or unemployable. Thus, employable is a person who is able and willing to work in a regular manner. The main concern here was to eliminate the "casual, undisciplined and unstable would-be-workers, or non-motivated poors, from becoming falsely employed and staying on the rolls".[3]

From these early days Gazier traces no less than six further definitions of employability each of which mirrors changes in the world market and changes in demands on the workforce. Two of these concepts are extensions of the first one. The "socio-medical concept of employability" emerged after the 1950s and was designed to handle rehabilitation of physically or mentally retarded persons. This kind of employability is defined as the distance between existing work abilities and specified work requirements. Thus employability can be a matter of degree and not just a question of either/or. The second definition, called "manpower policy employability"; includes further disadvantaged groups including welfare recipients, drop-outs, racial minorities and the poor in general.

Estes designed an employability scale within the framework of this definition of employability. He divides his Employability Assessment Scale, containing 50 items into 12 categories.[4]

1. years of education
2. language difficulties
3. health limitations

---

[3]   Gazier, 1999, p. 39; see also Philpott, 1998.
[4]   Estes, 1974.

4. legal barriers (driver's licence, conviction record, citizenship)
5. military status
6. age
7. motivation (belief in a work ethic, net earning capacity after job-related expenditures, cultural background, self-conception, work-shift preference, time on aid, ability to defer gratification, degree of perceived economic responsibility)
8. previous work history (years of employment, turnover rate, recency of employment, reasons for termination, availability and acceptability of experience, skills level, work habits)
9. transportation (public or private)
10. childcare needs
11. job market factors (unemployment rate in the skill area, seasonality and availability of jobs, union requirements, government job   subsidies, wage requirements, either excessive or competitive)
12. miscellaneous (discrimination problems, appearance (dress, grooming, physical attractiveness), housing problems, job hunting skills).

Each item can be graded along a scale of low, moderate or high, and the total sum gives the overall employability level. This scheme is in many ways comprehensive. It covers several items not noted above in the medico-legal context or in the educational context. Many of these items refer to formal qualifications, such as years of education and military status. In fact, only a minority of the items here refer to actual competencies (or incapacities) of the individual. Exceptions are language difficulties, net earning capacity and skills level. The references to competencies are mostly indirect. Among these indirect references are: years of education, health limitations, self-conception, time on aid and years of employment. It can be observed that motivation is given a high priority. The relationship of employability to the labour market comes out in the item: unemployment rate in the skill area.

I wish to mention three further concepts of employability which have come to the fore in the contemporary discussion. These are "labour market performance employability", "initiative employability" and "interactive employability".

The labour market performance employability was put forward internationally, says Gazier, during the 1970s. It is described as the future labour market outcome for a specified individual or group during a specified period, expressed in probability terms using some statistical model. In this version employability comes close to the notion of human capital, where the latter is understood as the individual productive ability as evaluated on the labour market. The initiative employability, on the other hand, can be defined as "the marketability of cumulative individual skills". This notion, says Gazier, includes not only human capital but also social capital, including reputation, informal ties and network connections.[5]

The interactive employability, finally, maintains the idea of individual initiative but it focuses on the disadvantaged persons and includes interactions between agents on the market. The Canadian Labour Force Development Board has expressed this idea in the following concise definition:

> Employability is the relative capacity of an individual to achieve meaningful employment given the interaction of personal circumstances and the labour market.[6]

In the same spirit the Confederation of British Industry (CBI) has defined employability thus:

> Employability is the possession by an individual of the qualities and competencies required to meet the changing needs of employers and customers and thereby help to realise his or her aspirations and potential in work.[7]

Here it is strongly emphasized how much one's possibility of getting a job is also dependent on the employability of other people. The employability of the individual at a particular moment is not only a function of his or her personal qualifications and the needs of employers. It is relative to the number of employable, not least the number of excellent, other job seekers. It is moreover relative to the opportunities, rules and institutions that govern the labour market.

Job Evaluation: the Criteria of Excellence

A further context where the issue of work ability is highlighted is that of profession evaluation. This kind of evaluation entails determining what competencies are necessary for fulfilling the tasks entailed by the professional jobs. These competencies are assessed on a scale of excellence for the purpose of comparison with other professions. One reason for making such assessments is to have an instrument for the setting of adequate wages for the members of the profession in question. This idea has been particularly encouraged by the trade unions in Swe-

---

[5] Gazier, 1999, p. 47.

[6] The Canadian Labour Force Development Board, 1994, p. viii.

[7] CBI, 1999, p. 1, cited and commented on in McQuaid *et al.*, 2005, p. 199.

den. An instrument for the purpose (the HAC model of qualifications) has been created by Andersson and Harriman.[8] The instrument was central in a comprehensive study of job evaluation by Rosenberg.[9]

The model for job analysis contains the following factors:

Knowledge and skills
    Education

    Ability for further learning

    Physical skills

    Intellectual skills (including problem solving, decision-making and strategic competence)

    Social skills (including empathy and cultural understanding)

Responsibility for
    Material objects

    Management

    People

    Planning, development, results

Exertion
    Physical

    Mental

Environment and risk
    Physical environment

    Risk of injury and disease.

The idea is that all occupations are in principle analysable along all these dimensions and that they can be weighed according to a scale from 1 to 5, where 5 refers to the most advanced degree. As an example Andersson and Harriman compare the occupation of assistant nurse with that of principal of a primary school. The assistant nurse scores 1 and the principal 4 on the scale of education, but the positions are the reverse with regard to physical skills. The assistant nurse scores 3 on the scale of responsibility for people, the principal 4 on the same scale. Concerning physical exertion the nurse gets 4 points and the principal 1. Altogether, all scores counted, the assistant nurse gets 32 points and the principal 45.

In a qualitative evaluation of the two professions it is said that the job of assistant nurse has its emphasis on physical and social skills. The

---

[8]   Andersson and Harriman, 1999.

[9]   Rosenberg, 2004.

main responsibility concerns people. It is both physically and mentally a heavy job. The physical environment is quite unpleasant and there is a great risk of being injured in doing the job. The principal, on the other hand, has to meet high requirements in general in the dimension knowledge and skills, with the exception of physical skills. Also the responsibility is comprehensive and covers several domains.

It is evident that the HAC list of competencies is more comprehensive than all the capacity lists used in the context of social insurance (with the possible exception of DOA, see Appendix 1). The categories of empathy, cultural understanding and responsibility are virtually non-existent in the social insurance case. They are included but not equally emphasized on the educational lists. It may be observed that the HAC model also comprises some environmental factors and not exclusively competencies.

CHAPTER 7

A Theoretical Analysis
of Work Content: Anselm Strauss

In their *Social Organization of Medical Work* Strauss *et al.* make a detailed investigation into the nature of medical work and attempt to trace a multitude of aspects of work, some of which are almost never noted in traditional descriptions of occupations or in pragmatic measures of work ability.

> We bring a sociological perspective to bear on the [questions of work]. Our perspective has been shaped by many years of observation in hospitals, these in turn preceding the four-year observational and interview study on which this book is based. The research reported on here was done on many different types of ward, in seven hospitals in the Bay Area of San Fransisco.[1]

The book deals with all kinds of medical work and all kinds of professions directly having to do with such work. Some professions come out more clearly than others in their analysis. The doctors are prominent, but so also are the nurses and the technical personnel. Much attention is paid to the high technology of modern medicine.

The medical scene described in the book is contemporary medicine, corresponding to the period 1946-85 in the USA. The disease panorama has by then already changed to chronic illness. Among the prominent characteristics of chronic illnesses are that they: 1. are long term, 2. are uncertain, 3. require large efforts at palliation, 4. tend to be multiple diseases, 5. are intrusive upon the lives of the ill and their families, 6. require a wide variety of ancillary services, 7. imply conflicts of interpretation and authority among patients, health-care staff and funding agents, 8. mainly require primary care and 9. are expensive to treat and manage.[2]

The authors observe that increased technological specialization and the complex bureaucratic health structures together have resulted in two crucial developments: first the fragmentation of chronic care, with

---

[1]   Strauss *et al.*, 1985, p. ix.

[2]   *Ibid.*, p. 2.

increasing possibilities that continuity of care will go awry, accompanied by accusatory cries of dehumanization; second the incorporation of new *workers* and roles to remedy the effects of fragmented care and dehumanization.

A distinction is drawn between a *course of illness* and an *illness trajectory.* "Trajectory" is a term used here to refer not only to the physiological unfolding of a patient's disease but also to the total organization of work done during the course of this unfolding. The complexities of trajectory work are added to by the new specialists (medical, nursing and technical) who are working on the patient's illness and having to relate to each other and to each other's work.[3]

One thing that is very significant for medical work, Strauss *et al.* say, is that it is work *on* as well as *together with* acting people. The patient can react and thus greatly affect the work, sometimes negatively, but the patient can also participate and ameliorate.

Strauss *et al.* distinguish between several types of work, some of which are crucially dependent on the fact that the objects of the work are human beings. The main categories are:

- Machine work
- Safety work
- Comfort work (where this includes consciousness of risks in relation to pain and suffering)
- Sentimental work
- Articulation work (monitoring, coordinating).

Other types considered less extensively are: error work, body work, information work and negotiative work.

Machine work involves monitoring machines and other equipment used in the medical work. This monitoring concerns safety, accuracy and efficiency. First, there is the monitoring of trajectory stabilization and change. Second, if the negative changes are drastic, then clinical safety is at stake and that is being monitored. Third, there may be monitoring along at least two other dimensions, neither strictly medical although each may greatly affect the medical course. One concerns the patient's comfort and the other the patient's "psychology" as affected by the machines and their operations.[4]

Safety work has already been mentioned under the category of machine work. There is, however, safety work outside the monitoring of

---

[3]   Strauss *et al.*, 1985, p. 8.

[4]   *Ibid.*, p. 61.

machines. Strauss *et al.* make a distinction between the notions of *danger* and *risk*. The former concept relates to the hazards of the illness itself, the fact that the illness might lead to grave disability or even death. By risk Strauss *et al.* mean the potential negative consequences of using technology and drugs. The authors also point to the possibility that the organization of health care may negatively affect the trajectory of illness.[5]

Comfort work. Under this heading the authors include the work done to eliminate or reduce the patient's symptoms (in particular pain and suffering) as well as such pain and suffering as can be the result of surgery or other treatments. Here one finds both the administration of pain-killing drugs and what the authors call soft comfort work, including the commonsensical and crucial holding of the patient's hand to sophisticated psychological techniques. The authors note that the workflow of the departments tends to complicate the amount and effectiveness of comfort work and that the hospital can be untidy, dirty and noisy.[6]

Sentimental work, which is the most original category of work introduced by Strauss *et al.*, has connections to comfort work and may partly involve similar techniques. However, sentimental work does not include direct intervention regarding symptoms of illnesses nor particularly with the alleviation of suffering directly caused by treatment. Like comfort work, sentimental work is, however, crucially dependent on the fact that *the object worked on is a human being who is alive, sentient and reacting.* The category of sentimental work can itself be divided into:

- Interactional work and moral rules
- Trust work
- Composure work
- Biographical work
- Identity work
- Awareness context work
- Rectification work.

The category of Interactional work focuses on the basic ethical constraints in medical work. The brutal doctor and nurse (or other medical worker) who refuse to give information to a patient do not fulfil their duties as professionals and thereby fail to do the proper interactional work. Composure work also has an ethical component. Many procedures and machines may expose clients to potential loss of composure

---

[5]   Strauss *et al.*, 1985, p. 71.

[6]   *Ibid.*, p. 107.

(for instance, loss of face and of self-control). The composure work is intended to prevent this.[7]

Biographical work includes, apart from anamnesis, the giving and receiving of biographical information. The ordinary diagnostic interview is an instance of biographical work that is always done but it does not necessarily concern the sentimental work aspects. However, consider a cancer case where the doctor needs to know a great deal about the patient's pattern of living in order to give proper advice regarding the patient's future life choices. Nurses continuously do biographical work, i.e. they try to get to know the patient better in order to help them and make interaction smoother.

Identity work entails working with the patient on matters of personal identity in order to keep his or her spirits up. It also involves helping the less gravely ill persons to face the realities of their physical conditions.

Awareness context work is the work done whenever members of staff withhold information which they believe will be difficult for the sick person to handle. Rectification work, finally, entails making apologetic or caustic remarks about the brusqueness, inconsiderateness or callousness of the offending staff member.[8]

Sentimental work is often invisible and quite rarely made explicit. There is no textbook about it. However, Strauss *et al.* note that there are institutional forms that permit or even encourage exchanges of information about recently performed sentimental tasks. There are, for instance, staff meetings and briefing sessions at which nurses exchange information about the conditions of various patients on the ward.

An important condition relating to the invisibility of patients' own sentimental work or that of their kin, is that the staff quite literally do not see this work. Articulation work involves managing and shaping a trajectory of illness. This kind of work has three levels:

- The doctor or head nurse makes an overview and plans the work
- The technical expert handles the necessary machines
- Different professionals perform the actual task coordination.[9]

Many of the different kinds of work support each other. Some are even preconditions of each other. However, it is clear that the different kinds of work can also interfere negatively with each other. Often the comfort and sentimental work has to be withdrawn in favour of some of

---

[7]   Strauss *et al.*, 1985, p. 136.

[8]   *Ibid.*, pp. 137-140.

[9]   *Ibid.*, pp. 143-151.

the necessary or allegedly necessary technical work. A number of conditions affecting medical production mitigate against its rationalization (competition between patients, unanticipated behavioural responses, the hospital's organization, and interaction between the various types of work).[10]

To all this is added patients' work. First, some of the patients' work is the mirror image of the staff's work: patients give urine, the staff take away the urine and send it to the lab. Second, some work is complementary to staff's work, such as maintaining composure in the face of procedural tasks. Third, work by patients may substitute for work that staff did not do but either were supposed to do or patients believe they were supposed to do. Fourth, patients do work that they believe is necessary, like monitoring for potential danger. Fifth, patients may rectify staff errors. This work quite often disrupts and changes the staff's plans and operations. Sixth, patients do the work that the staff cannot possibly do (for instance, giving information about allergy to certain drugs). Seventh, patients may engage in work that is outside the range of what staff may conceive of as the locus of their own work (for instance, deep identity problems).

Strauss *et al.* also highlight in an interesting way the work that is dirty in different senses of the word (physically dirty but also trivial, dishonourable, morally shameful, and discrediting work). Some work is dangerous. Other work is boring and unchallenging. Some work has low status, including what the hospital workers do when "they perform the lowly tasks without being recognized". This is similar to the case where the lawyer handles the less respectable legal problems of his or her clients.[11]

---

[10] Strauss *et al.*, 1985, p. 179.

[11] *Ibid.*, pp. 246-248.

PART II

AN ACTION-THEORETIC APPROACH
TO WORK ABILITY

CHAPTER 8

Some Action-Theoretic Preliminaries

General Remarks on the Contemporary Attempts to Characterize Work Ability

The characterizations of work ability and work content presented in these contemporary works are very diverse. They are diverse partly, but not only, because of their different purposes. The lists of abilities set forth in the medico-legal context, as well as in the psychological context, tend to be limited, mainly to physical and more technical capacities. It is evidently assumed that these limited lists are sufficient for the purpose of the enterprise. However, it is not at all clear that the authors of the classifications are right here. When one studies the notions of competence and qualification from the point of view of learning and development a further range of abilities comes to the fore. And more saliently, when one makes a meticulous analysis of what a job really entails, such as is the case in the work of Strauss *et al.*, the list of abilities will become even longer and encompass, for instance, a great variety of "sentimental" abilities. In my own analysis I will attempt to take account of the whole range of abilities and also add a number of further qualifications outside the ability sector.

In this chapter I will lay a general philosophical foundation for the study of human work ability as well as the study of other internal and external conditions for the performance of work. I will here include a variety of contexts, including the preparation for entering an occupation or a profession (education), seeking and getting a job, i.e. winning a competition for a job, keeping a job, i.e. fulfilling the tasks included in a job, temporarily leaving a job because of illness or injury, being rehabilitated to a job and having one's job evaluated in a comparison with other occupations or professions. My basic analysis will be general and cover human action in general. I will later turn to the specific aspects related to work ability.

The Complexity of Actions

Human beings are at least sometimes rational agents who plan their lives. They may even make fairly long-term plans entailing sequences of actions in order to reach a goal. Suppose that we have a person who wishes to take a university degree. In order to reach this goal the agent has to take examinations in a number of subjects, say politics, economics and philosophy. Thus the person must first read politics, then economics and then philosophy. This preliminary division can then be made more fine-grained. Studying politics may entail reading a certain number of books and writing a certain number of papers. This in its turn can be further divided into simpler actions and action-sequences.

In a way we can then say that we have a hierarchy of actions. On the top of the hierarchy we have the grand action of taking a university degree. Below that we have the actions of studying politics, economics and philosophy. Below these in their turn we have a further set of actions. This hierarchical relation is in ordinary language often indicated by two kinds of locution. The choice of one or the other depends on the perspective from which one looks upon the relation. If we look upon it from the perspective of the agents when they initiate the action-sequence we use the locution "in order to". The agents read books in economics in order to take an examination in economics. They take this examination in order to complete their degrees. The locution "in order to" indicates that the agent has more than one intention in performing his or her action.

But if we look upon the hierarchy from the perspective of the completed action we can use the locution "by doing". The agent completes his or her degree *by* taking an examination in economics. He or she passes the examination in economics by studying hard, etc. At the end of this hierarchy we reach a simple bodily movement or a sequence of movements. At this stage we cannot pursue the analysis further in action terms. When I lift my hand I do not do so by doing anything else. I just lift my hand. Such an action will in the following be called a *basic action*. (Basic actions can also be constituted of mental actions and omissions.)

Two fundamental mechanisms exist by means of which we can construct hierarchies of actions. One mechanism entails making sequences of actions, i.e. performing one action after another. The other mechanism entails the use of the external world and its causal and conventional machinery. The American philosopher Alvin Goldman[1] has coined the term "action-generation" for this mechanism. In the latter construction of a hierarchy of actions there is in fact only one *basic action* needed, namely one intentional bodily movement. The rest is produced by the environment. I will explain this phenomenon.

---

[1] Goldman, 1969.

Consider the following example. John starts the car by turning a key in the ignition. John turns the key by turning his hand rightwards. In this case we have only one basic action, viz. one intentional bodily movement. But at the same time at least two other actions are performed, the turning of the key and the starting of the car. Through the bodily movement a part of the external world is changed and a causal chain has been initiated. When the key is moved in the ignition the electrical circuit is closed, which has as its effect that the engine of the car starts. The basic action in question has *generated* two other actions.[2]

The mechanism behind the generation in my example was causal. The hand movement caused a number of subsequent states of affairs. This kind of generation is typical. This is what is involved in all actions that entail the creation of a new state of affairs in the physical world. However, causation – at least as understood physically – is not the only mechanism of generation available. It is also possible top speak of *conventional* generation. By this is meant the case where, for instance, a person by writing his or her name according to conventional rules can create a great number of different other actions, such as establishing a contract, opening a bank account or buying a house. In such a case there is also just one basic action involved, the movement of one's hand in writing. The rest is realized through the external "conventional" world.

The series of actions that come into being through action-generation will in the following be called *action chains*, as distinguished from *action sequences*. Action chains, where the whole chain is intentional, that is, that agent intends the final result to come into being, are called *accomplishments*. Action sequences, which are in a similar way intentional, are called *projects*. A good example of an action-sequence which is a project can be taken from our study-example. In reading one book after another in economics, the person performs a multitude of basic actions: picking up the first book, sitting down, reading page one, turning to page two, reading page two etc. It is typical that action-sequences require a long time to reach the final goal, in this case the degree.

Most action-sequences also involve action-chains. Many of the elements in an action-sequence involve the manipulation of the external world in one way or the other. Picking up a book, for instance, is not, strictly speaking, a basic action. The basic action involved is lifting one's hand. This means that most action-sequences are complex in two ways.

---

[2] For a detailed account of the notion of action generation see Goldman, 1969.

A Hierarchy of Actions for the Field of Rehabilitation: C. F. Vreede

The Dutch physiotherapist and philosopher C. F. Vreede[3] has devised a conceptual system designed to take care of some of the intuitions characterized above. He proposes a hierarchical structure called *DL* for daily living. There are three levels in this structure. On the lowest level is *ODL* (operations for daily living). On the next level is *ADL* (activities of daily living) and on top is *IDL* (ideas of daily living)

ODL denotes the physical or mental functional operations and appearances applied in *ADL*, insofar as they can be performed or experienced consciously. In practice consciousness need not, however, always be present. Examples of *ODL* are: bending one's knees, moving one's hands, and staring. There is a clear affinity between *ODL* and basic actions.

ADL denotes the actual intentional activities usual to an individual or group of individuals. For example: throwing at a target, walking to a place, concentrating on a subject.

IDL denotes the pursuits which subsume a value or common social purpose, in so far as they can be described concretely and can therefore be analysed in terms of *ADL*. For example: being a market vendor, playing marbles, dressing up in order to impress, listening to music.

This three-tiered concept of usual operations, activities and pursuits constitutes a hierarchical system. An *ADL* cannot be performed unless the required *ODL* are available, and will not be performed unless it forms part of an *IDL*. Moreover, *ODL*, *ADL* and *IDL* form a set of subsystems of increasing complexity, for an *IDL* always comprises several *ADL*, and an *ADL* in its turn comprises several *ODL*.

There is an obvious parallel here between on the one hand *IDL*, *ADL* and *ODL*, and on the other hand generated actions and basic actions. An *IDL* is performed by the performance of one or more *ADL* and the latter in its turn is performed by the performance of one or more *ODL*. Vreede does not, however, make my distinction between action-chains and action-sequences. Another difference is that Vreede restricts the notion of intention to the *ADL* level, whereas intention is present on all levels in my account.

A more crucial difference between Vreede's system and my own is that for Vreede all levels must in principle always be present. When somebody is engaged in an activity there is always some idea, i.e. an

---

[3]   Vreede, 1993.

IDL, some intention, i.e. an *ADL*, and some operation, i.e. an *ODL*. There is no free-floating *ODL*, for instance. A bodily movement is an *ODL*, according to Vreede, only within a complete *DL* context.

Conditions for Action[4]

There are a multitude of conditions that have to exist for an action to be realized. Apart from a bodily movement, a mental action, or an omission, there are many aspects of the external world that must be in order. The external world must provide the *opportunity* for the action to take place. And for the necessary bodily movement or mental action to occur the person must have the *ability* to perform it. For some conventional actions there is a further requirement. In order to perform certain institutional acts the agent must also be endowed with an *authority*. Only an authorized judge can sentence a criminal; and only a priest (or equivalent person) can marry a couple. The "can" here does not mean "is allowed to". It is a substantial "can" in the sense that unauthorized persons will not succeed in creating the desired results. The criminal will not be sentenced and the couple will not become married if unauthorized persons attempt to perform the actions in question.

When a person has both ability, opportunity and in special cases authority to perform an action, then we shall say that there is a *practical possibility* of this person's performing the action in question. Practical possibility is the strongest form of ability. If, for instance, John has the practical possibility of driving his car and tries to do so, then John will succeed in driving his car. Trying could then be used as a test for practical possibility.

I shall in the following focus on the notions of ability and opportunity and their interrelations. Abilities and opportunities are concepts that indicate *dimensions*. One can have more or less of an ability, and an opportunity can be more or less adequate. John can be a good driver or a bad driver, meaning that he has more or less of the ability to drive. A particular tennis court may provide a good opportunity to play tennis this year; last year, however, it was in poor condition and provided a bad opportunity.

Ability and opportunity are concepts that are logically interrelated in the following strong sense: when John is said to be able to drive his car, then this is so given a particular set of circumstances. John may be able to drive his car when the traffic is normal. He may, however, be unable to do so when there is a traffic jam. And, conversely, to take another

---

[4]   This whole section is a summary of my analysis in Nordenfelt, 2000, pp. 65-74.

example, when Sara is said to have an opportunity to play tennis, then this is so given a particular internal set-up in her case. The tennis court provides an opportunity to play tennis for Sara now that she is well-trained. Last year, however, when she knew nothing about tennis, the court would not give her any opportunity to play.

Thus there is no such thing as ability in isolation. And there is no such thing as an opportunity in isolation. A person's ability must be judged in the light of a certain set of circumstances. And a person's opportunity must be judged in the light of a certain set of conditions internal to his or her body or mind.

But if ability and opportunity are in this way related to each other, what sense can we give to the idea of enabling a person to do something? In ordinary discourse we say that it is the duty of the health care personnel to try to restore the person's ability to walk or to read. And normally we do not add anything about circumstances. Indeed, most of our ability talk is in absolute terms. We say about our fellow human beings that they can walk, drive cars, speak certain languages etc. Strictly speaking, this must be elliptic talk. There cannot be any absolute abilities of these kinds. So what do we mean when we ascribe *abilities simpliciter* to people?

We can discern two important interpretations of this mode of speech. They are not rival candidates. I think it is clear that in some cases one interpretation is the true one. In other cases the other interpretation is probably correct. According to the first interpretation, a person is said to have ability, given that *standard circumstances* obtain. According to the second interpretation, he or she is said to have this ability, given that *reasonable circumstances* obtain. Let me comment on both alternatives.

In most cases when I claim that John is able to walk, I mean that this is so, given that there is nothing unusual that would prevent the execution of his action. The weather should not be extremely bad, the ground should not be extremely rough, and there should be no direct obstacles preventing him from walking. Given the way the world normally is – and in particular the way John's immediate surroundings normally are – John is able to walk.

Situations occur when the idea of standard circumstances fails to account for our talk about ability. Consider the following case of a school-teacher in Iraq. He has been well-trained for his profession, he has a good talent for teaching and we would certainly describe him as a good teacher, i.e. able to teach young pupils. However, Iraq is a country that has for a long time been deprived of most reasonable opportunities. Most schools have been closed and there have been few if any possibilities of providing regular teaching. This has also meant that our school-teacher has not been able to teach.

This situation of deprivation has for some time been the standard situation in Iraq. Hence the school-teacher is unable, given standard circumstances, to teach. This is a strict application of the first interpretation. But certainly, we would say that he is capable of teaching. We must then have made a different presupposition. We must mean that he is able to teach, given *reasonable* circumstances.

There is an alternative interpretation. The term "standard" need not be limited to a particular time and a particular region. If "standard" is taken to refer to the global community, then the school-teacher must be said to be able to teach. He would succeed in teaching in most other countries. The situation in Iraq is non-standard. The distinction between standard and reasonable may nevertheless be important. There could be several contexts where we would call a particular circumstance standard while it is clearly not the statistically most common circumstance from a global point of view. For instance, much technological equipment exists which is standard in the prosperous world. We who live there take this standard for granted and judge the abilities of our fellow human beings from this point of view. Most of us in the rich world would fail to manage life without this equipment. We would be unable to live given the statistically most common circumstances. We are able to live, however, given what we consider to be reasonable circumstances, which are often deemed to be standard in the rich world.

The analysis of such factors as are needed for the success of actions can be made in a more detailed way than the notions of ability, opportunity, authority and competence allow. Moreover, given a classification of actions into *simple* and more *complex* ones, we can look at the differences between the numbers and types of factors needed for the various kinds of actions. In this section I will pursue this analysis in a more systematic way.

Consider now the conditions for a person's practical possibility of acting. These conditions differ, of course, depending on the type of action and whether we are talking about ability or opportunity. I shall first discuss conditions for *ability* and such conditions as hold for all kinds of action, in particular for *basic actions*.

I will first take into account the fact that actions are intended. A general ability to perform an action thus presupposes an ability to form the intention to perform the action in question. This indicates that certain mental preparation is necessary for a person to act. It is impossible for a person to intend to perform an action if he or she is completely unaware of the action in question. This kind of situation is not so common with basic actions as with many generated actions. (See the discussion below.) Still, the point is also relevant for basic actions. People are not aware of all the possible movements they can make with their limbs. Hence there are certain movements they will never intend to make.

Also, there are mental factors that may prevent a person from performing a particular action. The person may find an action so revolting that he or she would never intend to perform it. This again is more common with certain complex actions; most unethical actions, for instance, are complex actions. A further interesting case of mental prevention is the one where an agent is continually convinced that he or she is not physically able to perform the action in question. If this is so the agent will never form the intention to perform it. Another case is the one where the subject lacks the courage to perform the action.

Thus factors such as ignorance about an action, revulsion against it, lack of courage, or conviction of one's physical incapacity, will prevent the realization of the first stage of action, intending to act and setting about acting. These factors, which are not universally acknowledged in the context of ability, are of particular importance for the theory of health. Many types of mental diseases can be located in defects among the antecedents of intending. (I will return later in the context of work ability to the importance of one's perception of one's ability or inability regarding the actual performance of relevant actions.)

For the realization of the second stage of action, its actual performance and success, there are certain obvious requirements. When it comes to basic actions these requirements all concern the biological make-up of the agent. This make-up can be divided into various aspects. One is that the agent must not be paralyzed. Other aspects involve such things as that the muscle tissues be sufficiently developed and the joints function properly. Further factors have to do with the person's strength and perseverance. If the subject is very tired he or she may not succeed in performing even a basic action.

The condition of opportunity is easy to characterize in the case of basic actions. Here opportunity consists merely in the non-existence of external preventive factors. For instance, Sara has the opportunity to raise her hand if nothing physically prevents her doing so.

These, then, are the background conditions for the practical possibility of performing a basic action. Consider now a complex action. By definition, the performance of a complex action requires the performance of some basic action. A second requirement is that the complex action can *in fact* be generated, i.e. that the generating mechanism is in order. A third requirement is that the agent knows that there is a situation that constitutes the opportunity to generate the complex action in question. This entails either that the person has some causal knowledge, i.e. knows what happens, given a particular basic action in a particular situation, or that he or she has some conventional knowledge, i.e. knows of a particular action-generating rule and what it says about the required circumstances. (In some cases both kinds of knowledge may be presupposed.)

I will now collect these requirements (together with the ones noted above) into one schema. The following symbols will be used: A for an agent, *Acc* for accomplishment (action chain), *Pro* for project, B for basic action, and O for opportunity.

It is practically possible for A to perform an accomplishment *Acc* if, and only if,

(i) an action-chain, $B \rightarrow Acc$, given an opportunity O, is performed;

(ii) A believes that (i), feels no revulsion against performing *Acc*, and believes that he or she is physically able, given the circumstances, to perform *Acc*;

(iii) it is practically possible for A to perform B;

(iv) O is present;

(v) A identifies O.

I will now turn to the other kind of complex actions called *projects* (action sequences). The practical possibility of carrying out a project must involve the practical possibility of performing each action that is a member of some action-sequence constituting the project. (As I have said, there are often alternative ways of carrying out the project.) But the practical possibility of performing each member of a set of accomplishments does not suffice for the performance of the project. Again the agent must have a considerable amount of knowledge. I can summarize the items that he or she must know:

(i) The person must be aware of at least one action-sequence constituting the project.

(ii) The person must know what constitutes the opportunity for all members of this sequence.

(iii) The person must know how these opportunities are to be identified.

A further important element in the performance of some projects is the element of *coordination*. It is sometimes required that one can not only perform each of the basic actions or accomplishments involved in the project, but also coordinate them into a sequence with special properties (for instance, properties of time, force or elegance). For instance, to produce a melody it is clearly not enough to produce the right notes, one at a time. The components of the melody must be coordinated in a particular way for the result to be music.

I will express the requirements for carrying out a project in the proposed formal manner:

It is practically possible for *A* to carry out the project *Pro* if, and only if,

(i) an action-sequence *S*: *Acc*1 → *Acc*n constituting *Pro* is performed;

(ii) *A* believes that (i), feels no revulsion against carrying out *Pro* and believes that he or she is physically able, given the circumstances, to perform *Pro*;

(iii) it is practically possible for *A* to perform each of *Acc*1... *Acc*n, given their respective opportunities;

(iv) *A* is able to coordinate each of *Acc*1... *Acc*n in the appropriate way;

(v) the required opportunities actually arise;

and

(vi) *A* identifies these opportunities.

The Usefulness of this Analysis for the Case of Work Ability

What is the practical use of this exercise? One crucial point is that when we have the various conditions for ability we can then see in what various ways an action can go wrong. We can see that an action can fail to materialize because of a lack of opportunity, because of the subject's lack of understanding of the situation or because the subject dislikes the activity in question. To this can be added the subject's inability to perform the bodily movement or coordinate the bodily movements that are necessary for the completion of the action. (Several of these observations, in particular the ones concerning environmental factors, have also been made in the International Classification of Functioning, Disability and Health (ICF), see above in Chapter 1.)

Such observations are in their turn crucial for the rehabilitator. This person can then spot the adequate element in the chain that has gone wrong. But a further interesting observation is the following. A complex action can be generated in multiple ways. One can travel to a place in many ways. One can perhaps go by ship, by air, by train or by car. This is the case for the journey between Stockholm and Helsinki, for instance. Assume that there is a strike shutting down the airport. One of the modes of communication has thereby been broken. But the others still exist and the journey can be realized. Or consider an example from working life. A postman is used to delivering the post by bicycle. Suppose he injures one of his legs so severely that this way of transportation becomes impossible. The postman is thereby severely disabled with regard to his main occupational role. The traditional procedure of rehabilitation is the medical one, viz. trying to heal the injury and restore the postman's strength in his leg. But given our analysis there is a further way. One can try to find another basic action that can generate the desired complex action of delivering the post. In this case it is easy to see an alternative, viz. using a car.

On First- and Second-Order Ability

We may talk of ability of different orders. I will here distinguish between first- and second-order ability. So far, both my discussion and my characterizations have concerned first-order ability only. The notion of second-order ability will be defined as follows:

> Sara has a second-order ability with regard to an action if, and only if, Sara has the first-order ability to pursue a training programme after the completion of which she will have the first-order ability to perform the action in question.

Second-order *ability* is thus compatible with first-order *disability*, while the reverse does not hold. Sara may lack the first-order ability to earn her living in Sweden. She may, however, have the second-order ability to do so. She may be able to train to make a good living in that country.

Aristotle in fact notes the same kind of distinction by distinguishing between potentialities and actualities, as well as between different kinds of actualities.[5] What I here call a second-order ability can be actualized in two steps. First, the second-order ability can, through training, become a first-order ability. This is the first actualization. Then, the first-order ability can be actualized through action. This is the second actualization.

Note that the action of *training* must be given the same analysis as other kinds of action. When we ascribe to someone the first-order ability to follow a particular training programme, we must, as in the general case above, presuppose a set of standard or reasonable circumstances. We must moreover presuppose that it persists throughout the training process. Thus, a person who enters on a training programme, but in the end fails to acquire the desired first-order ability, need not lack second-

---

[5]   Aristotle, 1908, Book Д. 12.

order ability. First, the training programme may have been poor. This might indicate that the accepted circumstances did not obtain. Second, the subject may, after a while, no longer have intended to pursue the training in a proper way. This being so is still consistent with his or her having the second-order ability. Second-order ability may not turn into first-order ability if the agent does not consistently try to acquire the first-order ability.

Consider now the following case. Some subjects are afforded adequate training facilities, and they try to learn through the whole period designated for training. Nevertheless, after this period they still do not know how to perform the desired action. This indicates that the subjects do not have the second-order ability, at least not through the whole period of training, to perform the action. We could then say that they are *genuinely disabled* with respect to performing the action in question.

To summarize: persons have a second-order disability with regard to a particular action if, and only if, they are disabled, given accepted circumstances, with regard to consistently pursuing a training programme to acquire a first-order ability to perform the same action.

The notion of second-order ability brings us closer to the biologically founded capabilities of human beings. Nevertheless, it does not and cannot completely free us from the relationship of an action to an environment. To say that Sara has a first-order ability to follow a training programme successfully presupposes, as I have said, a particular set of circumstances. It may be conceivable that certain people who lack first-order ability could, if they were put into extremely advanced and extremely expensive training programmes, achieve the first-order ability desired. But if such programmes have not been offered, or if they have not even been designed, they cannot be taken into account in ascribing second-order ability to people.

Secondary Actions and Collective Actions

So far I have considered several aspects of actions performed by an agent and where the action ultimately rests on (or is generated by) a basic action performed by this agent. This means that initially a physical movement (such as a leg movement or a lip movement) occurs in the agent, or an intentional abstention from such a movement occurs in him or her.

I will now turn to a further class of actions where this is not the case. The actions I will introduce are *secondary actions* and *collective actions*. A paradigm case of a secondary action is the following. The captain of a ship gives an order to one of the mates to turn the ship in starboard direction. The mate fulfils the order and performs the physical operations necessary for turning the ship in the right direction. The mate has then turned the ship, but so has the captain according to common parlance. The legal responsibility lies wholly on the captain and therefore we need to ascribe the action to him. However, the mate is the person who has performed the basic actions necessary. (The captain's basic actions refer to his giving the order.) Thus the captain has not generated the action of turning the ship. Still, he has performed this action and he is held responsible for it.[6]

How can this phenomenon of secondary action be explained? Here a parallel exists between conventional generation of primary actions (i.e. actions generated by a basic action performed by the same agent) and secondary actions. The secondary action is dependent on the existence of a convention. A conventional rule exists to the effect that the action performed by the mate counts as an action performed by the captain. Another way of expressing this phenomenon is to say that the action of the mate constitutes the captain's action. This situation is common in many highly regulated societal hierarchies, in particular in the armed forces. I will coin the term "secondary generation" for this case.

One may argue that the phenomenon of secondary agency may appear within one and the same individual. Consider the king who signs a letter. As a person he performs the basic action of moving his hand and the generated action of signing a letter. But since he also has the authority of being a king his signature counts as the promotion of a general. But this action is only performed secondarily by him in his role of a king.

The idea of a secondary action constituted by a primary action can be further generalized to cover the phenomenon of *collective* action. We talk of collective actions when we, for instance, say that a government, a parliament or a society performs an action. These are secondary actions depending on one or more primary actions performed by individual agents. This time the secondary action cannot be attributed to a single individual, though, but to an abstract body or a collective. I will explain the mechanisms that can be involved in the following.

Consider first the institutional collective, such as a government, that makes decisions and performs acts of great importance. But what does it mean to say that a government acts? Can a government have reasons and intentions? The basic conditions for institutional acting are easy to line up. All the members of a government, in particular the prime minister, can in certain cases (and in accordance with strict rules) act on behalf of

---

[6]   See Copp, 1979, and Tuomela, 1995.

the government. This means that when, for instance, the minister of agriculture signs a decree on protection against mad cow disease, then this act counts as an act performed by the government as a whole. Sometimes more than one member of the government is needed for the government bill to be executed. The government may need to assemble and assent to a proposal. In the case of conflicting interests they may even have to vote. The action preferred by the majority of the government may then count as the act officially executed. In all these cases we have a constitutional relation regulated by laws or other rules to the effect that the action of a particular government member, under certain circumstances, counts as the government's action, or to the effect that the voting actions of the majority of the members of the government count as the government's action. I will tentatively call this kind of collective action an *institutional* action.

It is easy to find many parallels to the government case in ordinary working life. In most corporations a certain person, not necessarily the top manager, can represent the whole corporation and for instance sign a contract in the name of the firm. This then counts as an action performed by the firm.

The institutional actions may be contrasted with what I propose to call *brute collective* actions. Consider the following example borrowed from David Copp.[7] Three persons, Tom, Dick and Harry, together carry a piano upstairs in a house. None of them can succeed in carrying it on his own. The contribution of each of them is necessary for the transportation of the piano. Together their effort is sufficient for the enterprise. Here we can say that the collective consisting of Tom, Dick and Harry performs the action of carrying the piano upstairs.

Thus this is a collective action of a sort but it is quite different from the institutional action. In the typical institutional action normally only one person is "really" acting. When a minister acts on behalf of the government it is only the minister who performs some basic action, for example utters a sentence or signs a document by moving his or her hand. The other members can remain completely passive. The brute collective action presupposes a physical effort on the part of all members of the collective. All members of the brute collective perform some basic action of their own, i.e. they all (intentionally) contribute to the combined action.

In what sense can we say that the collectives have intentions and reasons? Can an abstract body have intentions? The answer is that the

---

[7]   Copp, 1979.

abstract body does not literally have an intention. The "real" intentions are properties of the individual agents, the minister, the manager, or Tom, Dick and Harry. Intentions can, however, meaningfully be attributed secondarily to collectives. I will explain how.

In the institutional case the minister has an intention to sign a decree. The intention is, however, peculiar. It must be an intention that has some reference to the collective, viz. the government. The minister must have an intention to sign a decree on behalf of the government. Tuomela has proposed the term "we-intentions" for this kind of intention. The minister adopts the position of the whole government and incorporates a we-intention in signing the document.[8]

This is anyway the requirement of the proper institutional action. This does not alter the fact that institutional actions can be defective in various ways. A minister may lack a we-intention and still by mistake or even deceitfully sign a document that receives the legal status of a government action. As a result, the whole government may become responsible for having performed the mistaken or deceitful action. This is an example, as with many other conventional actions, of a case where the existence of an action is not dependent on the existence of an intention to perform the action.

In a parliament or some other institution where we often have majority votes, the situation with reference to intentions is different. A majority and a minority normally have quite opposite intentions. In a sense, however, both the majority and the minority contribute to the resulting collective parliamentary decision. The only reasonable interpretation of this situation is to say that the we-intention of the majority counts as the intention of the parliament with regard to the decision in question. Observe, though, that this holds only with certainty for the final intention, viz. the intention to vote for a specific action. The reasons behind this intention (i.e. the intentions higher up in the intentional hierarchy) may vary a lot among the majority members of parliament. Assume that they vote for state economic support of the farmers in the northern region of Sweden. A few members of parliament vote for this proposal because they sincerely think that this will benefit the competitive strength of the whole agricultural enterprise in Sweden. Other members, in particular the ones who originate from the relevant region, think egoistically of themselves and intend to support their own economy.

It is clear that the ideas of secondary action and collective action have relevance for work ability. People in a leadership position can have

---

[8]   Tuomela, 1995.

actions done for them. These actions when approved can then be attributed to the leader. Similarly, people sometimes form work-collectives, either of a conventional or of a brute kind. The work ability of these people can then be dependent on their being able to enter the collectives.

On Ability, Know-How and Competence

Ever since the appearance of Gilbert Ryle's famous essay "Knowing How and Knowing That"[9] it has been commonplace to distinguish between theoretical knowledge, i.e. knowledge-that, and practical knowledge, i.e. knowledge-how. In having a piece of theoretical knowledge one knows that a set of propositions is true. In having a piece of practical knowledge one knows how to perform an action or how to reach a goal. This distinction is fruitful but not entirely clear. A fully satisfactory application of it requires a number of further clarifications. Since my presentation does not rely on the distinction I confine myself to the following remarks. Knowing-that and knowing-how, however further clarified, must be related to each other. In some cases knowing that something is the case may even be sufficient for knowing how to perform an action, and in many cases knowing a fact is necessary for knowing how to perform the action. Consider the following examples:

- Liza can count to one billion, but if she tries today she will probably not succeed because she is so tired that she will fall asleep after having counted to a couple of thousand.

- John can write a book on the nature of health, but he is at present not feeling well, so there is little chance that this book will materialize this year.

- Jenny can play football but she has broken her leg so she won't play any football this month.

Among my three examples the relation between knowing-that and knowing-how is perhaps strongest in the case of the arithmetician. This person's knowledge of a set of mathematical truths may be sufficient for her know-how. In the case of the author there is still a strong relation, but it seems quite plausible that some of the author's know-how cannot be translated into true propositions. In the case of the footballer most of her knowledge is of the practical kind and not translatable into theoretical knowledge.

But is knowledge, whether of the theoretical or the practical kind, ever sufficient for saying that the agent is able to perform a particular action? In answering this question, I will start with a case of a footballer,

---

[9]   Ryle, 1971.

where the grounds for doubt are the strongest. Are we inclined to say that a person can play football simply on the ground that he or she knows how to play football? Consider a former footballer, a 75-year-old man, who has ever since his active years worked as a radio commentator on football and has supreme both theoretical and practical knowledge of the game. In a perfectly understandable sense this person knows how to play football. But clearly this man no longer has the ability to play football, in the sense we are seeking. He has, as we say, lost the relevant skill. He is no longer well-trained; he cannot move quickly enough, he does not react quickly enough and he no longer has the required physical strength.

I will at this stage introduce what I take to be a crucial concept for my analytical task, namely the concept of *competence.* The competent footballer has both know-how and skill. In many areas of activity, perhaps ultimately in all areas, there is a combination of know-how and skill required for complete competence. This holds very clearly for painters, musicians and people who do handicraft. All these people need a skill to modulate and coordinate bodily movements that goes far beyond any kind of knowledge. But the same probably holds true to some extent for all enterprises.

To let the notion of skill also enter the mental field is crucial. In fact the distinction between the mind and the body is hard to uphold here. In the case of painters and musicians, similarly with athletes and circus artists, their training is as much a training of the mind as a training of the body. Their skill involves not only a trained body, that has strength and plasticity and is capable of rapid movement, but also a capacity for identifying more and more subtle nuances, whether it be in one's body, in one's task or in one's environment.

Let me summarize. I have identified an important notion of competence, constituted by know-how and by physical and mental skill. Supported by my examples I argue that the term "ability" and its verbal associate "being able" sometimes refer to competence and not to full ability. The person who counts has the competence for counting to a billion, but since he or she soon gets sick and tired of counting, does not succeed in doing so. The author and the footballer likewise have the competence for their respective tasks, but fail to realize them because of lack of attention, fatigue or injury.

In the case of full ability for a task F, therefore, the competence of a person must be supplemented with executive ability for performing F. In addition to having the competence the person must be healthy, in relevant respects, and must have the strength, patience and perseverance for accomplishing the task.[10]

---

[10] This section summarizes my argument in Nordenfelt, 1997.

CHAPTER 9

From Ability to Work Ability

On the Concept of Work

Introduction

A concept that is crucial and continuously used in this book is the concept of work itself. In spite of this my presentation of this concept will be quite limited. My subsequent analysis will not depend much on where exactly to draw the boundaries between work and other types of activity. Let me, however, in the following give a brief background to the contemporary discussion of the concept of work.

Engelstad divides existing definitions of work into four main categories: the socio-economic, the feminist, the Marxist and the anthropological ones. He himself proposes in addition a sociological kind of definition. According to the socio-economic concept work simply consists of all those activities that produce goods to be exchanged on a market. This could be seen as the narrowest conception of work. Engelstad does not formulate any exact feminist definition but cites the Norwegian feminist Waerness, who emphasizes the variety of care services mostly provided by women. Other feminists have in general highlighted the fact that work can involve services which do not result in goods that can be exchanged on a market.[1]

Karl Marx has discussed work in many places in his enormous production. The most classic definition of work is to be found in Marx 1890:

> Die Arbeit ist zunächst ein Prozess zwischen Mensch und Natur, ein Prozess, worin der Mensch seinen Stoffwechsel mit der Natur durch seine eigne That vermittelt, regelt und kontrolliert. [Work is primarily a cooperation between the human being and nature, a process where the human being through his activities mediates, regulates and controls his metabolism with nature.][2]

---

[1] Engelstad, 1984, and Waerness, 1979.
[2] Marx, 1890/1991, p. 162.

Engelstad underlines the fact that work, according to Marx, is intentional and builds upon a careful planning as regards means to chosen ends.

The anthropological definition is the most inclusive of the existing ones. Engelstad cites Wadel[3] who describes work as human activities which can be shown to establish, maintain or change valued institutions in society. These activities need not, however, intentionally be designed to achieve such results. Wadel's suggestion is thus in this respect completely contrary to that of Marx.

The sociological definition proposed by Engelstad himself is the following:

> Work is a goal directed activity which aims at the subsistence of individuals. The person who performs the activity is in principle replaceable.[4]

In this characterization Engelstad in a way comes back to Marx's proposal when he underlines the significance of supporting the survival of the individual in a given society. The idea of replaceability is interesting. By introducing this condition Engelstad excludes such activities as are completely private from belonging to the category of work. The act of bearing one's child cannot be performed by somebody else. Nor can the activities of enjoying oneself or maintaining personal relationships. Thus these are not work activities according to the sociological definition of work proposed by Engelstad.

In his dissertation Karlsson[5] provides a list of around 30 different definitions of the concept of work from the scientific literature. Many of these definitions are quite similar and have common elements. The notion of activity is central in almost all definitions. The notions of goal and need are frequent. So is the idea of work as a means of human subsistence. Work should according to this idea contribute to human survival and human welfare. This means that this ethical goal is indeed common in scientific definitions of work. The subject should work in order to survive and flourish through his or her salary but, more importantly, the results of his or her work should, according to these definitions, contribute to the subsistence and welfare of humans. Another important element in some conceptions of work is that work involves the utilization of nature for certain human purposes. Consider the following noted general characterization of work:

---

[3] Wadel, 1979.

[4] Engelstad, 1984, p. 13. My translation.

[5] Karlsson, 1986.

What is work? No definition is satisfactory because work relates to all human activities, and one would have to exhaust all such activities to exhaust the provinces of work. An oversimplified definition is that work uses the things and materials of nature to fashion tools with which to make objects, grow food, and control the living creatures and forces of nature to satisfy human needs and wants.

[...] Work has been defined as making things and has been related to needs. But making things and utilitarian work are not the only types of work. There are people who do not make anything – teachers, clerks, engineers, scientists, salespersons, nurses, lawyers, doctors, accountants, cashiers, secretaries, waiters and waitresses, guards, receptionists, typists, bookkeepers, and so on. Modern terminology uses the word occupation to identify work activities. It is a functional term describing what people do to "earn a living", emphasizing that it is work which sustains life. Thus, work includes both making things and performing services which are of value to oneself, as well as to others.[6]

A Pragmatic Position

I have already presupposed that working entails performing series of actions and that therefore almost all action theory is relevant to the theory of work. But work is of course a very special set of actions. I will here make a pragmatic restriction. The concept of work that is in focus in this book is *work for a salary*. I do not wish in general to exclude other activities, such as household work and hobby gardening, from the concept of work, but these will not be discussed in the following. The working conditions and the working situations to be analysed are such as are connected with being employed and the work in question is in the standard case paid for by an employer. The work performed by the employer him or herself is of course also covered by my analysis.

What is significant regarding the work as an employee is that it is more systematized than most other such activities. The employee is normally given a set of specified tasks which are elements of a much larger enterprise dedicated to a goal and administered by managers in an organization (private or governmental). The members of the organization are meant to support each other by making their contributions, efficiently and in the right order, to the common goal.

Ideally, but this certainly does not hold in general, the goal of an enterprise should be a goal in the common interest of a population, such as the production and delivery of food, building houses, providing transport, offering health care, education or culture in general. However,

---

[6]   Applebaum, 1992, p. x.

many paid activities are not in this sense in the public interest. Some of them are even detrimental, such as trafficking and the production and distribution of narcotic drugs. One might construct a concept of work that has the ethical element of a common good built into it. However, completely sticking to such a concept would only complicate the discussion in this book, which is mainly theoretical and not ethical. I will therefore not presuppose anything with regard to the quality of the goal of a job.

The Question of the Practical Possibility of Work

The standard notion in the context of analysing a person's conditions for performing his or her work is *ability*. But already here one can take advantage of the action-theoretic distinction between ability and *practical possibility*. The latter concept is an inclusive concept that also comprises *opportunity*. When a person has both ability and opportunity for performing a certain job then he or she has, per definition, the practical possibility of doing so.

To take an example. A teacher may have the general ability to teach but lacks opportunity because there is no school or there are no pupils available. The country may be at war, for instance. Or to take a less drastic example: a builder is in general able to build a house but lacks opportunity since his or her tools have been left behind.

The opportunity condition is also a matter of degree. One can have greater or lesser opportunity. The workplace can be more or less adapted to the kind of work required. The social climate can be more or less benevolent and inspiring. These factors will be the object of analysis later in this investigation.

The Idea of Basic Human Abilities

From birth we all have some biological and psychological preconditions for our future abilities. I have above called these *second-order abilities*. They are abilities regarding entering upon a training programme from which certain first-order abilities can follow. The latter notion has been defined in the following way: John has the first-order ability to perform an action F = def. John does F if John wants to do F and there is an opportunity for John to do F. When we say of a person who is 18 that he or she can in the future work as a doctor we are talking about this person's second-order ability. He or she can study and train to become a doctor and subsequently perform the work as a doctor.

The training programmes can be of several kinds. One can distinguish between on the one hand the standard life-training programme that almost all infants and children go through and on the other the special training which is a prerequisite for certain professions or occupations. The former training includes learning to walk and learning to speak one's native language. It also involves basic school-training, learning to read and count and learning the elements of subjects such as history, biology and geography. All this also entails basic social training. I will refer to the results of this education and training as the *standard basic competence* of an ordinary adult in a Western society.

Conditions of the Standard Basic Competence

Not all people even reach the standard basic competence. Behind this competence already lie a number of heterogeneous conditions. Let me attempt to list these.

Physiological or health conditions. The child must during its up-bringing for the most time have been reasonably healthy and have a minimal physical and mental strength. It must have been able to participate in the various training programmes.

Opportunity. There must have been some opportunity to participate. The basic external conditions for the training must have existed.

Intelligence. The child must have some minimal intelligence to achieve the basic competence.

Patience and Perseverance. Certain traits of character must exist. The child must be at least minimally patient, must understand and accept that results do not come immediately. It must also have at least some minimal perseverance and not abandon the programme because of the least obstacle.

Will and courage. A crucial condition for all action is that the agent wants and has the courage to act. I will in general separate such conditions from ability-conditions.[7] This distinction is difficult to uphold in all instances, as when the faculty of volition itself is damaged. A person can in extreme cases, such as in a state of severe depression, be totally deprived of an ability to want anything.

For many purposes we can regard the standard basic competence as a second-order ability for various occupations. It is from this competence that a person starts when he or she initiates a vocational or professional education. For certain menial jobs the standard basic competence is itself sufficient or almost sufficient for performing the tasks. Examples are jobs as cleaners, door-keepers or attendants. I underline here that I am talking about performing the job in at least a minimally acceptable

---

[7]   Other authors make contrary choices, see Ilmarinen, 2001b, and Brülde, 2008. Cf. also The Manpower Services Commission, 1982, see McQuaid *et al.*, 2005.

way. There is a great distinction between being able to do a job minimally and being able to do it well. (I will return to this distinction.)

Occupational Competence and Skill

What does the special training programme lead to? It leads ideally to occupational or professional know-how and skill, i.e. competence. The trained person can, in principle, do what the job requires. I will add some further conditions later.

What does the training programme contain? A few training programmes, including the ones for becoming a police officer, a fire fighter or an army officer, entail a lot of exercise where the basic physical and mental strength of the subject is developed. But all training programmes provide some theoretical knowledge in a number of disciplines. The theoretical knowledge also entails a related problem-solving ability required by the profession. The electrician must not only know the theory of electricity but must also be able to understand what has gone wrong when the light goes out in a house. To this can be added all the practical skills that are necessary for performing the job well. The electrician must, for instance, be able – in a manual way – to handle the technical problems involved in repairing a stove or installing a refrigerator. Practical and technical skills of some kind exist also in more theoretical professions. A history teacher must not only be able to give the pupils some knowledge of historical facts. These facts must also be presented in such a way that the pupils can assimilate them. This is the pedagogical skill.

A good occupational training programme should include much more. It should prepare the person for the various kinds of situations that he or she can meet with which may not be central to the vocation or profession. The programme should consider the social milieu in which the person will be acting. It should stress the importance of communicative ability and of ethical competence. The person will, in almost all vocations and professions, encounter other people and have dealings with them, in a curative, advisory or a commercial context. The programme should also prepare the learner for various stressful situations and help him or her tolerate disruption, complaints and other kinds of frustration. The training programme should also teach the learner to continuously seek new knowledge and develop as a professional.

If the training programme concerns an occupation that involves the care of human beings or leadership in an organization, certain requirements are deepened. Communicative ability will have a central role. To this can be added the ability to cooperate and establish deep contacts, to support and comfort. As a leader one must also acquire strategic competence, the ability to take decisions and the ability to take responsibility.

In certain positions, including the leadership ones, a development of character may be required. A leader must have a certain amount of courage and ability to tolerate certain complicated and stressful social situations.

The Conditions for Pursuing Training Programmes

Among the conditions for pursuing the vocational education or the training programme we can find substantially the same as for the basic standard competence.

Physiological or health conditions. The trainee must normally fulfil minimal health conditions and must have at least a minimal physical and mental strength. In the case of the really demanding professions such as the police, the fire service or the army these requirements are substantial.

Opportunity. The trainee must be given a fair opportunity to go through the programme. The arrangements must be in order and the person must have sufficient time and peace to fulfil the requirements.

Intelligence and talent. The trainee must at least be minimally gifted for pursuing the required tasks.

Capacity to cooperate. Since most contemporary courses of education and training programmes include group projects every member must possess a minimal capacity to communicate and in general cooperate with the other members.

Patience and perseverance. The requirements in this regard are much more pronounced here than when it comes to the conditions for the basic standard competence. The professional training programme is more systematic and much more focused than the ordinary training for life. In many instances the tasks are quite difficult and the learner may not be able to solve some of them in time.

Tolerance of stress and frustration. This introduces a new factor into the conditions. The subject must have a considerable tolerance of stress and must be able to accept frustrations in the process.

Will, self-confidence and courage. Again a crucial condition is that the subject has a standing intention to pursue the education or the training programme. This intention must not be blocked by a fear on the part of the subject with regard to the continuation of the programme. As soon as the will evaporates no action is pursued.

CHAPTER 10

On Work Ability and its Conditions

Introduction

As I have said, the occupational education leads to (or is intended to lead to) occupational competence. This competence has two basic knowledge components: theoretical and practical knowledge. Theoretical knowledge implies not only knowledge in basic subjects such as mathematics, chemistry and biology but also applied sciences such as ship technology, caring science or museum technology. Practical knowledge or *know-how* is knowledge about *what to do*, what concrete actions to perform in certain crucial situations and how to perform these actions. I distinguish practical knowledge and *skill* in the following way.[1] A person may have the practical knowledge to perform an action but still not the skill to do it. A pianist may have the practical knowledge to play a Beethoven sonata but at a particular moment not have the skill to do it, because he or she has not trained for the last couple of months. The pianist knows exactly "in the head" how the fingers should run and where to put an emphasis but will in practice not succeed in doing all this according to the formula. I will say that if a person has the theoretical knowledge, the practical knowledge and the skill required for a task then he or she has *competence* in the relevant respect.

I will in the following list some fundamental components of professional competence. It may be noted that these lists are mixed in the following sense. They contain both species of competences (or abilities to perform actions or complete tasks) and certain crucial conditions underlying such competencies or abilities. Among such conditions are various kinds of knowledge and also certain strengths and attitudes.

This distinction tends to be blurred by the fact that the term "ability" can be used in two ways. In the paradigm use of the general expressions "John is able to" or "John is capable of" these expressions are filled out with a locution referring to an intentional action on the part of John. We can say that John is able to teach French or John is able to build a house. Here teaching French and building a house are clear examples of inten-

---

[1] See my analysis in Chapter 8.

tional actions. Locutions exist, however, where ability can refer to mere dispositions. A child may be able to make a mess of a situation. A husband may be able to ruin his relationship with his wife. Here it need not be the case that the child and the husband actually intend to do so. The result may be an accident or at least an unintended result.

It can be useful to make this distinction also in the work ability context. Normally the abilities and capacities cited in the following directly refer to intentional actions. This holds for the ability to work hard or the ability to communicate. Ability in the mere dispositional sense appears, however, in the toleration and courage categories (see below). When a person tolerates the cold climate it is not a question (or not merely a question) of what the person intends to do. It is (at least partly) a question of his or her physiology and what the physiology permits. Similarly, the person who can tolerate a noise may have the same intentions as one who cannot tolerate it. The ability or capacity in these cases then refers to properties or dispositions of the person other than his or her abilities to perform intentional actions.

One might then wonder if one should include these dispositions in the same category of work abilities. I choose to do this since they are certainly relevant in the context. For one thing, the intentional actions involved in work tasks are dependent on many of the dispositional capacities. Capacity to tolerate a certain amount of noise and stress is a crucial condition for one's ability to perform most actions involved in work. Thus the toleration category may be seen as including basic conditions for action on a par with physiological conditions, such as muscular strength and lung function. Similarly, courage could be looked upon as a kind of mental strength.

The Competencies

I will first highlight the category of technical competence, which is perhaps the one mostly referred to in applied documents concerning work competence and skill. (See, in particular, the Norwegian, British, and Dutch lists of capacities in Chapter 2 and Appendix 1.)

Technical Competence

- Basic standard competence
- Developed physical and mental strength
- Developed intellectual capacity and talent
- Theoretical knowledge, including problem solving ability
- Practical knowledge, including problem solving ability
- Adequate skill.

I refer to the traits above as elements of technical competence. They are all to be seen as related to the specific vocation or profession. For instance, the theoretical knowledge and practical knowledge in question are knowledge as is relevant to the work tasks of the individual in question. The list is intended to contain the minimal set of elements in a person's competence to perform "technical" tasks, where these tasks do not require constant personal communication. Where communication and cooperation is necessary the list is completely inadequate. Since no job only entails purely technical tasks, but also involves some communication and cooperation, this list is always an inadequate one.

Observe here that I have summarized the technical competencies on a highly abstract level of description. It is clear that what I call developed physical and mental strength, intellectual capacity and talent, as well as adequate skill, incorporate a lot of specific abilities, some of which are specified in the Handbook of Human Abilities.[2] For instance static strength, namely the ability to use continuous muscular force in order to lift, push, pull or carry objects, is a crucial element in what I call physical strength. So is dynamic strength, namely the ability of the muscles to exert force repeatedly or continuously over a long period. Information ordering, inductive reasoning, as well as category flexibility, namely the ability to produce rules for the purpose of grouping things, are essential component abilities in what I call intellectual capacity. At the same time they are presuppositions for problem solving ability.

Practical Knowledge and Rules

I will further comment on the notion of practical knowledge in the work context. The concept of a *rule* plays a crucial role in the explication of this notion. To have practical knowledge is to a great extent tantamount to knowing the rules according to which a task or a series of tasks should be performed.

It is first instructive to consider a classical distinction between two kinds of rules, viz. *constitutive* rules and *regulative* rules.[3] A constitutive rule is a rule that defines a type of action. I have already noted that certain actions, the conventional actions, require for their existence a set of rules defining them. A move in chess is a proper move because of a certain rule saying that the movement of a certain piece in chess counts as a proper move if it is performed in a certain way given a set of circumstances (for instance that the other pieces are placed in certain

---

[2]   Fleishman *et al.*, 1995. These abilities are listed in Chapter 3 in this volume.
[3]   See Searle, 1969.

ways.) A regulative rule does not have anything to do with definitions; it only says what actions are allowed and what actions are prohibited in a certain context. The regulative rule is thus a rule in the ordinary sense of the term.

Practical knowledge involves knowledge of both kinds of rules. One must first know the defining rules in order to play a game at all. The same holds for a number of vocations that can in many ways be looked upon as sophisticated games. Being a judge or being an official in a governmental office entails in many ways grasping and managing the rules of these professions. Many of these rules are constitutive. Many legal and administrative acts owe their existence to a set of constitutive rules. In addition there are a number of regulative rules. Some of these are intertwined with the constitutive rules. A rule statement may at the same time define an act (for instance, the act of judging) and indicate when this act is appropriate. To follow the regulative rules is mandatory. To do something forbidden in a responsible position may entail ruining one's position in the office.

A further kind of rule is the *instrumental rule*, of which the *rule of thumb* is a species. The instrumental rule indicates what the worker should do in order to achieve the end he or she wishes to achieve and which is central to the vocation or profession in question. The instrumental rule is often based on theoretical knowledge, in certain cases scientific knowledge. The rules that the electrician follows when drawing a cable from one plug to another presuppose the laws of electricity, viz. a part of physics. The general law that states that an electrical current can only run through a particular closed medium lies at the bottom of connecting certain points by a cable. However, universal causal laws are not the only bases of instrumental rules. Modern philosophy of knowledge has abandoned the Platonic idea that all instrumental knowledge is in the end dependent on eternal laws derived from the basic sciences. Many instrumental rules have grown from the practice itself. This practice may be quite local and be dependent on configurations in the particular environment. No science, be it physics or some other natural science, comprises all such relevant elements. Therefore no universal scientific law can be applicable. The "quasi-law" that lies behind the instrumental rule is the result of many people's long experience in the relevant environment. Bertil Rolf[4] has given rich illustrations of such rules from the field of military planning.

---

[4]   Rolf, 1998.

General Competence

Here follows a list of competencies which are not specific to any particular vocation but which are nevertheless relevant for almost all vocations:

- Strategic ability, i.e. ability to plan one's work in a reasonable way
- Adaptability to new situations
- Ability to handle uncertainty
- Ability to take decisions
- Ability to take responsibility for the work done
- Communicative ability
- Ability to cooperate
- Ability to assimilate new knowledge
- Capacity to work hard.

These items of general competence are certainly desirable for members of all occupations and professions. They are necessary for people who aspire to advanced positions in their professions. Caring professions and leadership positions require, however, a certain further set of abilities.

Personal Competence

- Empathy, including

    ability to establish deep personal contacts

    ability to support and

    ability to comfort other people.
- Ethical competence, including knowledge about other people's rights
- Ability to take decisions with regard to human beings
- Ability to take responsibility for such decisions.

Under the heading of ethical competence (as well as under the general heading of empathy) I will include the sentimental work categories introduced and analysed by Strauss *et al.*[5] These categories include what Strauss calls interactional work and moral rules, trust work (build up trust), composure work (prevent loss of self-control), biographical work (get acquainted with the client's biography), identity work (keep spirits up) and rectification work (correct mistakes with regard to interaction).

---

[5]   Strauss *et al.*, 1985. See my presentation in Chapter 7.

I will here also list a number of abilities (or conditions of abilities) related to personality and character traits (of an ability type) which are necessary ingredients, at least to some minimal extent, in all occupations, but which are not commonly mentioned as included in professional competence. It is clear, though, that it would be better if all professional educations highlighted these as well as some of the personal competencies mentioned above.

Abilities Belonging to the Toleration Category

- Ability to tolerate stress and heavy work loads
- Ability to tolerate disruption
- Ability to tolerate complaints
- Ability to tolerate uncertainty
- Ability to tolerate frustration
- Ability to tolerate the physical environment
- Ability to tolerate the social environment
- Ability to tolerate criticism and opposition.

Some of these abilities are typically included in the concepts of *patience and perseverance*, which belong to the category of virtues. I will return to this category below.

The toleration category (in particular concerning the non-intentional variants) is crucial in the health context. It covers a certain element of the person's fortitude, viz. the strength to avoid illness and injury. The stress-tolerant person is able to avoid the burnt-out syndrome better than the less stress-tolerant.

Abilities Belonging to the Courage Category

A requirement of courage (where self-confidence is a central ingredient) is salient in particular with regard to crucial decisions to be taken by a leader, but it exists to some extent in all jobs. One has to have a minimal element of courage just to appear at the workplace and face one's work mates and other colleagues. Courage can be trained but perhaps less so than other features of one's competence.

- Having the courage to respond to criticism
- Having the courage to counter dangers
- Having the courage to take undesired decisions
- Having the courage to oppose unsuitable proposals from the leader ship.

Courage is an interesting character trait. I have here, in a preliminary way, treated it as a species of ability. So does Per Bauhn in his *The Value of Courage*.[6] In general, he says, courage is the ability to confront fear. He distinguishes between two species of courage: first, *the courage of creativity*, which is the ability to confront the fear of failure (this ability being directed by the agent's will to achieve), and second, *the courage of conviction*, which is the ability to confront the fear of personal transience (for instance, being sacked from one's job or being expelled from a community). This ability is directed by the agent's sense of moral responsibility.

What is lacking in this analysis is that courage must also contain an element of volition. The courageous person also has an attitude, an inclination. He or she has adopted a firm attitude towards a threat, and hence has a willingness to exercise this attitude. The person is willing to take a risk. This attitude may perhaps also be seen as a condition for the ability to confront fear.

Bauhn's two species of courage, that of creativity and that of conviction, seem both to be relevant to the analysis of work ability. The worker must have some minimal courage of creativity in order to start working at all. The worker must try to achieve and risk a failure. In some instances the risk of failure is great. A student working on a doctoral thesis runs a great risk of not achieving his or her goal. But this holds for all demanding jobs, such as doing professional sport, running a business and in general holding a leadership position. The courage of conviction is needed in situations of crisis, in particular when there is a situation of great danger and one has perhaps to act to save life or when the worker chooses to stand up to the boss and expresses a radically divergent opinion, thereby risking the job. Admittedly this kind of courage is rarely executed and perhaps not very common. From a societal point of view I would, however, claim that such courage is a desirable quality for any holder of a job. It is doubtful, however, whether all employers find it equally desirable.

A certain amount of courage, in particular the courage of creativity, is necessary for taking and holding a job. Observe that the mentioned clause from action theory with regard to the circumstances becomes much more particularized here. There is not really one standard circumstance for teachers, for instance. Different workplaces require more or less of theoretical and practical competence. And if we choose to consider different cultures we will encounter quite divergent requirements with regard to courage and the capacity to take responsibility.

---

[6]   Bauhn, 2003.

Other Virtues

In the discussion with regard to the British experiment of teaching basic skills it was argued by, for instance, Richard Smith,[7] that in many professions, not least the profession of teacher, there is a requirement of certain virtues, such as wisdom, reliability, honesty and patience. His main point was that such virtues cannot be taught on a special training course for the learning of skills. They belong to the deep personality of the person and they can at most be the object of the long socialization and upbringing that is provided in the good family.

How are we to look upon the basic virtues and their place in the structure of competencies? I think that most of the analysis required could partly parallel the one I have done with regard to courage. However, the virtues and other traits of character do not in general ontologically belong to the competencies as such. They are normally attitudes which can be seen as preconditions for certain competencies and abilities. Reliability and honesty are crucial virtues in relation to the whole work project. Reliability lies behind the fact that the work is done properly, at the right time and with great care. Patience is a precondition for the proper continuation of the work in a context where there is much interruption and disturbance. Wisdom is the sophisticated virtue which only such persons have as are very experienced and have lived a long life. Wisdom presupposes some intelligence but is much more than intelligence. It involves a specific attitude towards mankind. It entails deep understanding of the human fate and of how humans can react and develop. I think it also entails an attitude of benevolence. The wise teacher, for instance, abstains from reacting harshly to a student who has done a bad job, when he or she understands that the circumstances behind the failure were outside the student's control.

Possible Conflicts Between a General Societal Norm for Work Ability and the Demands of Employers

One can wonder whether the competencies and other capacities that I have tentatively listed here are self-evident qualifications for all kinds of jobs. (I am now disregarding the fact that not all competencies are equally relevant for all kinds of jobs.) One can, in particular, wonder whether there is an identity between what could be called societal requirements and the demands of employers. Does the ordinary employer want the employee to excel in all the respects mentioned?

---

[7] Smith, 1987.

In many ways the requirements and desiderata will probably coincide. The employer certainly looks for a technically competent, hardworking, enthusiastic, socially and ethically competent worker. In the interview study referred to in the FEU context above[8] the employers listed the following desirable properties of the young people to be employed in their businesses: versatility, initiative, pride in job, good personal relations, listen to instructions, wide viewpoint, seek work when slack, quality conscious, good time keepers, ask questions, methodical and neat, report faults, remedy the problem. As noted before, many of these properties have to do with personality and virtue and not with mere competencies.

It is clear, however, that the employer often also looks for qualifications outside the competence/virtue sphere. As is noted by Abiala[9], some people in the service sectors get their employment to a high degree on the basis of qualifications other than competencies in the sense analysed above. Many certainly get it on the basis of their general personality and experience, but many also get it via personal contacts or on the basis of their sex, age and looks. This indicates that there are other factors than traditional competencies that are crucial to a business. The success of a company may be dependent on other features of the personnel, features that might be attractive to potential customers and draw them to the business in question. In an extended sense one might perhaps say that the waitress in a restaurant who is good-looking has a specific crucial competence: she has the competence to attract customers, and this is a competence that is highly praised by the employer.

So far there is, however, no direct clash between what may be said to be general societal expectations and the expectations and demands of an employer. But there exist potential clashes. This comes up with regard to a particular virtue which may have different interpretations in different contexts. I am thinking of the virtue of *loyalty*.

The employer in general wants to have loyal employees. By this he or she normally means persons who are loyal to the enterprise and its aims. This entails standing up for the firm, defending it against competitors, perhaps even in an improper way. To some employers the person who compromises with his or her ethics for the sake of the firm is to be preferred to the really ethical person. The latter may be prepared to reveal that the firm does not have pure motives or that it has indeed performed immoral deeds, for instance by taking part in corruption or fraud.

---

[8]   Chapter 4 in this volume.

[9]   Abiala, 2000, p. 57.

Moreover, it may not be completely attractive for a manager of a company to have an employee who is brave enough to criticize the leadership of the company in various respects. In this regard, however, the picture is probably mixed. Many employers are certainly grateful to a competent employee who has discovered some fundamental mistake in the production that must be rectified for the future success of the company. And there are employers who can tolerate and even appreciate criticism for unethical conduct if this conduct is evidently detrimental to the spirit of the company. But few employers are particularly interested in employees who are consistently observant and critical with regard to the operation of the business.

This observation reveals an interesting tension between the requirements of an excellent and ethical member of society and an excellent employee in a company.

On the Importance of Interaction

Above it was noted that all ability is related to a task or a set of tasks. The tasks in various professions differ enormously. Compare a builder with a university professor; a sailor with a clerk in an insurance company; a farmer with a broker, or a cleaner with a pilot. There are salient differences between these occupations and professions. I will now focus on a special topic, namely to what extent the tasks in these occupations or professions involve changing moving targets and environments, in particular if they involve interaction with other people.

In some occupations the objects of manipulation are fairly stable and not continually changing. A carpenter works with nails and pieces of wood; a cleaner gets rid of dust and dirt which certainly builds up over time but is fairly constant at a particular moment. It is different with people who deal with a moving or a changing target. A captain has to handle a ship that is struggling with the unpredictable sea. A pilot has to handle an aeroplane that may be affected by serious meteorological conditions. And such changes in the task are especially salient when the object consists of living biological matter. A hunter must pursue the animal prey and adapt his or her behaviour to the movements of the prey. The surgeon who operates on an abdominal cancer may have to face a complication in terms of a haemorrhage in the abdomen and, as a result, the focus of the operation has for a period to be changed.

A special subcase of the moving target, which is particularly relevant in several professions and occupations, is when the target is an *acting human being*. The work involves a great deal of human interaction that deserves a particularly careful analysis.

We may consider some types of events that can occur during a working day. Some of them are very frequent and have to be dealt with continually. In diaries written for the present project by a travelling salesman and a pre-school teacher the following stories can function as illustrations. (The stories have been shortened and slightly modified.) The sales representative presents the following story:

I am an agent for a company that sells musical instruments. I spend most of my time travelling between customers and potential customers. Much of the time I drive my car on my way to various places, talking on the phone with customers and suppliers.

Tuesday morning starts at 6:48. I wake my children and take them to their school before my own work can start. I do the first things at home. I turn on my computer and check the mails from last night. I answer these. The first telephone call comes at 9 o'clock. A customer wonders when I can come and see him. I then pack all my things for today's journey. I include three guitars that I intend to demonstrate for the shop owners. I have to pack every day now during the winter. It is dangerous to have the instruments in the car overnight, partly because of the risk of theft but also because of the risk that the instruments will be damaged by the cold and the humidity.

The first stop is at a shop in the neighbouring town. When I enter the shop the owner is on the phone. I walk around and I notice that the owner has not bought the most recent articles from us. That annoys me. I had hoped that he was a faithful customer. However, when he arrives to chat with me it works well. I explain the advantages of our products and tell him that we have some reasonable campaign prices, and he finally decides to buy some of our products.

At 11.15 I am on my way to a meeting that I have not prepared and not announced. This is not usual. However, I am particularly interested in this customer. He has an exclusive shop and it has some prestige in this part of the country. As I might have expected the meeting is a failure. The owner is not interested and he is certainly irritated that I arrive without having booked a time for a proper meeting. I suddenly feel depressed. I fear that I have lost this crucial customer.

I get back to the car and my travels. I keep talking to people on the phone. Some other clients make me happier. I realize that I will be selling more towards the end of the week. This journey is long, too long, it takes two hours. When I arrive at the next town I go out with the customer to a restaurant and have a meal with him. We discuss our business at the restaurant. He has had some experience of some of our products and he tells me about it. A few things have gone wrong so I need to talk to the maker of the instruments on the phone. It seems as if my message gets through OK.

It is getting late and it has started snowing. I feel stressed. It will take another two hours before I get home and I have no snow tyres. I have to drive slowly, all the time talking to people on the phone. At last I arrive home, now quite exhausted.[10]

The pre-school teacher has had the following experiences:

When I had just arrived at the school I got the information that one of my colleagues was off sick and could not come to work. The remaining workforce had to convene and plan the day in a new way. We were considering whether we should call in a stand-in or whether we could manage reasonably well without her. We finally decided to call in another colleague.

I was standing at the entrance when a boy came in who wanted to tell me about a journey he had done together with his parents. I had to interrupt him immediately because a mother and her daughter entered. The daughter was very tired and the mother had to tell me the reason. The girl had fallen asleep very late. She now did not want her mother to leave. She started crying when her mother had to leave. It was very difficult for me to comfort the girl. The mother and the daughter had a habit of waving to each other when the mother was standing outside the window. This time the mother was very stressed since she had to hurry to her job. The mother first forgot about the waving and the girl was unconsolable. Finally, standing by the car the mother remembered the waving and the girl could gradually come back to herself again.

Later that day a boy rushed out from the playroom. He was desperate because the others had refused to let him join in the game. They were playing dad, mum and child. The boy wanted to be the dad but the others had refused. There was already a dad in the game. He had come in too late, they said. On the other hand they had said that he could be the elder brother or the grandfather of the child but the boy had not liked this proposal. This is a very typical situation. I have to reflect on such situations. I am not certain that the boy came in too late. Perhaps he has been refused before so that he does not dare to enter until it is becoming too late. It is difficult to know how to handle these situations.[11]

Other work incidents with human beings involved can be much more dramatic and even dangerous. A female social worker can have in front of her a client who asks for social benefit. The social worker refuses since she considers the arguments of the client to be too weak. As a result the client becomes aggressive and threatens to hurt her. The woman is terrified and calls for help. When she is left alone she remains for some time sitting still and is completely unable to continue her job.

---

[10] Swedish salesman, Diary, January 2007.

[11] Swedish pre-school teacher, Diary, November 2006.

The social worker has here not only to endure the situation but also to cope with it in a successful way by averting the threat. In many service occupations there are similar incidents that occur. Customers in a restaurant can be drunk or they can become aggressive so that the work in the restaurant is severely impeded for some time. Children in a school class can be disorderly and make life hard for their teachers. Not to speak about what can face a soldier at war. Being a soldier is in many countries a paid occupation.

But we need not only consider such dramatic events. More or less demanding incidents can occur in all jobs where human interaction is central, and they have to be coped with. It is also crucial to note that in many occupations these interactions are continual, as in a hospital, a restaurant and a school class. The continuous coping is a particular strain for people in occupations related to such workplaces.

So far I have been talking about interaction between the subject and the object of interaction, often a customer or a client. Interaction, however, is crucial also in the relationship between the subject and his or her colleagues or other collaborators. Here conflicts may be even more frequent than in the case of subject and customer or client. There are cases of abuse of power by a manager in relation to a subordinate, or cases of unsound competition between colleagues on the same level in a hierarchy. To these we can add simple cases of genuine dislike.

In certain workplaces, such as (to take the same examples as above) a hospital, a restaurant and a school, human beings other than clients and colleagues can enter the arena in several ways. The professional in such places may constantly interact with a great number of people. He or she is then not just acting with the people as a static background, but is also constantly influencing them and is influenced by them. The professional may give signals of various kinds to those around. He or she may sound tired, irritated or perhaps even arrogant. These signs are taken up by the people present, be they colleagues, clients or just observers, who may respond in a way that creates further tension in the interaction. Thus the agent influences those around and is influenced by them. The influence is in this case negative. The professional makes the environment unsuitable as a fruitful arena for work.

Abiala has made a comprehensive study of interactive phenomena with regard to several service occupations. Among the people involved were shop owners, salesmen, receptionists, waiters, tour guides, barbers and chauffeurs. She finds that the nature of the client contacts was crucial for success. There are many obstacles to overcome in these contacts. First, she notes that the professional often has to play a subordinate role. The service worker is not equal to the customer or client. The latter can often behave extremely rudely without any negative consequences for him or her. The professional, on the other hand, has everything to lose if he or she does not behave perfectly. Abiala writes:

> But in the public world of work, it is often part of an individual's job to accept uneven exchanges, to be treated with disrespect or anger by a client, all the while closeting into fantasy the anger one would like to respond with. Where the customer is king, unequal exchanges are normal, and from the beginning customer and client assume different rights to feeling and display.[12]

Many of the service workers in the study performed by Abiala emphasize that there are many awkward customers. It appears that people often lose their normal maturity and competence when they become service customers. Abiala notes that there seems to be a culture of rudeness that is permitted in the context of service provision.

We may also recall the observations made by Strauss *et al.*[13] in their analysis of patient work in the health care occupations. Patients' work may be complementary to and supportive of staff's work when it comes to maintaining composure, and work by patients may substitute for necessary work that staff cannot do or have forgotten to do. But patients' work may also be complicating, as when the patients complain or rectify staff errors. Such work quite often disrupts and changes the staff's plans and operations.

But interaction certainly is not only negative. The relationship practitioner-client/customer is normally positive and the same is often the case among colleagues. Let me – mainly considering interaction between colleagues – distinguish between some sub-cases. One case is that of *encouragement*. A boss is friendly to his or her subordinates and encourages them in their work. A second case is that of concrete *support*. A person at a workplace for instance helps a colleague to manage a problem. He or she may actually perform the required operation or supervise the colleague. The third and most interesting kind of interaction, in the work ability context, is that of genuine *cooperation*. Here the members of a work team take part in a collective endeavour where one member has to perform operation *A* and another member operation *B*. Building a house is a salient example. In the building of a house the various workers have to come in at specific stages. The people who excavate the earth must start, the workers who lay the foundations must come after and the carpenters and platers come in later. In this case there is a strict order. The actions of the members of one occupation presup-

---

[12] Abiala, 2000, p. 111.
[13] Strauss *et al.*, 1985.

pose those of the members of the other. Cooperation can of course also be of a looser kind where one action can support another but where the latter does not strictly presuppose the former. Moreover they can be completely contemporaneous.

In my example of building a house the relation between the professional actions is one of physical prerequisites. In many instances there are conventional or institutional requirements. A legal process, for instance, requires a certain order of actions, performed by holders of different positions. A salient example is the criminal legal process, where there is a strict order from police to prosecution to the court. One institution must be consulted before the other according to strict rules.

For some cases my analysis of collective action can be relevant to the characterization of cooperation in work. Builders who carry material together or the crew of a ship who together transport a substantial load of material from one place to another perform collective actions to which they all make a contribution. These are collective actions in the physical sense. People who cooperate as members of a board or a committee and who take a common decision thereby perform a collective action of what I call the institutional kind.

The Will as a Condition for the Execution of Work

A general question has been lurking during my whole analysis of competencies for work. What is the place of the will? Is it not crucial for anything to be done that the subject has motivation and is in the first place interested in doing the job required? And what is the relation between the will and the set of competencies? Shall we say that it belongs to one's competence that one not only has the ability to work hard but is also willing to do so or that one not only has the ability to tolerate criticism and opposition, for example, but also is *willing to* tolerate criticism and opposition?

In addition to all the abilities arguably included in a worker's general competence for a job we must in a more systematic way add the requirement that the worker wants to do the job. The requirements concerning volition are multifold. The worker must be willing to

- Take the job in the first place
- Fulfil the requirements of the job (including the codes of conduct)
- Keep this willingness over time.

In order to do the job well there is also a requirement of a certain basic enthusiasm for the job. The worker must be genuinely interested in the job and in the success of the firm or institution of which he or she is a part.

In the standard action-theoretic analysis, to which I have adhered, there is a firm distinction between the categories of volition and ability.[14] A man may want to do his work but be unable to do it because of a lack of competence or for reasons of health. Or he may be perfectly able to do it but completely lack the will for it. Indeed, the concepts can be defined in terms of each other. Consider the following standard analyses:

John has the practical possibility of doing F = def. if John wants to do F, then John does F.

We can recall that the notion of practical possibility includes both ability and opportunity. Ability is the "inner" aspect of practical possibility. Opportunity is the "outer" aspect of practical possibility.

John is able to do F = def. if John wants to do F and John has the opportunity to do F, then John does F.[15]

So a want is a distinct condition for performing one's job, parallel to ability and opportunity. But can we completely uphold the distinction between want and ability, and is it preferable to uphold it in all instances? It may first be observed that a want or a series of wants is a *necessary condition for the acquisition* of most abilities. I have already noted that most abilities are acquired; some, the most basic ones, are the result of ordinary upbringing, others are the result of special training. But in most cases there are actions of an exercise type that the subject has to perform in order to acquire the ability. To perform these actions the subject must have – at least in a minimal sense – wanted to perform them. Hence all acquired abilities are the result of intentional, willed actions. Some abilities may also be by-products of intentional actions.

We must further distinguish between specific wants and the *faculty of volition*. It is meaningful to talk about the faculty of volition in the case where a person is completely apathetic and does not perform any actions at all. Here no specific will is lacking; what is lacking is the function of the whole apparatus of will. In this case it seems reasonable to talk about a lack of ability due to ill health. And this lack of ability resides in the faculty of volition.

Certain virtues, attitudes and other character traits, such as courage, patience and interest, are, as I have noted, composed of a mixture of abilities, conditions for abilities and volition. Hence, including such

---

[14]   See Chapter 8 in this volume.

[15]   A terminological point: I take the term "will" as well as "volition" to be the most generic terms for this category. Wishes, wants and intentions are species of will. They are differentiated according to their strength with regard to issuing in action. An "idle" wish is the weakest form of will. An intention is the strongest form. An intention issues in action unless the agent is directly prevented from performing the action.

virtues among the abilities entails including certain volitions also among the abilities.

Whatever our decision with regard to the relation between the concepts of ability and will, motivation in terms of a general willingness to accept a job and perform it well is certainly among the crucial factors qualifying a person for a job. And qualifications, as I will note further in the next chapter, need not all be of an ability or competence kind.

CHAPTER 11

On Other Conditions for Work

The Notion of Qualification

A notion sometimes used in the context of occupations and professions is that of qualification.[1] How should it be differentiated from competence? Ellström uses the term with the connotation of a competence that is objectively required by the tasks of the profession in question and/or what is formally or informally required by the employer. As I noted in my review of Ellström, his notion is still of a competence kind. I find it more fruitful here to use qualification as a generic concept more inclusive than competence. Qualification thus includes competence, but also contains some further items. I noted what these could be in the context of employability[2]. Years of education (which is not the same as real competence), language difficulties, health limitations, legal barriers (having a driver's licence, a conviction record, a certain citizenship) and military status may enter as qualifying or disqualifying factors. In the Catholic Church a woman is not qualified for being a priest. A man is normally not qualified for being a model of women's clothes. A person under the age of 18 is unqualified for most occupations or professions regardless of his or her abilities. A certain certificate is needed for a person to qualify for many jobs. A person lacking a certificate but who is as competent as the holder of a certificate is normally not qualified for the job. We might summarize the conditions mentioned here as *formal conditions* for entering an occupation or profession. It is typical that the formal conditions are crucial precisely at the stage of starting a job. At later stages they normally play a minor role.

In her study of service workers Abiala[3] discovers that many people in the service sector get their employment largely on the basis of qualifications other than competencies in the ordinary sense. In a questionnaire the people in the study group claimed that the following qualifications had been particularly important for their employment. The

---

[1] See Berner, 1985 and 1989; Ellström, 1992.

[2] See for instance Estes, 1974.

[3] Abiala, 2000, p. 57.

numbers refer to per cent of the study population (altogether 870 people):

- Personality 88
- Experience 65
- Personal contacts 56
- Sex 46
- Age 39
- Education 36
- Looks 19.

Race is clearly also in practice a factor of qualification in some communities. Research in the USA into the importance of so-called "soft skills" in the service economy has found that many employers perceive black men as inadequately qualified for the work required.[4] According to these employers black men lack, in general, the desired attitude, behaviour and demeanour necessary for secure employment.

The Notion of Authority

A notion related to that of qualification is that of authority. Authority may be viewed as a special sort of ability, viz. a conventionally stipulated ability, which comes with the acquisition of a certain position. The authority grants that a desired outcome can be realized. Only a police officer can arrest a person. Only a judge can sentence a criminal. Only a professor can examine PhD students. Here, as in the case of a certificate, there are rules saying when something is possible. If a person who is not a police officer grabs another person the action can never count as an arrest. Similarly, when a person other than a professor signs an examination document, this counts as a void action. Authority may be seen as a formal condition for the execution of certain tasks. If qualification in general is tied to the moment of employment, authority may be seen as tied to the execution of a profession.

Health, Aging and Executive Ability

To this shall now be added the crucial factor of *executive ability*, where health plays an essential role.

One can wonder why executive ability or health is an additional factor to the previously mentioned ones. I have already stated that the practical possibility of action is constituted by ability and opportunity.

---

4   Tilly and Moss, 1996.

To what can health add? Is health a factor of opportunity? Indeed, health can be viewed as an "inner" opportunity. The state of the body gives the person an opportunity to act (in the case of health) or prevents the person from acting (in the case of ill health). This is hardly a natural mode of speech, however. One may instead say that what I have so far summarized as competence items do not add up to a *complete* set of conditions for ability, given standard or otherwise reasonable circumstances. It is not always sufficient for a person to be willing, completely competent and formally qualified for an action to come about. One must also have a particular strength that is often lacking in the case of ill health. I will push this analysis further.

When the competent electrician catches flu and does not go to work he or she does not, in general, lose the competence to do the work of an electrician. The basic competence is there all the time. What has happened normally is that the person has lost the strength to *execute* the competence during a short period. He or she has an aching body and has become very tired. The executive machinery is damaged. *Executive ability* is thus a notion to be added to our instrument in order to catch all the conditions for work action.[5]

Observe that ill health (in particular when it involves subjective suffering, such as pain, fatigue or anguish) also may strike against the person's *perception* of his or her work ability. In an informative study Schult et al.[6] studied two groups with comparable basic physical status. In one of the groups the participants abstained from work altogether mainly because of their subjective assessment of their status, whereas the other group attempted to do some work at least part-time. It emerged that the second group scored better than the first one in most relevant respects, including subjective quality of life. The general mental attitude of the group that remained at home in fact reduced their work ability considerably, much beyond what could reasonably be expected given their physical status. The perception of one's work ability is thus in itself a considerable causal factor with regard to the ultimate work ability.

A disease or injury strikes primarily, I would argue, against the executive ability. It does not typically affect the overall competence. This is possible, however, when we deal with certain serious and, in particular, enduring diseases. A neurological disease may reduce a person's intelligence as well as other aspects of his or her personality. A chronic

---

[5] Brülde and Tengland, 2003, have particularly emphasized the role of executive ability in health.

[6] Schult et al., 2000.

and serious disease of whatever kind will after a period reduce the person's talent for the job. He or she will inevitably forget both theoretical and practical elements involved in the competence. In addition, aspects of tolerance and courage will fade away. Thus ill health may in certain circumstances strike in a more basic way than just affecting the executive ability, i.e. the physiology of the person or the energy of the person. Ill health, in particular severe and chronic ill health, may certainly also affect a person's willingness to perform a job for a shorter or longer period.

The Dynamic Character of Work Ability; Aging

Work ability is clearly not static but changes, sometimes dramatically, over time. Ilmarinen[7] and his colleagues have particularly studied the changes related to aging. The typical evolution when an individual grows older is that he or she loses certain crucial capacities. The most important changes in mental functions, Ilmarinen contends, are the weakening of precision and the speed of perception. These changes concern the entire human system for processing information, including the sensori-perceptive system, the cognitive system and the motor system.

It is interesting to note, however, that many mental functions in fact improve over the years. Some cognitive functions, such as the control of use of language and the ability to process complex problems, improve with age. There are other qualities that come with a long life's work experience that substantially enhance the old person's general work ability. Ilmarinen points to the following crucial qualities of the elderly workers: ability to deliberate, ability to comprehend and reason about a complex system and better verbal command.

To this can be added certain qualities outside the traditional sphere of ability, for instance a higher degree of wisdom, stronger commitment to work, more faithfulness to the employer and a higher motivation to learn.

A Summary of a Person's Internal Conditions for Work

I can now summarize the general properties necessary for the tasks of a job. I have mentioned several items within the overall competence for the job. Moreover, I have added the notions of qualification, authority and executive ability, which together with competence constitute the person's full ability. I have also indicated the necessity of the factor of

---

[7]   Ilmarinen, 2001a.

volition, viz. the interest in the job and willingness to perform it in all its aspects.

Let me then collect a person's inner conditions for work into the following seven major categories:

1. Overall competence for the job, including knowledge and skill. I have suggested that this competence should be divided into technical, general and personal competence.

   The overall competence also includes factors such as:

   a. Toleration of physical, psychological and social aspects of the job.

   b. Courage with regard to taking up the job and fulfilling the demanding tasks of the job.

   c. Virtues necessary for fulfilling the tasks of the job (examples: honesty, loyalty, perseverance and carefulness).

2. Other qualifications for having and performing the job.

3. Executive ability to perform the job.

4. Willingness to take and perform the job.

The Environment as Enhancing and Restricting Ability

I have already noted that every kind of ability is related to a set of circumstances. In many instances we refrain from mentioning such circumstances. This is when we presuppose that a set of standard circumstances or reasonable circumstances exist. We often take such circumstances for granted.

In some cases, however, the right circumstances are not there. There is no opportunity for the agent to perform what he or she wishes to perform. This obviously also holds for the case of work ability. The worker who is perfectly able (in all the senses discussed above) to do the job may be prevented from doing it because of non-standard or unreasonable circumstances. There may simply be no job available or the agent may have been sacked. We should also consider the case where there are legal constraints. The tasks to be performed by the agent may be illegal or otherwise condemned by society.

A further possibility is that there are so many disturbing factors at the work place that it is impossible to complete the tasks. The physical environment (in terms of cold, noise or pollution) may be disastrous. Or the psychosocial environment (in terms of high demands, other kinds of stress, or unfriendly attitudes) may be intolerable.

The psychosocial environment can be demanding and stressful, as I said. We can note that some of these stresses are of a *normative* nature. I here wish to distinguish between various cases. First, we have the one where as a matter of brute fact a manager demands something (perhaps unreasonable) of a worker. Second, we have the situation where there is an agreement (still perhaps unreasonable) between employer and employee with regard to the fulfilment of a difficult task within some limited period. The inability to perform such a difficult task should not be regarded as a genuine *disability* if the environment is unreasonable. If we were not to make a distinction between reasonable and unreasonable environments then everybody might be considered disabled in some contexts. There is for everybody some type of environment such that it will prevent them from performing their job properly. Third, we have the case where there is a normative consensus in society that the proper job performance requires certain measures. This is then the case where the agent who cannot fulfil the task must legitimately be judged to be disabled with regard to doing what he or she is expected to do.

Karasek and Theorell have made great contributions to the research about demanding environments. Their results indicate that the picture of environmental influence is more complex than one might first imagine. It is not only the strain or demand that stresses the worker. An even more crucial factor is what the environment allows in terms of decision latitudes and control. The authors say: "the most adverse reactions of psychological strain (fatigue, anxiety, depression and physical illness) occur when the psychological demands of the job are high and the worker's decision latitude in the tasks is low".[8]

It is the combination of high demands with low control over environmental circumstances that is particularly detrimental. Control does not primarily refer to control of other people but rather to control of the working situation. It entails both skill discretion and decision authority. Skill discretion refers to the skill acquired by the subject and which he or she uses in completing the tasks of the job. The decision authority is in line with the concept of authority introduced earlier in this chapter. Some positions entail an authority to take decisions with regard to certain issues. Sometimes but not always there is a match between the skills acquired and the decision authority attributed to the person.

Karasek and Theorell observe the following consequences of the negative combination of high demands and a low degree of decision latitude:

> What occurs in a situation of increased demands such as speed-up is not just the constructive response of arousal but the often hopeless, long-lasting, and

---

[8]   Karasek and Theorell, 1990, p. 16.

negatively experienced response of residual psychological strain, often appearing as aggressive behavior or social withdrawal.[9]

The authors illustrate how various professions are distributed along the dimensions demand and control.[10] Professionals such as doctors, bank officials, teachers and public officials are the people who often have to meet tough demands but also possess a high degree of freedom in choosing their tasks and planning their days. As a result the demands are not normally detrimental to their health. In fact the demands can often be seen as stimulating and in combination with good control as enhancing their health. But there certainly are limits and there are too high demands on some of these highly skilled people. Professionals such as architects, natural scientists, foremen and machinists also score highly along the control dimension but often have to meet lower demands. They are perhaps the most secure group from the health point of view. People like watchmen, caretakers and shop assistants are faced with low demands but have little control. They risk ending up in a passive and sedentary life. But the real risk group for illness includes firemen, nurses' assistants, telephone operators and waitresses, people who are highly stressed with little control of their work situation. These are the people who risk acquiring the most stress related illnesses, such as burnt-out syndromes and cardiovascular diseases. It is significant that the risk group includes many occupations that are typically held by women.[11]

These observations are crucial in the practical analysis of work ability. There is much to be done for the improvement of work environments. A person who looks unfit (and even believes him or herself to be unfit) for his or her job may seem so because of an environment which is unsuitable and ought to be altered in terms of demands and decision latitudes. Much rehabilitative work should be directed to environments. Also the agent him or herself should make an attempt to change the workplace for the better. In fact this factor could be included in the list of desirable abilities: to have the ability to influence the character of one's workplace.

When we talk about the change of environment we often have physical changes of a workplace in mind. Good examples of that are restructuring the building where the workplace is located, the instalment of new and adequate technical devices and the relocation of apparatus and

[9] Karasek and Theorell, 1990, p. 33.
[10] *Ibid.*, pp. 40-62.
[11] Further empirical evidence supporting the theory of Karasek and Theorell is given in Kristensson *et al.*, 2004.

people. But it can also, as the demand and control model implies, involve institutional changes, the change of a complete organizational structure (including the distribution of decision authority) or of a local structure. The subject may, for instance, need a new and more understanding boss.

To this list of factors we can add a further possible change that is contained in my action-theoretic analysis. This entails in a sense a *redefinition* of a work task or a whole job. Let me take a simple example. There are many jobs, in particular of an institutional kind, such as that of a lawyer, a manager of a firm, or a clerk in an enterprise, which frequently involve the simple act of signing one's name. A contract is drawn up, a bank account is opened and a business transaction is finally made through the person's signing his or her name on a relevant document.

Consider now a person who is authorized in relevant respects and who has chronically or at least for a long time lost the capacity to move his or her right hand and thereby lost the ability to sign a contract. This means a radical disablement to this person but perhaps also to the company. Many crucial tasks in the company cannot be performed. The rehabilitation of this person normally entails attempts to restore the basic physical competence of the hand (in the case of there being a hand left). But this may be impossible. The person may have become chronically disabled. Is there then no other way of reintroducing the capacity to sign contracts? Indeed there is. The act of signing a contract is a conventional action; it is dependent on conventional rules. And conventions can always be altered or modified. One can simply decide or agree between relevant firms and institutions that a particular person who cannot move his or her hand, is permitted to sign relevant documents in a new way, perhaps by clicking on a certain button on a computer after having entered via a code. In this purely conventional way the agent is now enabled to perform his or her daily tasks. Here we can see how elements in the basic action-theoretic analysis can come into play. A certain complex action can be generated by different basic actions with the same result.

It is typical, as I have done in this section, to emphasize the environment as *restrictive*. Giddens[12] has noted this as a shortcoming in several analyses of ability. However, as he notes and as I have noted earlier, the environment is equally much an enabling factor. No action, or almost no action, could be performed in a vacuum. A certain configuration of the world is necessary for an action to be performed at all. The

---

[12]   Giddens, 1979.

right configuration is quite often present. Most workers perform well in their environments; from this follows that they must have a working environment that is quite adequate and enabling. In spite of this, all workplaces can always be improved; the working environment can always be changed, adjustments can be made, so as to enable the worker to excel even more in his or her work.[13]

---

[13] For illustrations of this, see Johansson and Lundberg, 2004, and my discussion in Chapter 14.

CHAPTER 12

Environment Change and Changes in the Concept of Disability

Environmental changes in the sense of changes on the structural and cultural level can be crucial in a more profound way than I have considered above. They can influence the whole notion of work ability to the effect that certain categories of people who have previously had both the ability and the opportunity to work become disabled and have to rely on governmental support.

This possibility is well illustrated in a comprehensive historical project performed by Martha Blomqvist.[1] In this study Blomqvist demonstrates how the development of industrial capitalism in Sweden gradually excluded large groups of people from their workplaces, because they did not match up to the new demands. Among the persons excluded were blind and deaf persons but also in general crippled persons. Many of those persons (even the blind ones) were taken care of in the old agrarian society and could contribute to the work on a farm by performing simple tasks such as cleaning the stables and handling the animals but sometimes also taking part in the more advanced parts of farming. The crucial thing here was that they were members of small enterprises, often extended families, where all the people cared for each other. Therefore during the 19th century practically all people, including the ones with salient defects, were earning their living through work.

Industrialism brought with it a tremendous reduction of the number of farms, mainly within the period between 1900 and 1950. Many people had to reconsider their occupation and many tried to enter the competitive arena of a factory where people became anonymous and where one had to face demands of efficiency and precision that had been unheard of in the agrarian society. Instead of the close and understanding environment, where there was some margin of tolerance with regard to working times and efficiency, the workers were now faced with merciless demands of achievement. One was either employed or not. And if one was employed one should do exactly what was required.

---

[1] Blomqvist, 1990 and 2001.

People with some defect, even a minor defect, who had been perfectly capable within the old context, were now completely lost.

According to the 1927 unemployment assessment in Sweden the proportion of partially disabled unemployed people had doubled since 1909 (which was the first time of measuring unemployment in Sweden). More men than women had been affected. This is understandable since the surplus of workers from the farms consisted mostly of men. The level of female employment was still on a fairly low level.

The situation for these people who had recently become unemployed was worsened by the fact that the trade unions had negotiated an understanding with the Swedish Employers' Association to the effect that there could be no acceptance of a reduction of wages for the disabled. These people therefore lost a crucial weapon to compete. They could not enter the labour market accepting a lower wage as a compensation for less efficient achievement. Thus a single decision with regard to wages between the most influential organizations on the market entailed a changed definition of the notion of a disabled person.

It is interesting to note that the renowned couple Alva and Gunnar Myrdal were concerned about this development. They argued for the introduction of special units for the less "productive" part of the work force. And the trade union movement was requested not to interfere with such a development.

> If it does [interfere], it jeopardises its most fundamental social policy ideal, that of safeguarding the interest of working people. For even individuals who are not top-grade are part of this group or at least should be. A trade union movement that in this and other respects developed in such a way as to thrust aside the weakest and shield the strongest would become soulless – it would embrace its own destruction just at the point when it wields its greatest power.[2]

Confronted with the joined forces keeping the partially disabled people out of the working arena, the state eventually had to take measures. A new term "occupationally handicapped" was coined as a heading for the categories of the unemployed that could be considered for subsidized employment. Thus certain workshops or other workplaces were installed for partially handicapped people who could work there under particularly advantageous circumstances and with some salary.

> "Occupationally handicapped" was (and is) a purely administrative concept and allowed a flexible use of the subsidies. It included the traditional dis-

---

[2]   Alva and Gunnar Myrdal, 1935, p. 256.

ability groups, but also the less than precise category of "socially malad-justed", eventually renamed to "socio-medical disabilities".[3]

The observations made by Blomqvist can be transferred to the situation today. The industrial society is now gradually being transformed into an information society or a post-industrial society. Manual work is becoming rarer and practically all jobs involve some intellectual tasks, in particular the handling of a computer for the exchange of information. To this is added a change from individual to collective work. Many organizational changes involve the delegation of control over the work to work teams. The individual becomes to a higher degree a member of a collective, has to cooperate even more and has to negotiate with the collective about his or her tasks.

For many employees these changes are for the better. Job enlargement means more varied tasks, which makes work more interesting and reduces the risk for musculoskeletal injuries ... [But] for those who do not meet the ever increasing performance demands, or who for other reasons find it difficult to adapt to the new organisations, the changes constitute a threat however.[4]

The employers now look for people who can tolerate stress and excel under the demands of the new era. The workers must have some intellectual talent, they must be able to communicate and in general have great social competence. Moreover, they must have stress tolerance of a new kind. They must all tolerate the stress of competition and high demands from colleagues and employers.

---

[3] Blomqvist, 2001, p. 203.
[4] *Ibid.*, p. 206.

CHAPTER 13

Minimal Ability and the Ability of Excellence

In the context of work ability there is one distinction which is rarely made, but which I have alluded to in several instances in this analysis. This is the one between performing one's tasks in a minimally acceptable way and performing them in an excellent way. The former notion is central in the context of social insurance whereas the latter notion is crucial for an employer in the situation of employment and in the context of evaluating a person's achievements. As a preparation for the analysis of these concepts I will present the following considerations with regard to *performing an action and performing an action well.*

In many cases, not least in the context of education or health care, there is a need for distinguishing between performing an action and performing an action well. Situations exist where it is important to perform an action well. A father tells his son to wash himself properly. Or a teacher tells a student to perform well during a course so that she will get her degree. But what do "goodness" and similar terms refer to here? There is a battery of distinctions to be made.

Standards for Performing an Action

Different standards for action exist. I will first consider the basic idea of a standard by which one can say whether an action has been performed at all. As I have previously noted, there are a number of legally formalized conventional actions, where the results as well as other required circumstances are clearly stipulated in a formal definition of the action. The reasons for these stipulations are obvious. No doubt shall exist concerning when a couple are married, when a criminal has been sentenced, or when a will has become valid. Thus, such actions and their entailed results are defined quite precisely. Moreover, when there is a lack of clarity this is normally straightened out by a court decision.

The areas where standards have been well developed are law, administration and medicine. Minimal requirements exist, for instance, for being a county councillor. These are formulated in written instructions. If the instructions are not followed, the councillor is not really performing the job. To some extent health care institutions, in particular institutions of rehabilitation, have introduced standards for judging when a patient can be said to be doing such things as walking, talking and reading. Such standards are necessary in order to define the rehabilitating tasks. It is necessary to ask such questions as: what is the goal of the rehabilitation of this man who cannot walk?

An interesting difference in character exists between the legal/administrative standard and the medical standard. In the former case no doubt can come up as to whether the agent is able to do what is required; the question is rather whether he or she is willing to do it. In the medical case the whole focus is on the agent's ability. The former standard is there to enforce action, and if it is not done, to hold a person legally responsible. The medical standard is there to help health care personnel in their efforts to rehabilitate patients.

Standards for Action and Standards for Proper Action

My focus has so far been completely on the basic criteria for the occurrence of an action of a certain type. Under what conditions has a person closed a door, baked a cake, passed an exam, walked, talked or administered a county council? I have said that the answer to this question frequently requires the introduction of a standard. This holds not only for the set of conventional actions (where this must be done almost per definition) but also for many natural actions. The notion of a standard, however, has a ring of *normativity* about it. Our initial task, however, was factual. We wanted to know about the existence conditions for actions. How should this be settled?

In one sense the normativity about standards is no problem or at least no exception in relation to, for instance, what is the case in science. We certainly talk about standards in many scientific contexts. For the purpose of exact measurement, for instance, one has to introduce standards to be followed all over the world. There is, for instance, a standard metre, situated in Paris, which stipulates the notion of a metre. There are thousands of other stipulated definitions in science. One has to follow these stipulations in order to be talking the scientific language correctly. Thus on this level there is nothing particularly problematic about the action language.

But not only this kind of normativity is at stake in the case of action. The standard suggested for the county council administrators does not just tell us what are to be counted as actions or performance in their job. It also tells us what they are supposed to do as administrators. The instructions do not just contain *constitutive* rules for actions but also *regulative* rules.[1] Or the rules are at the same time constitutive and regulative. Not all of them need have this double function, of course. There may, for instance, be a lot of actions that are optional for the administrator. This double function of rules is common in the case of conventional actions. It is easy to illustrate this ambivalence from the field of games. The game of chess contains a number of constitutive rules, rules that define the different moves and also what moves can be made in what order. If a player does something that is not defined, this move is no move at all, no action at all within the game. But apart from being no move this non-action, which is still an action in the ordinary world, is forbidden. The player violates the spirit of the game. This double function of many constitutive rules is the reason why I suggest that they define what is to be counted as a proper action.

What is to be said about normativity in the medical context? I suggested that, for instance, rehabilitation personnel have to fixate their language in order to communicate properly. One way of doing this is to specify activities such as walking, talking and reading in terms of actions (for example walking 50 yards) or in terms of characteristics such as speed and balance in the performance of the activity. Such things could be standardized and itemized in classificatory lists. This is partly done in the ICF (International Classification of Functioning, Disability and Health). Is this at all different from the standardization used in science? Is it not the case that the health care personnel create their own technical language?

To a great extent this is the case. Owing to the different purposes in the different practices, differences in emphasis may exist. In health care an emphasis exists on the minimal standard for proper action. The person who cannot walk, talk or read properly has not fulfilled the minimal standard for walking, talking or reading which has been set up as the goal of rehabilitation. The question then is: minimal for what? The answer is that the purposes can vary somewhat. Sometimes this minimum is set at a very low level. If a person cannot perform properly according to such a standard then he or she may be entitled to care or further rehabilitation.

Quite a different kind of minimal standard exists when people apply to enter a certain sector in life, a school or a profession. A person cannot become an army officer, a sailor or a police officer unless he or she can perform certain actions properly. With regard to these professions the requirements are not really "minimal". Particularly strong requirements

---

[1] See my definitions in Chapter 10.

exist with regard to perception and physical abilities for these professions.

Let me conclude about the element of normativity in standards for action.

a. A basic sense of "standard" exists where the term only refers to the result of a stipulated definition.

b. In legal and administrative definitions of actions, the constitutive standard can also be regulative in the sense that the action in question is obligatory for, or at least expected of, a professional in the relevant sector.

c. In the health care sector a proper action (or rather: the ability to perform a proper action) can be what is desired or required for a certain purpose and be related to a person's right to care and rehabilitation.

Standards of Excellence

So far I have been discussing conditions for performing an action at all or performing a minimally proper action. But we can also evaluate actions along a scale of excellence. We can perform an action just in the way required, we can perform it moderately well, we can perform it well, and we can perform it excellently. Some actions can even be quantitatively measured along scales of excellence. This is particularly salient in sports. To run 100 metres in 11 seconds is to run moderately well, to do it in 10.5 is to run very well, and under 10 seconds is excellent. This scale is tuned to real athletes; other scales exist for ordinary people. Similar evaluations can be made within the fine arts. Artists can perform well along the dimension of aesthetic beauty or other dimensions relevant to the arts: being provocative, being interesting, opening people's minds etc.

A different kind of evaluation deals with professional excellence. This is quite often, but not universally, a utilitarian evaluation. A person does well in engineering, in plumbing, in health care etc., if the person promotes the good that the profession has been instituted for. With some professions, such as the scientist's, one is inclined to add that there may be an intrinsic value in performing the professional activity. This holds equally as much for the artist. We often talk about the intellectual value of science that is to be compared to the aesthetic value of art.

CHAPTER 14

The Contexts for the Assessment
of Work Ability

In the Introduction I noted the differences between the contexts where the notion of work ability is crucial. I started with the context of social insurance and disability benefits but went on to look into the notion of work ability in much broader contexts where the concepts of competence and skill have a central place. There are connections between all these areas and I will look closer into them. Let me start with the assessment of the excellent worker which is tantamount to analyzing the requirements for the excellent performance of a job.

The Excellent Worker: the Contexts
of Assessment and Recruitment

For a person to perform his or her job well many requirements must be fulfilled. The basic qualifications (in terms of authority and other qualifications) must be in order. He or she must have full technical, general, strategic and personal competence. The capabilities for toleration and courage must be present. Moreover the motivational or volitional faculties must function perfectly. Certain virtues such as honesty, loyalty and courage must be present. The person must be willing to cooperate with and support his or her colleagues and must be empathic towards the clients. In short, the person must be enthusiastic about his or her work. These are the inside requirements. However, to succeed the person's environment must be in order. The workplace must be excellent, not just tolerable, both physically and psychosocially. The person's colleagues must be cooperative and supportive in their turn and the bosses must be positive in their attitudes to the whole work community including the person him or herself. Also other environmental conditions, both physical and psychosocial, have to be advantageous.

There is a lot that can go wrong, then, in this machinery. Some of the factors have been cited in the basic action-theoretic analysis above. But they have to be supplemented and specified for the work case. In the following brief analysis I will start from the state of excellence with regard to a particular job and finally turn to the situation where the worker lacks resources for performing even a minimal level of his or her work.

First we can note that there is hardly any worker or workplace that reaches perfection on all kinds of scales. Even the best professionals and even the best workplaces have their faults. There is always something that can become better. This has one crucial and partly comforting consequence. There is quite a big margin of tolerance with regard to performance of work and also the quality of the workplace in most societies and contexts. One cannot make a workplace better than what is reasonable in the particular country and environment. The requirements as to security are perhaps exceptions to this. They should be particularly stringent and no compromise can be tolerated in this respect in any context.

The assessment as to the worker varies of course a lot between workplaces. But in most contexts a person can be considered to be an excellent worker even if some of his or her skills are far from perfect and even if some of these skills have deteriorated in a salient way. This holds in particular for senior representatives of a profession. The senior worker normally loses some of his or her specific skills but this is normally compensated for by the fact that the workplace as a whole includes other young people who can do the technical job and in particular by the fact that the senior worker has normally acquired a certain element of wisdom with regard to how things should be done. His or her empathic and in general psychological skills may have improved considerably.

Thus the notion of an excellent worker tolerates a lot of varieties in most contexts, at least when we have to do with big workplaces where the total amount of work to be done can be distributed across the whole workforce. However, there is a limit. A competence can deteriorate so much that we say that the holder of a certain position no longer meets the requirements for being an excellent worker. A case can appear when the employer who needs an excellent person in the position has to sack the individual or at least move him or her to another position in the enterprise.

It is crucial to note that a set of competencies can be lost for several reasons which are not necessarily included among the maladies or disabilities in the socio-medical context. Nor need the loss of competence be due to ordinary old age. It is a simple fact that all human beings if they do not exercise or keep up a specific occupation after a time lose the necessary capacities.[1]

---

[1] This is sometimes compensated for, however. See the observations by Ilmarinen described in Chapter 11 in this volume.

The criterion of excellence crops up in particular in the context of recruitment. There may be a competition between several people, where all applicants have more than a minimal competence for the relevant job according to the list of qualifications. The list may say that the employee must be able to fulfil at least the following tasks along a number of dimensions: problem solving, socializing, taking responsibility for persons, working hard with a high degree of concentration. Some of the applicants may excel, and the employer will then pick the individual who stands out in this competition.

The Context of Education

The British skills project attempted to establish what employers really need with regard to the various occupations. But what does an educational programme really aim at? Does it aim at producing excellent workers on the top level according to the various dimensions of qualification discussed above?

This is hardly the case. Most courses of occupational education provide a basic platform of theoretical knowledge and some practical knowledge in the occupation in question. It is worth consulting Dreyfus[2] and Benner for the analysis of the educational case. Dreyfus has developed a conceptual framework for specifying degrees of competencies in professions. Benner has applied this scheme to the profession of nursing. Benner identifies four levels of competence. Stage 1 is the *novice.*

Beginners have had no experience of the situations in which they are expected to perform. To give them entry to these situations and allow them to gain the experience so necessary for skill development, they are taught about the situations in terms of objective attributes such as weight, intake and output, temperature, blood pressure, pulse, and other such objectifiable, measurable parameters of the patient's condition.[3]

The second stage is the one of the *advanced beginner.*

Advanced beginners are ones who can demonstrate marginally acceptable performance, ones who have coped with enough real situations to note ... the recurring meaningful situational components that are termed 'aspects of the situation' by Dreyfus.[4]

Stage 3 is called *competence.*

---

[2] Dreyfus, 1980, and later; Benner, 1984, and later.

[3] Benner, 1984, p. 20.

[4] *Ibid.*, 1984, p. 22.

Competence, typified by the nurse who has been on the job in the same or similar situations two or three years, develops when the nurse begins to see his or her actions in terms of long-range goals or plans of which he or she is consciously aware. The plan dictates which attributes and aspects of the current and contemplated future situation are to be considered most important and those which can be ignored.[5]

Stage 4, finally, stands for *proficiency*.

Characteristically, the proficient performer perceives situations as wholes rather than in terms of aspects, and performance is guided by maxims. Perception is a key word here. The perspective is not thought out but 'presents itself' based upon experience and recent events.[6]

It is clear that there is no education that could aim at proficiency in this sense. Proficiency, by definition, presupposes at least five years of practising the profession in question. The formal basic education seems to aim for the stage of advanced beginner (at least when we talk about the basic education of fairly complicated professionals such as the ones in health care). The student has after the education acquired a fair amount of theoretical knowledge. The student has also had some practical training so that he or she, after a brief introduction at the first workplace, can at least minimally handle the daily situations. This is by convention considered to be sufficient for entering the profession. For the higher levels much more practice and perhaps specialized courses are required.

This of course does not preclude the existence of particularly talented individuals who can reach excellence in a very short time. Thus there is a case for talking about excellence also among persons being recruited to a job for the first time. But this may be seen as excellence in relation to the level of competence as described by Dreyfus and Benner.

To Do one's Job Minimally Well: the Context of Sickness and Disability Benefits

Where is the limit of minimal ability to perform one's job? This is the sixty-four-thousand million dollar question that plagues social insurance authorities and companies, as well as medical doctors who give the "diagnosis" of inability to work.

There is certainly no ultimate theoretically sound answer to this question. The answer must be completely normative and will differ from

---

[5] Benner, 1984, p. 26.

[6] *Ibid.*, p. 27.

workplace to workplace, from position to position and from situation to situation. For reasons that I will expand, this situation is inevitable. However, some states of health stand out in a salient way. There are human conditions such that the bearer cannot possibly do any work at all. A person may be in coma or in such general pain or anguish that no reasonable action can be performed at all.

But if we exclude such extreme cases there is much reason for hesitation. A complicating factor with regard to the social benefit assessment is the following. A person may be quite capable of going to work and doing some work but may be strongly advised not to do so for medical reasons. A doctor may consider that the person's disease is such that any work or exertion may put his or her *future* health in jeopardy. Thus the person may be legitimately sick-listed although he or she is not strictly disabled from working. A similar point must also be made with regard to the requirements made with regard to healthy people. The work requirements must not be such that the healthy person puts his or her future health in jeopardy. The reasonable environment must fulfil such a basic condition.

Leaving also this case aside there are various considerations that make the limit of minimal health blurred. A particular job contains a variety of tasks. Some of these tasks may be highly demanding, whereas some are less demanding. The person may feel ill on a particular day when he or she is expected to fulfil a difficult task. Assume that we are considering a man who is a pilot and is expected to make a transatlantic flight with 200 passengers. It seems out of the question for this person to perform the task given his illness. Thus the pilot must abstain because of illness. However, if the illness happens to occur on a day when very little is required, then he need not be absent from work despite having the same degree of illness. It may be a day without any flights and only very light office work is required of him. Then there is no need for sick listing or any need for his absence from the same workplace. (A very special exception here is when there is a risk of contagion in connection with a disease.) In a sense, then, we must construe the medical disability as completely related to the various tasks of the occupation. If the tasks happen to be demanding, then the probability of disability is high, when they are less demanding the probability becomes lower.

The situation is different when we consider absence from work for a long period, the case where the illness or disability is chronic. Then one must consider both the extremely demanding and the less demanding periods. One has to take the whole spectrum of tasks into account. There are two principal directions for dealing with this kind of case. One alternative is to say that the person, given that the working circumstances are considered to be reasonable, is disabled from performing his or her job even in the minimal sense. Since some activities are essential for the profession, like flying an aeroplane in the pilot case, then the person who cannot perform these activities at all is genuinely disabled and must be absent from the job as long as the disability prevails.

However, there is another, much more positive direction, which should also be proposed from a rehabilitative perspective. The pilot is normally a member of quite a big company that has among its employees people from different professions with various tasks. Some of these tasks would benefit from the experience of a pilot. Thus the disabled pilot could temporarily or for all the foreseeable future be allocated to quite different tasks, for instance within the security department of the company.

Johansson and Lundberg[7] have made an interesting investigation that offers support for some of my observations in this chapter and further substantially qualifies the idea of minimal ability for work. They asked a population of respondents to what extent they could adjust their work tasks to their present state of health. Their specific questions were the following: 1. Can you do necessary work and postpone the rest? 2. Can you choose among work tasks? 3. Can you get help from workmates? 4. Can you work at a slower pace than usual? 5. Can you take longer breaks? 6. Can you shorten the workday? 7. Can you go home and do work later? 8. Can you work without being disturbed at the workplace? 9. Can you work from home?

These questions indicate that some employees (normally in cooperation with their employers) can create changes in the conditions for work, i.e. change the opportunities for work, so that the requirements for minimal ability can vary considerably from situation to situation.

Most of the results of Johansson and Lundberg's studies were expected. The more opportunities to adjust, the bigger the proportion of the population had no sickness absence and the smaller the proportion was off six days or more a year. But it was also evident that people with higher positions had more opportunities to adjust, and this together with their normally more stimulating work contributed to their stable work ability.

---

[7]   Johansson and Lundberg, 2004.

The Importance of Hierarchy for Requirements of Minimal Ability and Ability of Excellence: the French Example

Berner[8] describes a discussion among French labour researchers which has a bearing on my distinctions between different levels of ability and competence. Although Berner's analysis pertains to a debate from some decades ago it is still relevant and runs across national boundaries.

The French researchers note that there is a crucial distinction between setting up competence requirements for ordinary workers and formulating such requirements for professionals high up in the hierarchy of jobs.[9] In the case of workers there is often a good correlation between the, normally, technical requirements and what is expected of the worker in actual practice. The worker is expected to do something concrete, to build a house, to put together a car, to transport material to a particular place and so on. It is imperative that he or she can perform these things in a very concrete and substantial way.

In the case of higher civil servants, managers and people in other top positions there is a much looser relation between the "requirements", if such are formulated at all, and what one could expect of the person. The functions on the top level are much more indeterminate. A person on the top level can excel in many different ways. In an employment situation a person can appear who may demonstrate talents which are somewhat unexpected. A man who is basically an engineer and who applies for a technical job in a firm proves at the same time to be a linguist, being proficient in several languages. He is then considered to be extremely suitable as an export director of the firm. He knows very little about economics but this is considered to be compensated for by his personal and extraordinary linguistic talents. Other people can provide support when it comes to the technical economic issues.

The job of regional governor in Sweden is quite an indeterminate one. The person holding the office can by and large choose his or her own way of doing the job. What is expected is that he or she should represent the county in the best way and enhance its position in the Swedish arena in as many ways as possible. On this abstract level, then, there is a requirement. However, the concrete execution of the job can vary enormously. Since the governor cannot deal with all areas of activity, he or she has to choose. It is then natural and indeed desirable that the governor concentrates on matters that he or she happens to

---

[8] Berner, 1985.

[9] Berner here uses the word "qualification".

know something about. This can be the fight against criminality, support of local enterprises, or enhancement of cultural or sports activities. As a result two governors can in their everyday practice turn out to do very different things. They thereby execute very different competencies in the same type of job.

It may be noted, therefore, in the context of assessing whether a person has a minimal ability for performing his or her job, that in vocations where the content of the job can vary so much, there is much greater latitude in finding alternative tasks within the same type of job.

CHAPTER 15

On Definitions of Work Ability

I have now reached a stage where it may be useful to offer abstract definitions of work ability.[1]

Per-Anders Tengland proposes some alternative definitions of work ability. First he pays attention to such work ability as is related to a certain profession and a specific set of tasks.

A person P has complete (specific) work ability if, and only if, P has the work specific manual and intellectual competence, and has the physical, mental and social health that is required to fulfil the tasks and reach the goals (with some requirements of quality) which typically belong to the job in question (or which can typically be performed by someone in the occupation), given that the physical, psychosocial and organizational work environment is acceptable, that is, is such that most members of the same occupation (with similar competence) can be expected to fulfil the tasks in this environment.[2]

Later he also generalizes to talking about general work ability in the following way:

A person P has general full work ability if, and only if, P has the physical, mental and social health that is required to perform any work such that all people (of the same age and sex) could typically perform it after a short period of training, given that the physical, psychosocial and organizational environment is acceptable, that is, such that most adult individuals are expected to fulfil the tasks in this environment.[3]

Tengland also adds a definition that acknowledges the work ability of people with some defect or disability that somewhat reduces the full work ability.

A person P has relative (specific) work ability if, and only if, P has the work specific manual and intellectual competence and has the physical, mental and social health which is required to fulfill certain adapted tasks and reach certain (to the disability adapted) goals, and the physical, psychosocial and

---

[1] For a summary of work ability definitions, see Ludvigsson *et al.*, 2006.

[2] Tengland, 2005, p. 30. My translation.

[3] *Ibid.*, p. 30. My translation.

organizational work environment is especially advantageous, that is, it is particularly adapted to the limited ability of the individual.[4]

Let me now scrutinize these offers in the light of my previous analysis. Since Tengland has particularly focused on the health conditions, his specification of the competence requirement is not comprehensive. He confines himself to talking about manual and intellectual competence. Many authors, including myself, have introduced competencies of other kinds, including social, psychological and ethical ones. I have also mentioned general competencies, such as strategic ability and capacity to work hard. My picture also contains a certain set of non-intentional abilities, such as toleration, courage and other work-relevant virtues.

Tengland's definition can easily be modified by simply omitting a specification of the competencies and including other qualifications. Thus the person must have *the work specific competencies, other qualifications and the health conditions needed for the fulfillment of his or her work tasks.*

Tengland's definition of general work ability requires some comments. He relates this ability to what all people could typically do after a short period of training. This presupposition is problematic in the light of what I said about the *basic standard competence* in Chapter 9. Not all people have that competence and cannot therefore be expected to fulfil most jobs. A solution is to relate the general work ability only to people with basic standard competence or to abstain from talking about a completely general work ability and instead relate a person's work ability to a set of jobs on a specific level of competence. The Government Official Report SOU 1997 discusses the question of competence and acknowledges that in many cases of rehabilitation further education has to be provided for a new suitable job, but in some cases also for a return to the old employer. The old job may have changed character because of new demands.

Tengland relates the judgment of an individual's work ability to what most people could achieve with regard to the tasks in question. It is crucial to note that the report SOU 1997 explicitly goes against such a proposal. When the reduction of a person's work ability is to be assessed, this should be performed in relation to the person's own history, what he or she was able to do before. This means that the individual's work ability should not be related to any absolute norm, nor to what most people can do, nor, indeed, to what the most talented people can do.

---

[4]   Tengland, 2005, pp. 32-33. My translation.

A further presupposition made by Tengland is to relate work ability to jobs *actually existing* on the labour market. This is certainly in line with what is current praxis today. The report SOU 1997 discusses this presupposition in some detail.[5] The authors are eager to point out that it should really mean *normally* existing. Some jobs, for instance traditional secretarial jobs, are now gradually disappearing because of the IT revolution, resulting in a situation where most administrators do all their office work themselves. Such jobs as are fading away should not be considered as normally existing. The labour market should also be considered to be limited to the territory of the nation. No person should be expected to move abroad to take a job.

A possible point of view is to relate the person's work ability to a *conceivable* labour market. If the economic conditions in the country had been better and there had been a demand for building workers a particular person might perfectly well have been one. According to such an absolute conception of work ability this person should be considered to be able to work.[6]

It is clear that the definition of work ability should also acknowledge the variety of means by which work and workplaces could be adjusted to a person's state of health. Also circumstances at a work place which are in general reasonable may be too harsh for a person with a somewhat reduced ability. Simple changes or simple allowances in terms of post-poning more difficult tasks or letting a person work from home might enable the individual to work in a significant way.[7]

Let me summarize my observations with regard to Tengland's defini-tions and propose an alternative definition of my own. I here only specify for the case of specific work ability.

> A person *P* has complete (specific) work ability if, and only if, *P* has the work specific manual and intellectual competence, strength, as well as tol-eration and courage, relevant virtues, other qualifications and has the physi-cal, mental and social health that is required to fulfil the tasks (or alterna-tives within a set of tasks) and reach the goals (with some requirements of quality) which belong to the job in question, given that the physical, psycho-social and organizational work environment is acceptable to *P*, or can with adjustments easily be made acceptable to *P*.

---

[5] Swedish Government Official Report, SOU 1997, pp. 195-197.

[6] Hultgren, 2000, pp. 20-23, discusses this issue.

[7] Consider here Johansson and Lundberg, 2004 and 2006.

PART III

WORK ABILITY AND MEDICAL CONDITIONS

CHAPTER 16

On the Requirement of Disease as
the Cause of Disability Regarding Work

International Considerations

In a comprehensive report de Boer *et al.* make a comparison between the long-term disability arrangements in 15 countries (Belgium, Denmark, Finland, France, Germany, Hungary, Ireland, Italy, the Netherlands, Norway, the Russian Federation, Slovenia, Spain, the UK and the USA). This comparison also involves the basic conceptual frameworks used in the various countries.

The core notion is the notion of disability in respect of work. In the Netherlands, which functions as the reference country in this analysis, the basic definition is as follows:

> As a direct and medically statable result of disease or impairment, a person is unable, fully or partially, to earn with customary labour the income of a comparable healthy person. Customary labour refers to all possible jobs for a person. Disability refers to earning capacity. Disability can be accepted after 52 weeks of sick leave and after employer and employee have shown sufficient evidence of trying to get the employee reintegrated.[1]

(There is a problem with the terminology here. De Boer *et al.* oscillate between the terms "disability" and "earning capacity". In the definition above "disability" is in fact defined in terms of earning capacity. However, the two concepts need not be identical. They are clearly separated, for instance, in the Norwegian legislation.)

De Boer *et al.* make a useful comparison between the Dutch definition and the ones of the other 14 countries. Their findings can be summarized thus:[2]

Cause of disability: Most definitions entail that the incapacity should have resulted from a medical condition, such as disease, impairment or injury. However, not all countries require that the medical condition should be medically or, in some other sense, objectively verified.

---

[1] De Boer *et al.*, 2004, p. 17.
[2] *Ibid.*, 2004, pp. 18-19.

The concept of disability: There are differences in the exact definition of disability. Some identify disability with loss of capacity for work, or as a loss of capacity to earn income, or simply as anatomical injury. The first formulation, loss of capacity for work, is the most common one in the examined countries.

Time perspective: Many countries explicitly state the expected time duration of the incapacity in the definitions. The most common explicitly stated minimal time duration is one year.

One fundamental aspect investigated by de Boer *et al.* concerns the operationalization of the concept of disability. Should one in assessing a person's work ability in a theoretical way consider what a person could do, by studying certain criteria, or should one consider what the person in fact does? With the exception of Norway and Denmark all countries propose theoretical methods. Mainly the methods include determining the presence of certain diseases or impairments. In some countries (Belgium, Italy, Russia and the USA) such strictly medical methods are the only ones used. In other countries (Ireland, Spain, Slovenia and the UK) functional methods are used, entailing the determination of specific losses or reductions of gross functions, such as walking, standing and concentrating. In yet other countries the focus is on rehabilitation. This means that the gravity of a disability is assessed in terms of the expected time for rehabilitation. Logically, however, this method must be secondary. It must have been decided whether something is a disability in the first place, before a consideration about rehabilitation comes to the fore.

The assessors of disability are in all countries academically trained doctors. In many countries the medical assessors must also have a further education and training in the area of disability evaluation. The courses can vary in length between a few days and four years. Six months is a common duration. The assessor could be identical with the curative doctor in most countries. Exceptions are, however, the Netherlands, Belgium and Spain, where the medical assessor of disability is a different person and the curative doctor is consulted only in special circumstances.

The Netherlands has in general the most elaborated system for disability assessment. Apart from the specially trained assessor, the employer plays a major role when it comes to sickness benefits and rehabilitation. The employer and the employee are jointly responsible for the reintegration of the employee in the case of sickness.

In addition, if the employer has a clear interest in the decision about disability, he/she can make an appeal to the social insurance agency. If the employer is not satisfied with the ultimate decision of the social insurance agency, an appeal can be made to the administrative law department of the

District Court. Decisions made by this court can be appealed to the Central Court of Appeals.[3]

The Dutch Procedure for Disability Assessment

The Dutch procedure for disability assessment is implemented in a way that is almost unique in the world and worthy of a fairly detailed description.[4] To qualify for a disability grant a claimant has to experience a loss of earning capacity of at least 35%, due to health problems. The object of insurance is earning capacity, defined as the personal income from wage work before the onset of a 2-year period of (partial) sick leave. The calculation can be illustrated by the following example. A person used to earn 20 euros an hour. It is estimated that he is still able to earn about 12 euros an hour. The resulting degree of disability will be assessed at 60%.

What is assessed in the Dutch system is thus earning capacity. The earning capacity is assessed in an evaluation involving the contribution of two kinds of professionals. An insurance physician is involved in estimating the claimant's current ability to function. An insurance physician is employed by the insurance authorities and is never identical with a treating physician. A labour expert has the duty to establish the type of job a person could still perform in order to estimate the amount of money to be earned were he or she to perform the job. The physician uses the functional capacity list described in Chapter 2. Hereby the physician assesses the nature and extent of limitations of functioning, activities or participation (using the ICF terminology). If the physician has established that a person is no longer able to perform his or her former work, the labour expert has to find out what other common jobs in the Netherlands this person could still perform given his or her present limitations. Using the types of jobs the assessor finds applicable, he or she has to show the amount of money that the claimant could earn by performing such jobs. The expert is helped by a national database of common jobs, CBBS (Claim Assessment and Monitoring System). The base contains descriptions of 7,500 jobs. Each description refers to a unique job in a unique company, containing information on qualifications required, work demands, working conditions and the salary paid to the employees in the particular company. The information in the database is continuously kept up to date by 25 job analysts.

---

[3] De Boer *et al.*, 2004, p. 26.

[4] There is no such description available in English. My presentation is based on information given by Dr Henny Mulders of the Dutch Workers' Insurance Authority (UWV), who is one of the creators of the Dutch system.

The final judgment of the claimant's work status is made by the labour expert. However, in complex and ambiguous situations the labour expert makes his or her judgments together with the physician.

The Norwegian Case

The Norwegian family doctor Hans Magnus Solli has made a thorough investigation of the Norwegian system for determining eligibility for disability benefits.[5] The basis for evaluations in Norway has been the National Insurance Act [*Lov om folketrygd*] of 1966, which included the acts on rehabilitation and disability benefits of 1960. The National Insurance Act was revised in 1997. There are two crucial elements in these laws containing the fundamental conditions for assessment.

1. The individual whose status is investigated must have a disease, injury or defect.[6] The act on disability benefit of 1960 demanded objective findings. Later law texts did not require such findings. Also mental illness may entitle a person to disability benefits.

2. The ability to earn an income must have been permanently reduced by at least 50%. This disability must be caused by disease, injury or defect. The reduction of ability, understood as properties of the individual as an isolated entity, should be a result of a disease, injury or defect. Social and economic problems should play no role with regard to the eligibility of compensation.

Solli argues that the law has traditionally used two models for determining the existence of disability in the medical sense. One, and the most obvious, model is what Solli calls the *biomedical unicausal model*. By this he means that the significant disability must have an objective, physiological or biochemical cause, typically a somatic disease or an injury. This idea, Solli claims, is based on the prevalent medical hypothesis, existing at least since the days of the discovery of bacteria and other microbes, that for every disease there is a single cause, at least a single fundamental cause. Although this idea is continuously being contested it is still flourishing. It is, says Solli, also well established in the social insurance context. However, here the causal relation is, strictly speaking, not between a specific causal agent and a disease, but between a disease and a disability.

Solli relates the story of how the conception of disease has been developing in the contemporary Norwegian insurance system.[7] The so-

---

[5]   Solli, 2007.

[6]   In the following I will sometimes use the term "malady" as a general label for these three conditions. See Gert *et al.*, 2006.

[7]   Solli, 2007, pp. 237-246.

called Kjönstad commission from 1977 came to the conclusion that there is no universal definition of disease. As a consequence, the commission says, one cannot tie the notion of disability in the insurance context to a medical concept of disease. However, in a governmental decision of 1991 the concept of disease was narrowed down to accord better with the medical understanding of disease. Here it is claimed that the cause of a disability should be a medically accepted disease category, although not necessarily an organic disease. This decision proved, however, to be a problem for people with chronic pain and people suffering from fibromyalgia (at the time not yet accepted as a medical condition). In the case of these persons it was not possible to demonstrate a somatic cause. On the other hand they were frequently very ill and disabled. It therefore seemed simply merciless to deny them the right to social benefits on the ground of a non-existent disease. As a consequence of this "crisis" the Social Security Tribunal [*Trygderetten*] ordered a report from a group of experts who were to make a further analysis of the concept of disease and give recommendations in this regard. The resulting Consensus Report of 1995 contains a serious discussion of the matter. The committee experts acknowledge that there have been two major concepts of disease in the history of medicine. One concept is value-neutral. According to this concept diseases are separate, objective units to be described by medical science.[8] This concept has now been rejected as "unsustainable", the experts say. The other concept is value-laden and relational. It defines the concept in the following way: "Disease is a value-laden and relational concept which is determined by the relation between medical science, the suffering and the resources of the individual and the requirements and expectations of society" (my translation).[9]

The experts found the latter concept of disease to be the only reasonable one. They seriously doubt that medical science will ever be able to find an operational characterization of disease for the purposes involved in insurance medicine. The search for "objective" signs is futile, they claim. There will always be a certain type of patients, now often diagnosed as suffering from fibromyalgia or fatigue syndrome, who are evidently seriously disabled but in the case of whom one will not find any obvious physiological or in general somatic condition. Excluding this category of patients from sickness or disability benefits would constitute an inhuman measure taken by the state.

---

[8] Cf. Chapter 17, the bio-statistical concept of disease.

[9] The Consensus Report, 1995, p. 13; Solli, 2007, p. 441.

The Social Security Tribunal accepted the relational concept of disease as described in the Consensus Report and in practice refused the old unicausal model. A person who is clearly disabled with regard to work must from the point of view of the insurance system be judged to be ill (and have a disease) even if there is no objective finding, i.e. even if no somatic disease has been discovered.

The 1997 law still says that the concepts of disease and injury should be scientifically based and generally accepted in medical praxis. These conditions need not, however, in accordance with the Consensus Report, entail that the disease has a salient organic basis. There may be illness without somatic disease. However, no other cause, for instance of a social or economic kind, even if its contribution to the disability is salient, should count in the determination of disability benefits.

Solli mentions also a further model, *the scale model*, which has sometimes functioned as a supplementary model to the mono-factorial one.[10] The scale model should primarily quantify the level of *impairment* of the individual. Impairment is a concept that is broader than both disease and injury and primarily refers to the losses of physical function that may be the effects of disease and injury.[11] The idea of the scale model is to specify the degree of disability in quantitative terms. Say that a man has a fractured thigh bone and that it is broken at a particular point of the thigh. The table should then in principle inform the investigating doctor what degree of disability this impairment of the person amounts to. The normal idea is to give a percentage, from 1 to 100. Say that the impairment in this case is assessed as a 50% disability. Like the unicausal model the scale model (in its initial versions anyway) is based on the assumption of "objective" findings. The impairments measured are all observable organic impairments.

The paradigm for a scale evaluation is today the American Guides to the Evaluation of Permanent Impairment, whose latest edition is from 2001.[12] The Guides indicate for every listed impairment, for instance *diabetes mellitus* type 1, where hyperglycaemia or hypoglycaemia occurs frequently despite conscientious efforts of both individual and physician, that the impairment of the whole person should be judged to be between 21 and 40%. Another example: a person with *causalgia* with a swollen and aching leg, and where the pain is constant despite treatment, is assessed to have a 40% impairment of the whole person.

---

[10]   Solli, 2007, pp. 210-214.

[11]   The notion of impairment is more precisely defined in the ICF. See Chapter 1 in this volume.

[12]   Cocchiarella *et al.*, 2001.

The scale model has in Norway been spelt out in detail for one kind of maladies, viz. for industrial injuries and some occupational diseases. It was used during the 20th century for industrial injury compensation and is still in use there. The National Insurance Act provides a table for disabilities by means of which the injured organ and the degree of impairment may be specified.[13] It is interesting that this table also explicitly acknowledges posttraumatic stress disorder as an impairment. This is in accordance with the enlarged set of criteria of illness (and impairment), proposed by the Consensus Report and accepted by the Social Security Tribunal in 1994, which includes conditions such as chronic pain without "objective findings", i.e. illnesses without disease. Otherwise the scale model seems more to be a general model of thought when disability benefits are concerned. It is, for instance, only implicit in the Norwegian textbook on welfare rights written by Kjönstad and Syse.[14] The model is not, however, a model for quantifying disability in the more holistic sense proposed by the WHO in their International Classification of Functioning, Disability and Health (ICF). Solli himself claims that a quantified measure of degree of impairment related to separate diseases or injuries cannot determine the overall disability of the person. A specific impairment can have an impact on one person which is so different from the impact of the same impairment on another person that the impairment itself cannot function as a reasonable criterion for decisions in the medical insurance system.

Although the ICF opens the door to the whole complexity of activities and participations (and their limitations) it is still encapsulated in the medical way of thinking. The causes of activity limitations or participation restrictions should, if they are to be taken seriously in a medical context, be diseases, injuries or defects. Solli wants to go beyond that and proposes a modified model for the evaluation of disabilities which he calls a *complex functional ability model*.[15]

Solli notes, and I think he is correct here, that the social insurance agencies cannot reasonably always require the existence of a disease, injury or defect as the cause of an activity limitation or a participation restriction, in order to grant economic compensation. Solli mentions two cases where there may not be any obvious malady causing some activity limitation. First, there is the case of *mental illness*. A mental illness proper has per definition no obvious somatic cause. The mental illness displays itself on the activity level. It may consist of compulsive or

---

[13]   The National Insurance Act, 1997.

[14]   Kjönstad & Syse, 2005.

[15]   Solli, 2007, pp. 463-465.

irrational behaviour. The criteria for such illnesses exist so far only on the activity level and not on a body function level. The second kind of case is the general case of *illness without disease* (see below for the terminology here). A person who has widespread chronic pain or is otherwise obviously incapacitated but has no recognized somatic diagnosis has an illness, Solli argues. Thus this person should be entitled to some benefit.[16]

The Swedish Case

Some Elements in the Legal Development

The Swedish National Insurance Act (originally from 1962 but many changes and additions have been made later) states in one of its central paragraphs that economic compensation will be given to a sick-listed person if, and only if, his or her work ability is reduced by a disease or injury by at least 25%. This statement is loaded with presuppositions. One of these will be the focus of this chapter. The Social Insurance Agency should be able to determine whether reduced ability is due to a disease (or comparable medical condition) and not to some other phenomenon.

What does the Act say about the notion of disease? The first blunt answer is that it contains no definition of disease. In the preparatory works of the Act some statements were made which are still considered to be valid. According to these a disease is what "according to ordinary language and common medical understanding" is considered to be a disease. "Every abnormal bodily and mental state of an individual which does not belong to the normal life process should thus be classified as a disease" (my translation). These statements were however not to be taken as binding. Every case should be assessed with due consideration of the special circumstances which exist.[17]

During the 1980s and the beginning of the 1990s certain changes of application of the Insurance Act had taken place among physicians and insurance administrators. The criteria for granting sickness compensation had then in practice become somewhat loosened (without any formal change in the Act) so that people with general life problems that were disabling could be included. There was in fact a Government Official Report which in a rather radical way attempted to make the

---

[16] For further support of this conclusion and for a further analysis of the functional ability model, see Chapter 17 in this volume.

[17] Swedish Government Official Report of the Commission of Social Care, SOU 1944:15, p. 162.

criteria more inclusive. It was proposed that, apart from diseases, also certain other states of "insufficiency" that may be caused by "life problems" should be included.[18]

It is interesting to follow the reasoning presented in the report. Here the experts acknowledge the difficulties that people can have in adapting to the working life of modern times. They refer to the new information technology, to high specialization in today's work tasks, and to the restructuring of many workplaces. The working situation has become more demanding. Many people simply cannot cope and they are threatened with losing their jobs. Their life problems may be such that they are in practice disabled from working.[19]

In such a situation, the report says, sick-listing can in fact play a crucial supportive role. The subject, although he or she has no salient somatic disease, may be seriously disabled and must be helped. To be sick-listed and be absent from the workplace for a short period may in fact in itself have a rehabilitative effect. Moreover, the employer and the subject's nearest and dearest may as a result become more understanding of the subject and adapt their demands to the new situation.

The report continues:

> Even though it is crucial to have, as a guiding principle, a medical concept of disease that is as clearly defined as possible, it may from the point of view of social insurance be reasonable to consider as equal to disease such psychosocial states of insufficiency as cause a reduced working and functional ability. Such a change is in fact just an adaptation to the application of the concept of disease that is currently already in use today but it will provide improved conditions for a more just and equal application.[20]

The report, however, never brought about a change in the law, though it may have influenced the continuation of a more liberal praxis current until the middle of the 1990s.

A governmental bill acknowledges that the concept of disease has in practice continually become enlarged.[21] There is now, it says, a new and more liberal view with regard to disturbances during pregnancy, problems in connection with operations, and states of fatigue and grief, in particular in connection with the death of a close relative. The government, however, proposes a counteraction to this liberal praxis and as a result the National Insurance Act is made more precise through the legal

---

[18]   Swedish Government Official Report, SOU 1988:41.
[19]   *Ibid.*, p. 281.
[20]   *Ibid.*, p. 282, my translation.
[21]   Swedish Governmental Bill 1994/95:147, p. 20.

changes acquiring force in 1995. It is said that in the assessment whether an individual suffers from a disease or not, there should not be complete disregard of the labour market, or economic and social circumstances. The right to compensation should presuppose that the reduced work ability is caused by a disease or a medically comparable state. On the other hand the changes in the Act in 1995 explicitly include some conditions, the "medically comparable" ones, which had before formally but not in practice been excluded. These involved defects, impairments and disabilities. Such conditions are normally static and not *processes* as was the defining term regarding diseases in the Act.

A report which prepares the 1995 changes in the Act underlines the importance of strict medical criteria.[22] The committee members, who wrote the report, show their understanding of the difficulties involved in assessing many individual cases. They express, however, their hope that the medical criteria will become much clearer and more concrete in the future. They also draw the conclusion that many people who have hitherto received social benefit will cease to be entitled to such benefit. The committee emphasize that these people should not be left to fend for themselves. They should instead become the objects of other political measures within the domain of labour market policy. Thus a special requirement is imposed on the affected authorities to cooperate and unite their efforts.

From 1995 the National Insurance Act contains the following paragraph:

> In the assessment of whether there is a disease or not no regard shall be given to labour market, economic, social or similar circumstances.[23]

In the explication of this paragraph it is said that the distribution of sickness benefits shall presuppose that the subject's disability is dependent on a disease or a comparable medical state. A similar view is expressed in the Work Injury Insurance Act according to which the assessment of work injuries should not be related to the present situation on the labour market.[24]

Although no consideration should in principle be given to labour market, economic or social circumstances, it follows from the stepwise decision procedure (see below) that there must be some such consideration. A person who has the possibility, after rehabilitation, of getting another job at his or her old workplace is entitled to compensation

---

[22] Swedish Government Official Report, SOU, 1995:149.

[23] The Swedish National Insurance Act, 1995, Chapter 3, 7§, my translation.

[24] The Work Insurance Act, SOU 1998:37, p. 213. For a discussion see Hultgren, 2000, pp. 22-23.

during the rehabilitation period even if he or she would be able, without any rehabilitation, to manage another job which occurs on the market. The right to get compensation will then become dependent on the fact that the employer has resources and is able to offer other work tasks to the insured person. This puts the unemployed persons in a disadvantageous position. Commentators have questioned whether the legislators really intended to create this injustice.[25]

Let me summarize the present praxis with regard to the medical requirements for sickness benefits. There is now a much stricter attitude. In principle, the claimant must suffer from a medically verifiable disease. General life problems, even if they are obviously disabling, are not entitling criteria. Moreover, physiological conditions which belong to the normal life process, such as pregnancy (without special complications) cannot be classified as diseases. It is only when such complications as can be considered to be pathological occur that the disease label can be used. Such cases include threatening miscarriage, multiple child pregnancy and RH immunization. However, there are cases when a pregnant woman who does not have the strength to work, without having a diagnosed disease, is still awarded economic compensation.

Infertility is considered as an abnormal bodily state that does not belong to the normal life process. Therefore both the man and the woman fulfill the criteria of receiving sickness compensation if they are prevented from working during the infertility investigation or during treatment for the condition.[26]

The guidelines from 2004 do not explicitly comment on the cases of grief and fatigue related to the loss of a close relative. It seems clear, though, from the Act that, in principle, ordinary grief can never entitle to sickness benefit. However, if the state of grief is prolonged and in fact turns into a state of depression then the "ordinary" reaction has turned into a state that is medically classifiable. Thus, the case can be treated as a case of disability due to disease.[27]

As we saw, in the new paragraph that was put into the Act in 1995 the assessment of work ability shall not depend on labour market, economic or social considerations. In principle, thus, a sickness benefit should not be awarded to a builder just because the economic situation for this occupation happens to be bad. In such a case the work authori-

---

[25] See Westerhäll, 2006, pp. 107-108.

[26] *Försäkringskassan* [Swedish Social Insurance Agency], 2004, pp. 10-13.

[27] Observe, however, that the Swedish Government Official Report 1997:166, p. 189, contains a clause stating that grief can entitle to sickness compensation even without there being a diagnosis of a pathological condition.

ties should come in and use the measure of unemployment benefit. However, a connection to the labour market comes in from another angle. When it comes to the assessment of whether a person has reduced working ability or not, in the sickness insurance context, the judgment should be related, according to the law, to such jobs as currently normally exist on the labour market and not just to the subject's present job. And this entails that the assessment must be made in relation to a continuously changing labour market.[28]

The Decision Procedure

Decisions with regard to social benefits are taken by the Swedish Social Insurance Agency [*Försäkringskassan*] mainly on the basis of a document issued by a medical assessor. This assessor is normally the doctor who is assigned to be the curative doctor of the applicant. The doctor should, besides giving a medical diagnosis, also give his or her opinion of the applicant's degree of disability, mainly with regard to the applicant's regular job but also with regard to other jobs normally existing on the market.

The Government Bill 1996/97:28 describes a model of seven steps, each involving a major question, in order to structure the work for judging about sickness benefits, the need of rehabilitation, and special measures of rehabilitation. The Social Insurance Agency has until now adopted this model for its assessment procedure. The steps are the following:

Step 1: Can the applicant perform his or her normal work after necessary treatment and convalescence? If yes, there will be a sickness benefit, if no turn to step 2.

Step 2: Can the applicant perform the present work tasks after some period of rehabilitation or adaptation of the tasks? If yes, sickness benefit and rehabilitation benefit are granted during the period of illness and rehabilitation. If no, turn to step 3.

Step 3: Can the applicant perform and be assigned other tasks by the present employer without extra measures? If yes, benefit is granted during treatment. If no, turn to step 4.

Step 4: Can the applicant be assigned other tasks by the employer after having gone through rehabilitation and further education? If yes,

---

[28] For useful introductions to the Swedish system of sickness listing and regulations with regard to social insurance, see Järvholm and Olofsson, 2002 and 2005. See also the discussion in Westerholm and Bostedt, 2004, and Westerholm and Lindenger, 2008.

benefit is granted during treatment, and rehabilitation benefit can be provided during a period of up to one year. If no, turn to step 5.

Step 5: Can the applicant take and perform other jobs which normally exist on the labour market? If yes, there will be no benefit. The applicant is able to take a job. If there is no job available the applicant has to approach the authority for employment insurance. If no, turn to step 6.

Step 6: Can the applicant take up and perform other normally existing jobs on the labour market after some rehabilitative measures? If yes, the applicant will get sickness and rehabilitation benefit for a period up to a year during treatment and rehabilitation. If no, turn to step 7.

Step 7: Is the disability of the applicant expected to last for ever or at least for more than one year? If yes, the insurance authority should, after a thorough investigation, change the sickness benefit to early pension (*sjukersättning* or *aktivitetsersättning*).

It is crucial for all these steps of assessment to be made at all that the claimant has a disease or comparable medical condition. Moreover, it holds for every step in this model, that if the claimant can take a job or do some work, for instance if he or she is assigned new tasks by the regular employer, then he or she is not entitled to any economic compensation even if the disease (or other medical condition) continues. It is of course here presupposed that the disease does not constitute a danger for the individual's rehabilitation.[29]

It should be noted that the Swedish system for rehabilitation and the granting of sickness benefits is at present, summer 2008, under radical revision. In a Ministry Communication 2008:3 the Swedish Government proposes a so-called "Rehabilitation Chain" in three steps according to which certain crucial decisions shall be made at particular time points during the period of rehabilitation. The plan is that this new legislation will come into force on July 1, 2008:

1. When a person has had reduced ability to work, and has had sickness benefit, during 90 days the authority shall consider whether the person can earn his or her living in some other position at the present work place. This entails a reconsideration of the case according to the first four steps in the above mentioned model.
2. When a person has had reduced ability to work, and has had sickness benefit, during 180 days the authority shall consider whether the person can earn his or her living somewhere else on the regular

---

[29] *Försäkringskassan*, 2004, pp. 48-75. For a legal analysis of the decision procedure see Westerhäll, 2006, pp. 105-109.

labour market. This entails a reconsideration of the case according to steps 5 and 6 in the model.

3. When a person has had reduced ability to work, and has had sickness benefit, for one year he or she shall in principle lose the benefit. (Certain exceptions to this legislation exist.) Instead other regulations, for instance regarding disablement pension, will take over.

Some Recent Research on Sickness Absence and Sickness Presence in the Swedish Context

As I noted in the Introduction, sickness absence has been exceptionally high in Sweden at least since the end of the 1980s compared to all other European countries. In 2003 on average 14% of the Swedish population were absent because of sickness. The cost for sickness compensation that year amounted to not less than 12 billion euros.[30] Women have had a higher level of sickness absence than men. This gap has widened over time and the rate of absence was in 2002 77% higher for women than for men. This difference is evident in all age groups. However, the pattern of diseases does not differ between the sexes. Musculosceletal diseases caused about 1/3 of the sickness absence for both men and women between 1999 and 2002. Mental disorders are the second most common causes of sickness absence. Another finding is that manual employees have higher sickness absence than non-manual employees.[31]

A recent dissertation on sickness absence and sickness presence attempts to trace the causes of the growing sickness absence and also to understand the paradoxical fact that many people go to work in spite of illness.[32] Gun Johansson demonstrates that parallel to a high degree of sickness absence there is a surprisingly high sickness presence at work. This shows that the health problems of the Swedish population are much more prevalent than the absence statistics indicate.

For the purpose of elucidating these matters Johansson adopts a specific conceptual framework for the analysis. This framework contains among other things the distinction between the notions of disease, illness and sickness. Roughly this distinction amounts to the following. By a disease is meant a condition, normally a somatic condition, diagnosed by a physician or other medical expert. The disease is a physiological malfunction, typically an infection, a mechanical breakdown or a physical degeneration. The term "illness" refers to subjective experi-

---

[30] Hogstedt *et al.*, 2004.

[31] Johansson, 2007, p. 1.

[32] Johansson, 2007.

ences of negative signs and symptoms. The term "illness" is also often used to designate the subject's overall perception of his or her negatively affected bodily and mental state. An illness may but need not be caused by a disease. The fact that an illness can exist without a corresponding disease is, as we have seen, a crucial problem for the sickness insurance authorities. The term "sickness" refers to the social role taken by a person who has acknowledged his or her disease or illness.[33]

Illness experiences are the typical causes of sickness absence. Illness is normally the only way for the subject to get to know about a disease. The person "feels ill", is in pain or is exceptionally tired and decides to abstain from work. Such feelings are also the typical reasons for a person to seek medical assistance and thus get sick-listed.

Although illness normally functions as the reason for sickness absence the illness cannot, strictly speaking, be referred to in the medicolegal assessment of entitlement to benefits. As we have seen, the Swedish physician should in principle find the "objective" signs, the objective disease in the human body.[34]

However, many people who experience illness – in particular if the symptoms are not too pronounced – ignore their troubles and are present at their workplaces. The data that Johansson provides are significant enough. Data from a survey from 1997 show that 38% of the women and 35% of the men had, in spite of illness, attended work several times during the year preceding the survey. In 2001 these proportions had risen to 56% for women and 50% for men. Many factors contributed to this sickness attendance at work. Frequently the explicatory factors are negative. There may be low replaceability and small resources at the work place. Time pressure can be another reason. The individual feels forced to attend and to fulfill specific tasks.[35]

However, there may also be positive reasons. Johansson puts a lot of emphasis on the concept of motivation. Many of the sick people who still go to work are very motivated for doing their job. They find the job interesting and they are eager to enhance their career in the organization or the company. This means that the sick attendants often tend to be the ambitious workers or professionals for whom work has the highest priority.[36]

---

[33] This distinction is further analysed by Twaddle and Nordenfelt, 1993.

[34] Cf. the similar Norwegian development described above.

[35] Johansson, 2007.

[36] Johansson, 2007, discusses the concept of motivation in some detail. She puts motivation, as I myself do, outside ability and argues against the choice of Ilmarinen, 2001b, to view motivation as a part of ability.

CHAPTER 17

Towards an Analysis of the Notions of Disease and Medical Condition

The Purpose of This Study

There has, as I indicated in the last chapter, been a continuous controversy about the place of the notion of disease or medical condition in the assessment of sickness or disability benefits. Some commentators, mainly representing the medical field, have underlined the importance of "objective criteria". The cause of the applicant's problem should be an objectively statable disease (injury or defect) and nothing else. Other people who are involved in the process have said either that it is very difficult to determine the borders of "objective" diseases or that there may very well be cases of serious ill health that should warrant economic compensation, but where there are no salient diseases responsible for such ill health.[1]

The sixty-four-thousand-dollar question is: Are there objective criteria of the presence of disease, injury or defect? Or must decisions in this area be made on other, more pragmatic, grounds? Should we in fact make decisions from case to case? But is such a procedure compatible with the demands of justice? I will face these difficult questions in this part of the book. I will first present a fairly comprehensive analysis of two contemporary theories of disease. In Appendix 2, I will add an analysis of a third theory, put forward by the philosopher and psychiatrist Lawrie Reznek, which, in a way, lies between the two presented here.[2]

One reason for paying so much attention to this question is that the statements of the law on the notion of disease are so brief and therefore unsatisfactory from a theoretical point of view. Another reason is that there is now, 2008, a far-reaching philosophical and scientific discussion about the basic concepts of disease, injury and disability. It seems to be timely to introduce these analyses into the medico-legal context. It is true that no one has so far come up with any easy answers. The issue is

---

[1] Cf. Westerhäll-Gisselsson, 1983.
[2] Reznek, 1987 and 1991.

controversial and there are at least two fundamentally different points of view with regard to these concepts. But the fact that the issue is so controversial indicates something crucial for the medico-legal context: there are no simple and universal "objective" criteria by which the assessing doctor can show that a particular disability is caused by a disease. The judgments must be made in each individual case and they can only in certain salient cases be made with "objective" certainty.

Introduction to the Theories

The controversial issue in all philosophical analyses of health and illness is whether there is any place for values or subjectivity in these medical concepts. Some theorists indeed claim and argue that the medical concepts are value-free and descriptive in the same sense as the concepts of atom, metal and rain are value-free and descriptive. To say that a person has a certain disease or that he or she is unhealthy is thus, they claim, to objectively describe this person. On the other hand this certainly does not preclude an additional evaluation of the state of affairs as undesirable or bad. The basic scientific description and the evaluation are, however, two independent matters, according to this kind of theory.

Other theorists claim that the concept of health, together with the other medical concepts, is essentially value-laden. To establish that a person is healthy does not just entail a certain amount of objective inspection and measurement. It presupposes also an evaluation of the general bodily and mental functioning of the person. A statement that he or she is healthy does not merely imply certain scientific facts regarding the person's body or mind but implies also a (positive) evaluation of the person's bodily and mental state.

The first of the theories to be discussed is representative of mainstream medical thought. This is the bio-statistical theory of Christopher Boorse.[3] The second, my own theory, is holistic and argues that the notion of disease presupposes a positive notion of health which itself is partly of a normative character. Lawrie Reznek's theory has a largely medical starting-point but contests many of the ideas forming the bio-statistical theory. Some of its conclusions are therefore similar to those of the holistic theory.[4] My presentation here is a shortened version of two analyses published recently.[5]

---

[3]   Boorse, 1977 and 1997.
[4]   Reznek, 1987 and 1991.
[5]   Nordenfelt, 2001 and 2006.

A Brief Outline of Two Theories of Health and Disease

Conceptual analysis will never get off the ground unless it has a purpose. Sometimes disagreement between theorists can be found to be due to their diverging purposes. I will list here three possible alternative purposes.

1. Investigating how the terms "health" and "illness" are commonly used in medical practice. Here are subdivisions in accordance with what communities of medical practice we are referring to (doctors, nurses, occupational therapists, etc.).

2. Creating a consistent theory of health and illness concepts which is as close as possible to one or more of the actual uses.

3. Creating a theory of health and illness concepts which without being extremely close to any of the current uses will serve the purpose of medical practice, or any of its subcategories, better than the current conceptual systems do.

Alternatives 2 and 3 are important philosophical purposes. Alternative 2 is an explicit purpose of the American philosopher Christopher Boorse whose theory will be discussed below. He claims that he has formulated a theory which essentially captures the way doctors use the terms "health" and "disease." To capture this use is also a partial purpose of my own. However, I am also interested in capturing how lay persons use these terms. I wish not only to construct a conceptual theory which is reasonably close to the general use of terms such as "health" and "illness", but also to contribute to the amendment of the prevalent medical conceptual network. My view is that the current conceptual network is deficient. For instance, notable ambiguities pertain to the use of "illness", where that term is sometimes used synonymously with "disease" and sometimes not. Such ambiguities, as well as other unclarities, do not contribute to the good of medicine.[6]

According to Boorse health is conformity to *species design*. Health is the case when all organs and tissues, as well as mental faculties, function in accordance with the design by which the organisms of the species in question maintain and renew their life. A disease, according to Boorse, is a type of internal state which is an impairment of normal functional ability (as statistically determined) or a limitation of functional ability caused by environmental agents. Given this definition of disease, health can also be characterized as the absence of disease.

---

[6] Nordenfelt, 1995 and 2001.

With this general description as a background, Boorse presents the following definitions:

1. The reference class is a natural class of organisms of uniform functional design; specifically, an age group of a sex of a species.

2. A normal function of a part or process within members of the reference class is a statistically typical contribution by it to their individual survival and reproduction.

3. A disease is a type of internal state which is either an impairment of normal functional ability, i.e. a reduction of one or more functional abilities below typical efficiency, or a limitation on functional ability caused by environmental agents.

4. Health is the absence of disease.[7]

In contrast I call my own theory a *holistic theory of health*. I consider health to be the primary concept in the web of medical concepts. My notion of health is characterized in the following action-theoretic terms:

A is completely healthy if, and only if, A is in a bodily and mental state which is such that A has a second-order ability to realize all his or her vital goals, given accepted circumstances.[8]

If the person's (second-order) ability is reduced in accepted circumstances, then that person is to the same extent ill. Diseases, injuries, and defects form a common category of *maladies* which have similar definitions. For the case of diseases, I propose the following characterization: "*D* is a disease-type in environment *E* if, and only if, *D* is a type of physical or mental process which, when instanced in a person *P* in *E*, would with great probability cause ill health in *P*."

In the following the two theories will be more fully presented.

The Bio-Statistical Theory of Disease: Christopher Boorse

The goal of the *bio-statistical theory of disease* (*BST*) is to analyze the normal/pathological distinction.[9] When the term "disease" replaces the term "pathological", it is intended to capture the whole range of pathological phenomena including defects, injuries, growth disorders, etc. In order to characterize the modern Western concept of disease, Boorse proposes a modern explication of the ancient idea that the normal is the natural when he says that health is conformity to species design. In modern terms, Boorse says "species design is the internal

---

[7]   Boorse, 1997, pp. 7-8.

[8]   Nordenfelt, 2001, p. 9.

[9]   Boorse, 1997.

functional organization typical of species members, which (as regards somatic medicine) forms the subject matter of physiology: the interlocking hierarchy of functional processes, at every level from organelle to cell to tissue to organ to gross behavior, by which organisms of a given species maintain and renew their life".[10] All conditions which are called pathological by ordinary medicine constitute disrupted part-function at some level of this hierarchy.

Virtually the whole of this theory, Boorse maintains, is applicable to mental health. This presupposes that human psychology is divisible into part-processes with biological functions. Biology should then be understood as a general science of life embracing species-typical physiology and species-typical psychology.[11]

An Investigation of Boorse's Project

Boorse says that his account "defines a theoretical concept of health, not a practical one. It aims at a pathologist's concept of disease, not a clinician's, and still less at any social or legal category".[12] What is, then, the procedure by which we should find out the nature of pathological disease? One might have expected that Boorse would consult pathology textbooks. He occasionally does so. But this is not what he refers to when he describes his purpose. Instead, he refers to *medical classifications*. His idea, then, is the following: In medical classifications of diseases many entities are classified which are normally called diseases. We should see what is distinctive about these entities, and we should try to produce a general theory that neatly covers these entities and nothing but these entities. We should not exclude the discovery of future diseases. Indeed, once we have a general theory, we can use this theory as a criterion for the inclusion of new categories in the set of diseases, and thereby in the classification of diseases.

On Medical Classifications of Diseases and Related Conditions

The medical classification *par préférence* is the International Classification of Diseases and Related Health Conditions, ICD, Tenth Revision.[13] This classification is used worldwide. It is published by the World Health Organization (WHO), and it is continually revised by the

---

[10] Boorse, 1997, p. 7.
[11] *Ibid.*, pp. 13-14.
[12] *Ibid.*, 1997, p. 11.
[13] ICD, 1992.

WHO. Almost all contemporary national classifications of diseases and related problems are based on the ICD.

I will now strictly follow the logic of Boorse's procedure. To get the pathologist's notion of disease I will attempt to extract it from the ICD. The ICD classifies the acknowledged diseases in the world into seventeen main categories. The ground for division is traditional, and it does not, as has been shown many times, fulfil elementary logical requirements. This need not concern us. We should look at the species and see whether they fit the Boorsian theory of disease. The next step is to consider how these species in their turn are characterized in comprehensive textbooks.

I will use the well-known disease of asthma as my paradigm. In the ICD, asthma is a species of the genus Diseases of the Respiratory System. Strictly speaking, it is divided into two species, J 45 and J 46, the second having the label Acute severe asthma. Ordinary asthma has in its turn four variants: allergic, non-allergic, mixed and unspecified.

For a comprehensive definition of asthma, I consult *Harrison's Principles of Internal Medicine*, Fourteenth Edition. Under the heading "Definition" the paragraph *in toto* runs as follows:

> Asthma is a disease of airways that is characterized by increased responsiveness of the tracheobronchial tree to a multiplicity of stimuli. Asthma is manifested physiologically by a widespread narrowing of the air passages which may be relieved spontaneously or as a result of therapy, and clinically by paroxysms of dyspnea, cough and wheezing. Asthma is an episodic disease, acute exacerbations being interspersed with symptom-free periods. Typically, most attacks are short-lived, lasting minutes to hours, and clinically the patient seems to recover completely after an attack. However, there can be a phase in which the patient experiences some degree of airways obstruction daily. This phase can be mild, with or without superimposed severe periods, or much more serious, with serious obstruction persisting for days or weeks, a condition known as status asthmaticus. In unusual circumstances acute episodes can cause death.[14]

One striking thing about this characterization is that it covers a great deal of ground. A basic patho-physiological element is in it, but this is only a fragment of the characterization. It contains also a story of clinical evolution in terms of symptoms and signs, and it says something about prognosis. Thus the description is quite comprehensive. The urgent question now is: What belongs to the ontology of the disease of asthma? What sort of entity is it? The most reasonable interpretation of the text would be to say something like the following: the disease of

---

[14] Harrison's Principles of Internal medicine, 1997, p. 1419.

asthma is a complex process, initiated by a hypersensitivity to various stimuli, manifesting itself physiologically as a narrowing of air passages, and clinically by paroxysms of dyspnea, cough, and wheezing. The patient can experience these symptoms for short or long periods. Moreover, therapy is already mentioned under the heading "Definition." Such a description is rather far from the purified "pathological" story that Boorse presents.

Consider now some species of disease found in the *ICD* which involve complications of another kind. The *ICD* contains several states or "disorders" which are really only deviant or abnormal, be it in a statistical or some other sense. Consider, for instance, E 30.0 "Delayed sexual development"; E 66 "Obesity"; R 11 "Nausea"; R 25.0 "Abnormal head movements", and in general everything which is covered by the title Symptoms, Signs and Abnormal Clinical and Laboratory Findings, such as: R 45.2 "Unhappiness"; R 46.0 "Very low level of personal hygiene"; R 51 "Headache"; and indeed R 46.7 "Verbosity and circumstantial detail obscuring reason for contact". The mentioned conditions seem far from being instances of statistically subnormal functioning in relation to survival. They are just abnormal or undesirable, or else, as with the last condition, completely irrelevant to the person's gross functioning.

Preliminary Conclusions Concerning Boorse's Project

My analysis in the preceding paragraphs has scrutinized Boorse's version of conceptual analysis. Since Boorse purports to work quite close to the empirical field – that is, purports to characterize the concept of disease held by most doctors, at least implicitly, I have tried to support my analysis by using textbooks. This is relevant since Boorse has pointed out a clear criterion for identifying what doctors mean by the term "disease": diseases are such entities as are classified in medical disease classifications. A natural procedure, then, is to take examples from such classifications and see to what extent they fit the abstract characterization.

The first result of our investigation is that diseases as classified are not the kind of "pure pathological" entities that Boorse's theory asserts. They contain several elements apart from the saliently pathological ones, including experiences and disabilities. Boorse's theory, then, is not directed towards mirroring the richness of disease concepts, and is not concerned with the fact that the defining characterizations of all major diseases contain a whole spectrum of features, including the patient's experiences. It is instead directed towards finding some common denominator, a *sine qua non* of all diseases. This common denominator is dysfunction, understood as dysfunction in relation to individual survival or species survival.

However, we have already seen that examples exist of disease entities, as classified, which do not fulfil the *sine qua non* criterion. Most classified disease entities refer to or contain some kind of dysfunction, where dysfunction is taken in a wide sense. Mental diseases often entail disability pertaining to the individual. According to the Diagnostic Statistical Manual (DSM)[15] they should always do so. Disability is a notion with clear connections to dysfunction, but it is not identical with dysfunction. Insofar as dysfunction is related to disability, it need not be a question of a dysfunction in relation to survival. The sociopath's inability to follow moral rules in our society is hardly bound up with any organic dysfunction relative to survival. To maintain Boorse's position we must make the following extremely strong claim: All human disabilities, whatever individual or societal goals they may be related to, are ultimately dysfunctional in relation to the goal of individual or species survival. Or, put in other terms: All human disabilities lower, at least to some minute extent, the probability of the survival of the individual or of the species. I wonder how this strong contention can be supported. Most of all I wonder why it is necessary to make such a strong statement in order to construct a viable theory of health and disease.

My conclusion is that Boorse has hardly succeeded in producing a descriptive theory of the pathological notion of disease, given the criteria he has suggested for grounding and testing such a theory.

The Argument from Repair

In Boorse's first presentations of his theory he did not consider the importance of the environment for human functioning.[16] All physiologists and biochemists know that, depending on the circumstances as well as the individual's food-intake and movements, the functioning of the human body will vary. A person who is standing in the cold will be freezing, a person who has just eaten a lot of food will have a lot of intestinal activity and a person who has just been exercising will have an extreme increase of heart and lung functioning. All these changes in the functioning of the human body are considered to be "normal". But they are statistically normal only if we make this concept a very complex one and calculate the statistically normal functioning given all conceivable circumstances.

Such a calculation is, however, in principle feasible, so this observation is not automatically a blow to the bio-statistical theory as such. One

---

[15]   DSM, 1994.

[16]   Boorse, 1977.

can say that the functioning of the heart of the athlete who has just run 100 metres (and whose pulse is 180) is normal given the particular circumstance of this athlete's 100-metre race. It is more interesting, however, to extend the argument to really harsh circumstances. Consider the case of an ordinary infection. Microbes invade the organism. The immune defence system is triggered and starts its combating work, terminating in the annihilation of the microbes. This work of the immune system is "statistically normal" given the particular circumstances of the microbe-invasion. The snag is, however, that this "statistically normal" work of the reparative system is what constitutes the major part of the illness, as experienced by the individual. It is the repairing work that causes the pain and the fever, not the microbe invasion as such. The paradoxical conclusion of this argument then is: the immune response to the infection makes its statistically normal contribution to the individual's survival. Thus this state of affairs is healthy. On the other hand, a situation of this kind, perhaps involving pain and high fever, is nevertheless a typical instance of human illness.

There are conceivable moves to be made here. Boorse has chosen one that I consider inadequate. His proposal is that the calculation of the normal functioning of the human body shall only take into account "statistically normal circumstances", thus presumably excluding "dangerous" circumstances.[17] But how much is included in the span of statistically normal circumstances? We risk including too little. A 100-metre race is hardly a statistically normal circumstance to most people. Yet it is hardly a dangerous circumstance. And we risk including too much. There are many types of circumstance that are extremely common in some parts of the world but which are still dangerous. I have been told that 90% of some African populations have the Bilharzia disease. The existence of the Bilharzia worm is therefore statistically normal, at least in a great part of the world. So what should be the reference basis of the statistical calculation?

Another move is to say that in the case of the infection the "real" disease precedes the repairing work of the immune system. The real disease would then be constituted by the "damage" done in the cells invaded by the microbes. I do not doubt that there are cases of infection where there is great damage caused to central systems of the body in the sense that their function is reduced below typical efficiency before the start of the immune response. Therefore I do not doubt that the biostatistical approach will capture many instances of diseases as intuitively understood. I doubt, however, that it will capture all instances. Immu-

---

17   Boorse, 1997.

nologists have told me that in some cases it is sufficient that microbes are present and start infusing their toxins, for the immune system to start its work. Hardly any damage to the tissues need be present before the infection begins.

Making these observations one can wonder whether the statistical approach is the most reasonable approach to the philosophy of health and illness. If, in several cases, it is the statistically normal response of the organism to an external threat that causes the symptoms that we in ordinary discourse associate with illness, then one can wonder whether the conception of statistically normal functions is an adequate basis for a theory of disease and health.

The Argument from the Clinic

This brings me to a further critical argument against the bio-statistical conception. I call it the argument from the clinic and it is an argument that lies behind the Reverse theory of disease and illness.[18] Consider the following, hopefully plausible, story with regard to the emergence of the concepts of illness and disease.

In the beginning there were people who experienced problems in and with themselves. They felt pain and fatigue and they found themselves unable to do what they could normally do. They experienced what we now call illnesses, which they located somewhere in their bodies and minds. Several people came to experience similar illnesses. This led to the giving of names to the illnesses, and hereby the presence of the illnesses could be efficiently communicated. These were the phases of *illness recognition* and *illness communication*.

The people who were ill approached experts, called doctors, in order to get help. They communicated their experiences to the doctors, via the illness language. The doctors tried to help them and cure them. In the search for curative remedies, the doctors did not just rely on the stories told by the people who were ill. They also looked for the *causes* of the illnesses within the bodies and minds of the ill. This meant in the end that they initiated systematic studies of the biology of their patients. This was the phase of *search for the causes of illnesses.*

As a result of these studies the doctors found some regular connections between certain bodily states and the illness-symptoms of their patients. They formed hypotheses about causal connections between the internal states and processes and the illness-syndromes. They designated these causes of illnesses *diseases.* And they invented a vocabulary and a

---

[18]   Canguilhem, 1978; Fulford, 1989; Nordenfelt, 2001.

conceptual apparatus for the diseases. This was the phase of *disease recognition*.

4. Once the diseases were recognized, a new and independent research could be established. The diseases as biological processes could be studied in their own right and irrespective of their connections to human suffering. This was the phase of *biomedical research.*

The point of my story-telling is that in the beginning there is always a problem conceived by a subject. The problem is a vital problem, one that concerns the subject's living a reasonable life, but it does not necessarily concern a threat to the person's life, growth or reproduction. The problem quite often concerns pain or other kinds of suffering, such as depression or extreme fatigue. And the subject believes that this problem has some kind of internal (biological or psychological) cause. This is the standard condition of the patient who is seeking help in a health-care situation.

The focus of attention is thus the illness – the problem as perceived by the subject. I therefore consider illness to be the primary concept from the point of view of conceptual development. From the concept of illness we can derive the concept of disease, i.e. the internal state which causes (or tends to cause) the illness. But observe here how the diseases are identified. They are identified on the basis of an illness-recognition. A discovery of the disease presupposes the occurrence of an illness. (Hence the expression "Reverse theory of disease and illness".)

Given this interpretation we arrive at a definition of disease which is far from the Boorsian bio-statistical one. A preliminary definition of disease would thus be: Disease = df. a bodily or mental process which is such that it tends to cause an illness (understood as a state of suffering or disability in the subject). This conclusion leads me to introduce a theory of disease that is a rival to Boorse's bio-statistical theory.

An Action-theoretic Theory of Health and Disease

The Central Place of Disability

Suffering and disability are not novel concepts in the history of medicine or health care. They are central in the clinic but they have not consistently been used in the theoretical characterization of basic medical concepts such as disease and pathology. In the history of philosophy of health, however, we can find the ideas of suffering and disability in the writings of certain authors. The locus classicus is Galen's formulation in his *Ars Medica* (The Art of Medicine) written in about AD 190.[19] It runs: "Health is a state in which we neither suffer from evil nor are hindered in the functions of daily life". Thus, health is here understood as the opposite of illness.[20]

There are alternative ways of using these phenomena in the construction of theories. Either one uses both kinds of concepts, as Galen does and as Reznek does, and says that illness is constituted both by suffering and by disability, or one focuses on one of them for the purpose of definition.[21] In my own analysis of health I have focused on the concept pair ability and disability, since I find it to be more universally useful then the concept pair well-being and suffering. (Observe that this holds only for my analysis of health, not for my analysis of welfare or quality of life, where the mental concepts of well-being and suffering play a fundamental role.)

At the same time we realize that there is a strong connection between suffering and disability, where suffering is taken to be a very general concept covering both physical pain and mental distress. A person cannot experience great suffering without evincing some degree of disability. But the converse relation does not always hold: a person may have a disability, and even be disabled in several respects, without suffering. There are paradigm cases of ill-health where suffering is absent. As a consequence of this reasoning a number of theorists have used the notions of ability and disability as the central notions in the definitions of health and illness.[22]

An Analysis of Health in Terms of Ability to Realize Vital Goals

What, then, should a healthy person be able to do? Or, conversely, what kinds of disabilities constitute a reduction of the person's health? What disabilities are such that the health-care system should provide health care for the person? These questions are clearly not identical. The last question has a political overtone. The answer to it depends not only on conceptual analysis but equally on policy decisions concerning medical priorities. I shall not enter into a discussion of this here.

It is plausible to believe that whatever the adequate answer to the question of the nature of health should be, it will be an answer on an

---

[19] For a modern edition, see Galen, 1997.
[20] See also Temkin, 1963, p. 637.
[21] Reznek, 1987.
[22] Seedhouse, 1986; Fulford, 1989; Nordenfelt, 1995; Pörn, 1993.

abstract level, capable of being summarized in terms of certain general goals. The question to be put should then rather be formulated in the following terms: what are the goals that a healthy person must be able to realize through his or her actions? To me not all abilities can qualify if we intend to stick to ordinary intuition. My primary reason for refusing to include all abilities is that if we did include them we would not be able to differentiate between health and general strength and excellence of various kinds. A man who does weight-lifting and increases his muscle strength tremendously has not thereby improved his health, according to ordinary intuitions. He may have improved his health as a side-effect. He may have strengthened his immune system by his training, but that is different from the pure muscle strength. Likewise, a woman who practises languages a lot and becomes an extremely proficient speaker of several languages has not improved her health, according to ordinary intuition. Thus a set of excellence concepts should, at least in the first instance, be kept distinct from the concept of health.

What alternatives do we have, then, in our search for the peculiar medical abilities? Let me again list several alternatives, some of which have already been mentioned and can be easily dismissed.

The abilities of health are

(1) the ability to satisfy our basic needs

(2) the ability to satisfy our wants

(3) the ability to do "ordinary things"

(4) the ability to run our daily affairs

(5) the ability to make ourselves minimally happy.

(1) is too narrow if "basic needs" only refer to survival. (2) is both too narrow and too wide. We may have unrealistic and "mad" wants, or we may have too low a level of wants. (3) is, as I have just indicated, unclear. "Ordinary" has to be unpacked. (4) probably provides a good rule of thumb but has much of the unclarity of (3) in it. The question also remains whether health only has to do with our ability to do the ordinary and daily things. Do not some unusual, but yet important, things exist which healthy people should still be able to do? Should they not be able to get married, or be able to make a long journey, or, in general, to deal with the demanding and unusual complexities that life may contain? (5) is my attempt to cover a good deal of that ground which I think the health concept should cover. It has to be interpreted and operationalized, however, to be directly clinically useful. For the moment, I have no other proposal which has the merit of covering enough ground and also of being immediately operational.

Another aspect of ability has to be scrutinized in the health context. Abilities occur in layers, where one layer presupposes another, but not the other way around. One distinction which I have found crucial is the one between first-order and second-order abilities. I claim that the ability involved in health is of the second-order kind. What does this mean, and why do I claim this? A second-order ability is a "quasi-ability". If you have a second-order ability to drive a car, then it does not follow that you can actually drive a car, that you have the first-order ability. What the expression says is that you have the basic physical and mental resources to learn to drive a car, if you are given the proper instructions.

Why, then, do I opt for this quasi-ability in characterizing health? The reason is obvious. I do not wish to say that it is only those people who have been given the adequate training in different respects who have health. I wish to say that the person who has not gone to school and who has not become cultivated in other respects, can be as healthy as the highly cultivated person. This is so because the untrained person may have as good basic biological and psychological resources as the cultivated person. By emphasizing the second-order level as the more appropriate level for this defining purpose, I have pushed the concept of health more towards a person's basic biology and psychology.

My general proposal is thus the following: A is completely healthy if, and only if, A is in a bodily and mental state which is such that A has the second-order ability to realize all his or her vital goals given a set of standard conditions.[23] Let me now clarify and to some extent defend this proposal by commenting on the crucial clauses concerning vital goals and second-order ability. I will be brief with regard to the first clause and instead concentrate on the relation between health and second-order ability.

What are the vital goals of a human being? And is there just one set of vital goals? A vital goal of a person, I suggest, is a state of affairs that is necessary for this person's minimal long-term happiness. As a consequence of this interpretation many of the things that human beings hope to realize or maintain belong to their vital goals. More precisely, most states that have a high priority along a person's scale of preferences belong to his or her vital goals. Examples of such vital goals can be: taking an exam, getting married and having children, as well as simply maintaining elements in the *status quo* such as retaining one's job and remaining in touch with one's nearest and dearest.

---

[23] Nordenfelt, 2001, p. 9. I have here made a slight revision in relation to this formulation.

However, certain things that people happen to want do not belong to their vital goals. First we have trivial wants. People may casually want something, but if they don't get it, it does not matter much. Second, people may sometimes have counterproductive wants. They may want to get drunk, but getting drunk is not a vital goal. Instead of contributing to long-term happiness, being drunk contributes in the long run to suffering and thereby unhappiness. Third, we may have irrational wants, i.e. wants that are in conflict with other, more important wants. As soon as the agent acknowledges that there is this conflict, he or she normally realizes that the only candidates for vital goals are the more important wants.

On the other hand, some things that we do not want may be contained in our set of vital goals. The completely apathetic or lazy person who does not have any conscious goals whatsoever will soon realize that this creates suffering for him or her. This will be particularly salient if the person does not even seek food or shelter. It must certainly belong to this person's long-term minimal happiness to have these basic matters organized. Therefore such basic goals are among every person's vital goals.

A crucial observation to be made here, then, is that a vital goal of *A* need not be wanted by *A* at a particular moment. The notion of a vital goal is thus a technical notion partly distinct from the ordinary-language notion of a goal.[24]

I will now turn to the idea of health as a second-order ability. To be healthy, I have proposed, is to have the second-order ability to realize one's vital goals. Consider the following situation. A refugee from, say, an African country, has just moved to Sweden. In his native country he had his own business, which he managed well enough to sustain himself and his family. When he enters Sweden he is no longer able to lead such a life. He does not know Swedish culture and, in particular, the Swedish language so he cannot initially make any arrangements for establishing a business in Sweden. Whereas in his home country he lived relatively well, in Sweden he is disabled. But would we say that this man is healthy in his native country, and becomes ill upon entering Sweden? No, it seems more plausible to say that as long as he has the second-order ability to run a business in Sweden, then he remains healthy. This means: as long as the immigrant has the ability to learn the Swedish language and the ability to learn how to go about in our society, then he is a completely healthy person. In general, then, such disability as is solely due to lack of training is not an indication of illness. There is

---

[24] For a further discussion, see Nordenfelt 2001, pp. 63-74.

reason to speak of illness only if the acts of training have in turn been prevented by internal factors, in which case there is a second-order disability.

To this analysis of ability must be added a few remarks about the circumstances under which a person can be said to have an ability. It is evident that health cannot be the ability to reach vital goals in all kinds of circumstances. If that were the case then nobody would be completely healthy. There is always some conceivable circumstance in which one cannot reach one's vital goals. The outbreak of a natural catastrophe is one example. Another such circumstance is that a person is physically or legally prevented by other people from performing the actions necessary for the achievement of his or her vital goals. Nor could health be constituted by ability to realize one's vital goals given merely one kind of circumstance. If that were the case then almost everybody would emerge as completely healthy. Consider the case where an individual is almost completely dependent on the help of somebody else in his or her endeavour to achieve a goal. We can imagine a paraplegic person who is supported in his or her attempts to reach various destinations; a personal assistant may help in various ways and transport the person. If this were a case where it is true to say that the paraplegic person has the ability to travel to all necessary places, then we should ascribe health to him or her. This is clearly counterintuitive. Such a situation of extreme support is not one in which we assess a person's degree of health.

So how should these circumstances be defined? A first plausible idea is that the circumstances that we normally have in mind in a health assessment are such as are in some way standard in our culture. A person who cannot walk on an ordinary pavement is certainly disabled with regard to a standard situation. Likewise, to take an animal example, a dog that cannot run on an ordinary well-kept lawn is disabled. In both cases, unless there are other impediments, we can draw medical conclusions. The person and the dog are unhealthy.

The way we devise such a standard (which is normally done implicitly) is not via statistics. What is a statistically normal situation (in a geographical region at a particular time) may turn out to be an unreasonable situation. In certain countries the political and cultural situation may be such that it would be unreasonable to judge the health of its inhabitants given this situation. It may, for instance, be impossible to work as a teacher in Chechenya for a long time. But it would be unreasonable to say that the trained unemployed teacher in Chechenya is unhealthy for this reason. The circumstances in Chechenya are in this case unreasonable.

On the basis of this reasoning I have in some texts used the terms "reasonable" or "accepted" circumstances, instead of the term "standard" that has been adopted here.[25]

Consequences with Regard to Maladies

There is a special conclusion to be drawn from this approach to health and illness, in contradistinction to the bio-statistical approach. Although I have above underlined the differences between the two approaches, one must also observe that their respective conclusions are not totally at odds. Many of the diseases picked out by Boorse's bio-statistical theory would also be picked out by a holistic theory. A cancer is a disease for Boorse, as well as for myself. But the reasons differ: for Boorse a cancer is a disease because it makes a statistically subnormal contribution to the subject's survival, whilst for myself a cancer is a disease because it tends to create disability (and normally indeed suffering) in its bearer.

For the moment I will disregard the differences between the various holistic theories. I think all holists would agree that illness has its conceptual root in the notion of a *problem* with one's body and mind, and that, conversely, health is a state where there are no such problems and where one's life has a certain high quality.

But what happens to the notions of disease, injury and defect in this theory? I have in my historical sketch already indicated this. Diseases, injuries and defects are causes or potential causes of the reduced health of the individual bearers. But there is a relevant question here. How can we reconcile the holistic idea of health with the science of diseases dealing with general types such as "common cold", "cancer" and "tuberculosis", when there is some difference between the vital goals of individuals? Can a type of condition sometimes be a disease and sometimes not? How can a common cold be a disease if it does not always reduce the health of its bearer?

My proposal as an answer to this question is that a condition is a disease-type if, and only if, it is a type of process within people, most (but not necessarily all) instances of which actually compromise the health of these people. This can be interpreted in two plausible ways, the first of which is the following. Most but not all instances of the common cold actually compromise the health of an individual, say John. John sometimes has a cold which is hardly recognizable. In such cases we would still say that John has a disease, but that his health is not affected.

---

[25] Nordenfelt, 2000 and 2001.

In the other interpretation, which is crucial for the science of diseases, we consider the whole population, and say that a condition is a disease-type if, when occurring in many people, it would reduce the health of most of these people. Thus whatever the vital goals of the members of the population, the condition would reduce the health of most of its bearers. The notion of disease would then incorporate a statistical element. This is very different, however, from the statistical element included in the bio-statistical concept of disease. In my case the statistical analysis concerns people's ability to reach vital goals; in Boorse's case it concerns the function of bodily organs in relation to the survival of the individual and the species.

From this follows that we can have a science of diseases, and still allow for individual variations in the health of people. Both John and Sara can have colds that in traditional medical terms have identical descriptions. Only John, however, has reduced health, since the cold happens to affect mechanisms relevant to the realization of a vital goal of his, but the same cold does not affect Sara's ability to realize her vital goals.

But can we rely on frequency in order to determine the list of diseases? Do people have vital goals similar enough to allow the science of diseases? I think we can be reassured by making the following reflection. A great many maladies, probably the majority, cause pain, fatigue and general unease. Such sensations and moods have a tendency to affect all kinds of activity. Thus the differences in people's vital goals will play a small role. Both if you are an athlete and if you are an author you will be severely affected by pain and fatigue. You will be prevented from performing in the way you had expected and hoped for. Thus the conditions lying behind the pain and fatigue would be classified as diseases.

A Problem in Identifying Diseases given a Holistic Theory of Health

Let me now consider a basic problem which must be faced by every theorist of health who has an action-theoretic approach. How shall we distinguish between such disabilities as are due to diseases and such as are due to other kinds of weakness in a person? The excellence concepts, for instance strength, intelligence and endurance, have their negative counterparts, say weakness, idiocy and lack of endurance, which, given standard intuitions, need not be identical with, or due to, ill health. Still, a person's weakness, low intelligence, and lack of endurance can cause or constitute an inability to realize vital goals. We face a dilemma: we must either try to find criteria by which we can sort out such lack of excellence as is not due to a disease or malady (obviously,

174

lack of excellence may sometimes be due to a malady), or we must face the fact that we operate with a stipulative definition of health which covers more ground than ordinary language indicates.

But do ways exist to differentiate grave lack of excellence from ill health, and must we make such differentiations? I will take up the second question first. We have ordinary intuitions that persons can be weak, even extremely weak, or can have a low degree of intelligence, without their being unhealthy. Thus an ordinary-language argument exists for distinguishing between the two categories. Perhaps as a corollary of this, an institutional differentiation exists as well. A distinction is made in many cultures between on the one hand health care, which treats the ill, on the other hand the care of the disabled. This is a basic cultural distinction with great social and economic implications, and it warrants a good conceptual backing supported by a viable philosophy of health. A theory of health which just relies on the notion of internal second-order disability does not give this support.

What, then, distinguishes ill health from grave lack of excellence in our intuitive understanding? The answer must be that ill health, at least typically, is due to the occurrence of disease or some other malady, like a congenital defect. So, when a disability is due to a malady we have ill health, according to this intuition.

The question now is: can theories like my own, sticking to a Reverse view of health and illness, handle this intuition? The first impression might be that I would end up in the following circle. According to me, ill health is primary. First, we must identify the ill health; derivatively we can identify diseases, as typical causes of ill health. But does not the solution to my present problem presuppose that diseases can be identified independently of ill health?

My answer is that no problem need arise in principle. Diseases can only ultimately be identified via the observation of ill health and illness. When we have observed that a person has a disability, in my qualified sense, we can start looking for the internal cause of this disability, either a somatic or a mental cause. If this kind of cause proves to hold for similar instances of ill health in other persons, we have found a disease which can be registered in the medical classifications. Once we have found the disease-type, this disease can, as I have said, live a life of its own. We can describe the disease in physiological or psychological terms, without reference in this description to its disposition to cause ill health. We can, for instance, make a physiological characterization of it. We can, for instance, identify this disease-type in other individuals who have not, at least not yet, acquired a full-blown illness. In principle, therefore, we can easily distinguish between cases of disability with and without a triggering disease.

But a deeper question lurks. Can we conceive of a disability which does not have a cause, be it physiological or psychological? If we cannot conceive of such a disability, must not its cause be some kind of malady, for instance a disease or a congenital defect? Would not, then, the putative distinctions between disability *simpliciter* and disability due to malady vanish?

My answer to this is twofold. First, an understandable and proper distinction exists between such disabilities for which we have clearly identified internal causes, and such disabilities for which no such causes are to be found. This distinction is sufficient to warrant the institutional distinction between health care and disability care. Second, that all things, including disabilities, must have a causal background, does not entail that they must have a background in terms of clearly identifiable typical causes. Diseases, in my sense, are typical and previously categorized causes of disabilities. Disabilities exist which have no such typical backgrounds.

The line of reasoning I have followed here is certainly of great importance for the praxis of sickness compensation that is the central issue in this treatise. But I have not yet answered the question whether we should reserve the term "ill health" only for cases where the cause is a kind of disease or malady. When I discuss the social insurance case more concretely in sections 6 and 7, I will argue that there are further instances of ill health than the ones caused by a disease or some other kind of malady and for which the bearer ought to be entitled to economic compensation.

Some Practical Conclusions from the Analysis of the Concept of Disease

What conclusions can the sickness insurance systems draw from the present philosophical discussion on the notions of health and disease? Is there an "objective" procedure? And in such a case, would the objective procedure satisfy the desiderata that one could have with regard to the system?

A Medical Approach to Disease Identification

The bio-statistical theory comes closest to providing an objective procedure. It says that a disease is or causes a statistically subnormal contribution to the individual's survival. (The alternative that it only affects the survival of the species is hardly relevant in this context.) This contribution could in principle be calculated by theoretical means. Thus such a process in a person's body as fulfils these criteria would emerge as a disease and would answer the questions from the sickness insurance authorities.

The defender of this reasoning could also point out that the disciplines of clinical physiology and clinical chemistry make constant measurements of human functions and define normal or reference values for each function.[26] Persons whose functions fall within the defined reference intervals could therefore be classified as healthy, whereas persons who have some function that falls outside a specified reference interval must be considered to have a disease. Hence the basic *desiderata* of an objective procedure are fulfilled.

However, there are problems with this proposal (irrespective of the basic philosophical arguments against the theory as such). It is indeed true that the reference measurements made by clinical physiologists and clinical chemists define statistically normal ranges for human functions. However, they do not determine what is a *subnormal contribution to the individual's survival.* It should be observed that the bio-statistical theory does not only talk about normality and abnormality. It also makes a causal statement. The disease process is such, according to the theory, that its *causal contribution* to survival is less than what is statistically normal for a certain population. This contribution is not at all as easily determined as the normality of the function itself.

I can illustrate the problem by a simple example. Consider the reference interval for the human pulse. It is normally taken to lie between 60 and 80 beats a minute (when the individual is at rest and is not affected by any external disturbance). Every pulse outside this range is considered abnormal. But certainly it is not true to say that every individual who falls outside this range is unhealthy or has a disease. We can consider the extremely well-trained athlete who may have a pulse around 40 or even 35. In this person's case the low (and abnormal) pulse does not indicate a subnormal contribution to his or her survival. On the contrary, the athlete's pulse, in combination with his or her strong-beating heart, makes a supernormal contribution to survival. Bodily work that is less intense, therefore, is not subnormal in the sense intended in the bio-statistical theory.

But can one not calculate the causal contribution in another way? It is still a theoretical question, one might maintain, and there ought to be, in principle, a clear answer to the question. However, there is hardly any easy practical way to do this by simply measuring separate functions. A factor to be noted is that one function in the body can be compensated

---

[26]   Gräsbeck *et al.*, 1981.

for by another function with a normal or indeed supernormal, more comprehensive, function as a result. The fact that the athlete's heart pumps so efficiently can be seen as compensating for the low frequency of the pumping. Thus, it seems as if any characterization of a person's functions must take the gross function of the whole person into account. But then we have left the process of simple mathematical calculation and instead entered into clinical interpretation. And this is not what we had hoped for by invoking the bio-statistical theory for the objective determination of diseases.

The clinical interpretation involves a holistic judgment. Here the doctor assesses whether the organism or the person as a whole is affected negatively by any changes in his or her functions. But this entails the judgment of well-being and disability which belongs to another theory of health and disease.

But is there no alternative procedure within the bio-statistical framework for making an "objective" judgment? Isn't the science of pathology objective enough? Cannot the pathologist discern whether an organ is infected or whether there is a cancer tumour growing in a part of the body? And cannot these discoveries be made without making a general clinical judgment of the whole person?

Yes, indeed. There are certain salient pathological processes to be discovered. In the case of infections and tumours and several other cases we know that there is a great probability that the gross functions of the person will be affected by the infections or the tumours, if they have not already been affected. In the case of some types of cancer (and very severe infections) we can also say with confidence that they threaten the life of their bearers. They therefore fulfil the Boorsian criteria well. But can we say this of pathological conditions in general? Do they all reduce the probability of survival of their bearers? Do they not just increase the probability of subjective ill health and disability of their bearers? And I have already above, in my general criticism of Boorse's theory, seriously doubted that all human disabilities, be it even to some minute extent, must reduce the probability of the survival of the individual (or of the species).

Thus, it is certainly true that many pathological conditions can be "objectively" verified. But the idea that they should be classified as pathological conditions in the first instance must be based on a theory of health and disease. As I have argued, it is not evident that this theory should be a bio-statistical theory in the Boorsian sense.

Let me instead try the method discussed above, i.e. to consult the standard medical classifications such as ICD 10 or DSM IV (Diagnostic and Statistical Manual of Mental Disorders). Here we find lists and definitions of diseases and other medical conditions which at a particular time are accepted as pathological entities. It seems to be a very rational procedure to use such lists, in particular the ICD which is supported by the WHO, for the determination of a condition's status as disease.

I will certainly not question the value of such a method as a rule of thumb. However, there are complications attaching also to such a procedure. First, the classifications develop over time. Certain conditions enter a classification and others leave. This is frequently due to new medical discoveries but it is sometimes due to altered attitudes to the condition. A celebrated example is homosexuality, which for a long time before 1973 was considered to be a disease but which is now officially removed from the international disease classifications. The latter change was in fact made on the basis of a theoretical discussion about the criteria of diseasehood made by Dr. R. L. Spitzer. As a result of this discussion the later versions of the DSM were to include a general definition of mental illness:

> Each of the mental disorders is conceptualized as a clinically significant behavioral or psychological syndrome or pattern that occurs in an individual and that is associated with present distress (e.g. a painful symptom) or disability (i.e. impairment in one or more important areas of functioning) or with a significantly increased risk of suffering death, pain, disability or an important loss of freedom.[27]

The American Association of Psychiatrists, who voted for this definition whereby most of the sexual deviances disappeared from the manual of mental disorders, hereby accepted a holistic definition of health and illness, with affinities to my own definition.

Another way of describing this change is to say that there is a new societal valuation of the condition of homosexuality and some other deviances. A theorist who argues in this direction is Lawrie Reznek.[28]

Second, as was salient already in my discussion of Boorse's theory, ICD 10 contains a number of conditions, in particular within the category of Symptoms, Signs and Abnormal Laboratory Conditions, which are dubious as candidates for being diseases. I mentioned as examples: Unhappiness, Low level of personal hygiene and Verbosity. The two latter conditions cannot reasonably function as causes of such disabilities as could be assessed in the sickness benefit context. They must

---

[27] DSM IV, 1994, p. xxi.

[28] Reznek, 1991. See Appendix 3. For an analysis of the conceptual development around homosexuality, see Bayer, 1981.

179

themselves be symptoms of some more underlying conditions. Still, they are proper entries in the classificatory system. A blind trust in the classification therefore cannot do if we wish to find an "objective" foundation for the identification of diseases.

A Holistic Approach to Disease Identification

But what is the alternative? Can an action-theoretic approach give any help for the practical purpose at issue here? Observe that the starting-point for this approach is the existence of a disability. In the holistic theories we define diseases (and other medical conditions, viz. the *maladies*) as such types of bodily or mental processes as tend to cause a disability in their bearers. According to such theories there is initially no independent way of identifying them. Hence, if a condition tends to reduce people's abilities then it can receive the status of a disease type (or type of other medical condition such as a defect).

It seems obvious that this causal relationship is easier to determine than the one suggested by Boorse. It is, as I have said, difficult to understand exactly what is meant by saying that a process makes a subnormal contribution to survival. And even if we operationalize the meaning of this statement it seems impossible to determine it in many cases. Shall we say that a mild infection makes a subnormal contribution to survival? Hardly any mild infection ever leads to death. And if it does it would probably automatically be reclassified. There are thus no statistics to rely on. The only thing we can do is to make some plausible statement saying roughly: every condition which makes a person slightly weaker also increases the probability of death at least to some least minimal extent. But this seems to be a very roundabout procedure. The effect on the individual's well-being and ability is much more direct and salient. I find therefore that a concept of disease related to suffering and a reduced ability is much more practically viable than a concept of disease related to a reduced probability of survival.

But do we not reason in a circle if we define diseases through the identification of disabilities in the first place? How can we then distinguish between such disabilities as do not have diseases as their causes and such as have? As I have already indicated, this is quite possible. When a type of condition has been found to be a typical cause of ill health (i.e. a typical cause of reduced ability) then we have a disease type that can in principle live a life of its own. We can identify a new instance of the condition type without first observing a case of disability caused by it. And at a later stage, when we have a new case of disability, we can discover whether the disability has an instance of this condition type as its cause. Try an example. We observe in several individuals who have severe pain in their chest, who have difficulty in breathing and moving about, that they are suffering from a tissue death in the heart due to a lack of oxygen and nutrition. This condition is identified, defined and given the name of "myocardial infarction". Hence, we have the disease of myocardial infarction. Later when a doctor observes a person with the mentioned symptoms he or she can detect that these are caused precisely by a myocardial infarction in the individual. This person's disability, leading to a loss of work ability, is then found to have as its cause an instance of myocardial infarction. Thus the reduced work ability fulfils the criterion set up by the sickness insurance authorities.

But are there then any disabilities that do not have diseases as their causes? Do not all disabilities have some cause, and is it not always a malady? I have already treated this argument in my presentation of the holistic theory in section 4 of the present chapter. Diseases, in my sense, are typical and previously categorized causes of disabilities. Disabilities exist which have no such typical backgrounds. A person may be disabled at a particular time by a special configuration of internal factors, none of which belongs to an accepted disease category but which interact in such a precarious way that the individual becomes disabled.

This possibility then of course calls for a serious discussion about the reasonableness of the disease (or malady) requirement in the National Insurance Act. Is it reasonable to say that only such disabilities as are dependent on established diseases or maladies can justify sickness compensation? What about other obvious states of ill health which have inner causes (and we are now excluding factors such as laziness and lack of motivation)? Is it reasonable to exclude a person just because he or she suffers from something that is not (yet) part of the disease (or malady) classification? I would myself, on logical grounds, argue for including also these kinds of disabilities among the ones which justify sickness compensation.

One might argue that there is an institutional requirement to distinguish between sickness benefits and disability benefits.[29] The disability involved in sickness is, according to this reasoning, something different from "simple", often congenital, disability. The two categories also require different kinds of expertise for their assessment. There may then be good reasons for such a distinction. This can be granted but it need not of course entail that there should be a difference in the entitlement to economic compensation.

---

[29] I have argued in this direction in Nordenfelt, 2001.

Possible Guidelines for Establishing Sickness or Disability Benefits

What, then, is the upshot of this lengthy discussion about the notion of disease for practical work? Is the philosopher of any help? Or has he only muddled the matter to the extent that there is no way out?

The basic message of my analysis is to show that we cannot in any easy way rely on a "scientific" concept of disease. This is not an original conclusion. It was in fact drawn by the Norwegian *Consensus Report* from 1995. My contribution may be that I have argued in much more detail than the authors of this report. Moreover, the procedure proposed by Boorse and others to ground a scientific concept is, even if it were in principle accepted, impracticable. We can with regard to many conditions not know for sure if they lower a person's probability of survival. We cannot either (as a universal rule) take the shortcut via accepted lists of diseases in the current disease classifications. These classifications contain contested items, some of which, such as obesity or unhappiness, cannot be directly applied to the social insurance context.

So what could be done? I propose that the theoretical background should be a holistic concept of health and disease. Diseases should be defined in terms of their propensity to cause suffering and disability. This is also more practicable. It is much easier to determine whether something causes suffering and disability than to determine whether it lowers the person's probability of survival. With disability and suffering as a starting point one could then in the manner sketched by me build up a list of diseases. Now, such a procedure, if it should be taken very seriously, is extremely cumbersome and we cannot really reconstruct the whole medical conceptual framework that has developed over 2,000 years. This is indeed also completely unnecessary. Most of the work has already been done and it has been meticulously described in the good medical textbooks of the world. In these textbooks we can see that almost all entries, for the conditions that have hitherto been acknowledged as maladies, include clauses about the pain, other kinds of suffering and the disabilities that are typical for the condition in question. Consider as an example the case of asthma described above.

> Asthma is an episodic disease, acute exacerbations being interspersed with symptom-free periods. Typically, most attacks are short-lived, lasting minutes to hours, and clinically the patient seems to recover completely after an attack. However, there can be a phase in which the patient experiences some degree of airways obstruction daily.[30]

---

[30] Harrison, 1997, p. 1419.

Thus, by and large, the existing classifications of diseases contain those elements that the holistic notions of health and disease would require. But only by and large, there are exceptions (to be found for instance in the pathological classification SNOMED) and there are contested conditions.[31] The most celebrated ones exist among the mental illnesses. I noted above that most of the sexual deviations that used to belong to the accepted mental illnesses have now disappeared from the group of such illnesses and are not included in the ICD or the DSM. Moreover, some new items appear over time. Kutchins and Kirk have described in detail how certain new conditions have recently entered the DSM manual.[32] Some of these have even already disappeared. The authors note that the diagnoses of Sadistic Personality, Self-Defeating Personality Disorder and Paraphilic Racism that had been included in DSM III R were "voted away" from the list of mental disorders at the Board of Trustees' meeting in 1986.

However, the probability that the insurance authorities will come across the contested conditions is quite small. And, if and when they do, a cautious attitude would be recommendable. Here the thing to do is really to investigate the status of the disability. The authority must continuously ask the question: Is the presented case of purported disability really a disability caused by certain inner conditions of the person's body and mind, such as maladies or other dysfunctions, or is it a case of laziness or unwillingness (for which of course a deeper explanation can be given) or is it directly caused by external conditions?

It is evident that when we make a proposal of this kind, including cases of ill health without the requirement of a specific disease diagnosis, very strict requirements must be laid upon the notion of work ability. Work ability must be considered in quite a narrow sense. Let me refer to my analysis in Chapters 10 and 11. Our concept of work ability must primarily deal with *executive ability*, one's ability to execute one's basic competence. As I have argued, it is primarily the executive ability that is affected by disease. An infection may cause pain and fatigue, which means that one's capacity to work in general has been reduced. It does not however in the standard case affect one's basic competence.

However, certain serious diseases, for instance some neurological diseases, may affect also basic competencies. Brain damage may affect one's linguistic and in general cognitive competencies and lead to severe disability in a work context. Such cases must clearly also be included among the instances of ill health in this context.

---

[31] SNOMED, 2007.
[32] Kutchins and Kirk, 1997.

The virtues and the will, however, should be excluded. Unwillingness and laziness, which were my examples above, do not belong to the relevant category of ability. The person who is unwilling to go to work or abstains from doing so because of laziness is not unable to work in the relevant sense. There may be some exceptions to this rule, however. These are the cases when a person's unwillingness has as its ground a serious illness, such as depression or another mental illness.

A Comparison with Hans Magnus Solli's Model of Functional Ability

My analysis could be compared to the one conducted by Solli where he wishes to introduce a new way of thinking in the social insurance context.[33] We must, he claims, get away from the old models, the scale model and the biomedical unicausal one. It is, first, in practice impossible to rely on a basic medical condition or even on a basic impairment in order to assess the work ability of a client. As we have seen, not all clients have a somatic disease or a somatic impairment. There are also mental illnesses and other illnesses without disease. But, second, and more importantly, it is on another level, the level of ability, that the crucial decision must be made. It is the person who is unable to work, given reasonable circumstances, who should be entitled to public compensation, according to Solli. Whether this is due to an instance of a well-defined disease category is a secondary matter.

Solli presents his argument in a number of steps, starting with a complex theory of health and illness and ending with a new model of disability. Solli's definition of health runs as follows:

> Health in a holistic sense is characterized by good functional and general ability in relation to the environment, realization of life goals as well as well-being, harmony, the establishment of meaning and a relatively long life.[34]

A disease, according to Solli, is a bodily or mental condition that disturbs the holistic structure constituted by health. Solli thus proposes a characterization of health, illness and disease of the same holistic kind as I have advocated above.

The model of functional ability proposed by Solli takes as one starting point the conceptual system of ICF.[35] Here there is a distinction between three fundamental categories: impairments, activity limitations

---

[33] Solli, 2007.
[34] *Ibid.*, p. 265. My translation from the Norwegian.
[35] See Chapter 1 in this volume.

and participation restrictions. Impairments are problems in body function. Activity limitations are difficulties an individual may have in executing activities. Participation restrictions are problems an individual may experience in involvement in life situations. This conceptual system helps the physician as well as any other assessor to evaluate a person's degree of disability. Here one can find a classification of all categories of impairment, activity limitations and participation restrictions.

Given Solli's holistic definition of health which is activity-oriented, it becomes very natural for Solli to settle for the activity level as the crucial level for establishing work disability. The person who has a substantial activity limitation is the person who is disabled in the sense that is relevant for social compensation. Thus he starts developing a model of functional ability based on the notion of *substantial activity limitation.*

To introduce this notion means, says Solli, that the physician and the social insurance officer must – in addition to the traditional medical investigation, which is certainly not ruled out – also make an individual judgment of the client in question. This judgment should be based not on physical examination but on a specification of the client's specific needs, goals and ideals. Behind this suggestion lies the insight that an activity limitation is not just dependent on physical impairment but also on the kind of life that the person lives. This in its turn is dependent on the person's wishes, evaluations and goals in life.

From this follows that there must be a much more individualized assessment of disability than has hitherto been the case.

PART IV

ON ASSESSING WORK ABILITY: CONCLUSIONS

CHAPTER 18

On the Assessment of Work Ability

A General Procedure for the Assessment of Work Ability

This book contains, as will have become obvious, a theoretical analysis of the concepts of work ability and adjacent concepts, such as work qualification and work environment. It has not been central in my analysis (apart from the scrutiny of the medical concepts of disease and illness) to investigate the causes of working disabilities or, even less, to suggest measures for rehabilitation to work. Such a type of study belongs to the sciences of medicine and rehabilitation as well as the science of social work.

However, several of the theoretical observations in this book lend themselves to some basic reflections on rehabilitative work in the broadest sense of the word. I here have some support from an interesting Danish analysis that provides a method for analysing work ability and for proposing remedies.[1]

The analyses in the present book as well as the one by Jens Bang point to the multiplicity of factors lying behind the fact that a person actually goes to work on a particular day. Let me briefly rehearse the main factors. The person must have a practical possibility of performing the tasks involved in the work in question. This in itself presupposes a considerable set of factors. Some of these are physical and some are mental. Some factors concern the environment. Among the physical factors are the person's health and basic strength. The mental factors include knowledge and skill, tolerance as well as traits of character such as courage, reliability and honesty. A crucial mental factor is also the person's own expectations with regard to the tasks in question. Does the person really believe that he or she has the practical possibility of performing the required tasks? Even more crucial: what are the person's inclinations? Does he or she want to do what is expected of him or her at the workplace in question? To this should be added the status of the environment, not only the workplace but also other environmental factors, including human beings who may be colleagues, customers, clients or patients.

---

[1] Bang, 2002.

189

Assume now that a woman, Liza, does not go to work on a particular day, and assume that she is expected to be present at her workplace on that day. She is working as the manager of a boutique belonging to a big chain represented in most towns of the country. Assume also that we (as employers or external assessors) are in a position to evaluate the situation. We wish to understand why Liza is absent and, if possible, suggest some method for rectifying the situation. This is the kind of situation envisaged by the Danish doctor Bang and he proposes a list of questions to be put to the assessor.[2] I am partly inspired by Bang's list of questions but I will discuss the issue mostly in line with my own analysis in the present work.

The first general question is obvious. What is the reason for Liza's absence from work? We wish to make a diagnosis, but this is indeed not a medical diagnosis – such a diagnosis may enter the picture later but only secondarily. We must first be open to all alternatives.

1. Is Liza prevented from going to work by any *external circumstances*? Is there anything wrong with Liza's car? Has the public transportation system in the town broken down? Is the weather so bad that she must abstain from going out? Is there an urgent family matter that Liza must attend to?

2. Has Liza had an *accident*? Has she fallen on the icy pavement and hurt herself badly or even broken her arm? Has she been involved in a car accident?

3. Is Liza stricken with a *disease*? Has Liza caught a cold or flu? Does she have pneumonia? Or does she have more worrying symptoms, such as a pain in her chest so that she must see a doctor?

These three types of reasons are the typical ones and cover probably the majority of cases. They are also in a sense the clearly *legitimate* reasons for Liza's absence. The two latter items represent the typical medical cases. Here Liza cannot go to work because her work ability is reduced by injury or disease. But there may be further alternatives.

4. Is Liza *ill*? This is not exactly the same question as 3. Liza may be ill, as I have said, i.e. not feel well, without having any obvious disease. Her absence may still be "legitimate" in the sense that most doctors would accept her illness, since it is obviously incapacitating. She may be in great pain or she may be suffering from extreme fatigue.

5. Is Liza *depressed*? This is a question that need not be distinct from 4. Liza may be in a state of depressive illness which is

---

[2] Bang, 2002.

clearly on a par with other illnesses with respect to the person's inability for work. Liza's depression may on the other hand be of an ordinary reactive kind. Liza may be in a state of grief at the death of a close relative, a broken marriage or a ruined career.

6. Is Liza *in anguish or very worried*? This is a case that has several sub-variants. Liza may be deeply worried about a number of things and her anguish or worry may be so deep that she cannot consider going to work. She may be worried about the fate of her son who has disappeared in the Middle East. She may be worried about her job situation. She may be in conflict with some colleagues or even her boss. Or she may seriously doubt that she is competent enough for her job and fear that she will fail in her present position.

Items 5 and 6 describe contested states from the point of view of medical insurance. Most insurance systems struggle with these conditions. Intuitively, they do not fit into the medical pattern. On the other hand such states may affect the person's basic capacity as much as a standard medical condition. I have earlier argued that they ought, in principle in the severe cases, to be covered by the insurance systems.

The most important matter here is however not the question of insurance but the question of measures to be taken to remedy the situation. The measures should in most cases not be medical. Grief is not a medical condition but a basic human emotion which should be met by compassion and understanding as well as by practical help. If a person is worried he or she should be helped to assess the object of worry in a realistic way. What can be done to find the son in the Middle East? What is the nature of the job conflict? Perhaps there is an easy way of resolving it. Is Liza really right in her judgment of her own competence? Is she not too self-critical? She may be helped in sorting this out. The help here is of a sort to be provided by a fellow human being, a family member or a friend, perhaps in some cases by a therapist.

Does Liza at all *want* to go to her job? We must face the crucial question of Liza's basic willingness. Liza may abstain from going to her job and lack a will to go there for other reasons than the above-mentioned. She may just be fed up. She may have completely lost interest in her job.

This is certainly an illegitimate reason. However, if this is Liza's situation she may still be in need of help. She may have chosen the wrong job; she may have other interests that she ought to cultivate in her professional life. In fact, her situation may be such that an analytical schema of another kind is more applicable. This is what I will provide below.

Imagine now a different case where the analysis has further complications. We consider the case of Peter who has been absent from the
work arena for two years. He lost his job as an administrator on a municipal water board because of reductions in the municipal budget. He
has had difficulty ever since in entering the job market. He has made a
few attempts, has had some occasional jobs but has also been ill quite
often – with unclear diagnoses – and has had rather few working days
during the two year period.

Assume that we are participants in a project where Peter's work ability is to be assessed in order for him to find an adequate job. Here we
have to make considerations of more diverse kinds than in the case of
Liza, where the question is basically limited to a particular situation and
where the job in question is fixated.

1. What are Peter's *competencies* with regard to work? Here we must
   take Peter's whole educational and work background into account.
   What has he studied? What work experience does he have, i.e. what
   skills has he achieved? What has he shown in terms of general and
   personal competencies? What ability has he to work hard and what is
   his tolerance of disturbances and other impediments at work? How
   reliable as a worker has he proven to be?

2. What are Peter's *formal qualifications* with regard to work? What
   exams has he passed? Does he qualify for the proposed jobs in terms
   of age, sex, citizenship, language and other formal requirements?

3. What is Peter's own *judgment* with regard to his competencies? I
   separate this question from question 1 although the two are, as I have
   earlier argued, partially causally related. Peter's own judgment certainly influences his competencies. In a situation of rehabilitation it
   may however be crucial to identify Peter's beliefs and expectations.
   Does Peter believe that he is competent enough for the jobs that are
   presented in the project? Does he believe – and if so, is it in fact true
   – that he needs some further education? Has he lost track of crucial
   developments in the areas where he has his basic competence?

4. What are Peter's *interests* with regard to work? What does he want
   to do? Are his basic interests really in line with his previous education and work experience? And if he really wants to do something
   else, how feasible is this alternative? Is it realistic to expect that Peter
   could get the further education necessary in a reasonable time?

5. How *prepared* is Peter to enter upon a new course of education? Is
   Peter prepared to go in for a demanding educational programme?
   And is he prepared to enter a completely new work situation?

6. What is Peter's *health status* at the moment? Has Peter completely recovered from his previous illnesses? Has he taken part in any rehabilitative programme?

7. What is the state of Peter's *social network*? What is the state of Peter's family conditions? Does he have any personal back-up from family members or friends?

8. How advantageous are the *external* conditions for Peter's entering a new and probably demanding work situation? What is his housing situation? Where is his home located in relation to the suggested work-place? What is the transport situation?

9. What are the conditions at the *suggested workplace*? Are they such that Peter will probably cope with them? What are the physical conditions in terms of, for instance, temperature, noise and space? What are the mental conditions, mainly in terms of decision hierarchies and stress? What support will Peter have at the suggested workplace?

The answers to all these questions will most probably imply a list of problems. Very few of these problems are medical. The other problems require solutions of a very different kind. Some of them are educational in a broad sense. They concern efforts to raise the level of Peter's theoretical and practical knowledge as well as his skills. They also concern matters of formal qualification. Other problems are practical. They may have to do with logistics and with improvements of Peter's home situation and work situation. Yet other problems may be psychological. What can be done to raise Peter's self-confidence and willingness to encounter new challenges? All problems are in principle, although not always in practice, solvable if the right expertise is called.

On the Idea of Measuring Work Ability

I started the investigation in this book by noting some crucial features in the Scandinavian legislation about sickness benefits. I noted that the Swedish National Insurance Act (from 1962 and onwards) in one of its central paragraphs states that economic compensation will be given to a sick-listed person if, and only if, his or her work ability is reduced by disease or injury by at least 25%. In a similar way the Norwegian National Insurance Act states that a person who cannot perform more than one half of his or her work duties because of some medical disability is entitled to economic compensation. These statements presuppose that we should be able to measure a person's work ability in degrees.

But is the statement that a person *A* has work ability to degree 30% an unequivocal statement? Can such a statement be taken seriously in a decision about a person's sick leave and thereby about his or her economic compensation?

Although I have said much about the features of the notion of work ability I have not explicitly returned to the idea of measuring such ability. Can we now give this locution any meaning? Is there a way of calculating work ability in degrees and percentages?

In answering this question I will return to the scale method that has at times been proposed in the Norwegian system of sickness insurance and which has proponents in the American system. As I said, an assessment according to the scale model should result in a quantification of the level of *impairment* of the individual. Impairment, as it is understood here, is a concept that is broader than both disease and injury and primarily refers to the losses of physical function that may be the effects of disease and injury. Say that a man has a fractured thigh bone and that it is broken at a particular point of the thigh. The table should then in principle inform the investigating physician what degree of *disability* this impairment of the person amounts to. The normal idea is to give a percentage, from 1 to 100. Say that the impairment in this case is assessed as amounting to a 50% disability. The idea then is that the quantified degree of impairment could be transposed to count as a corresponding degree of disability.

The paradigm for a scale evaluation is, as mentioned above in Chapter 17, the American Guides to the Evaluation of Permanent Impairment, whose latest edition is from 2001.[3] The Guides indicate for every listed impairment, for instance *diabetes mellitus* type 1, in the case where hyperglycaemia or hypoglycaemia occurs frequently despite conscientious efforts of both individual and physician, that the impairment of the whole person should be judged to be between 21 and 40%. A person with *causalgia* with a swelling and aching leg, and where the pain is constant despite treatment, is assessed to have a 40% impairment, to mention a different example.

The scale model has in Norway been spelt out in detail for one kind of maladies, viz. for industrial injuries. The National Insurance Act provides a table for disabilities where the injured organ and the degree of impairment may be specified.

A pure scale model has never been applied in the Swedish sickness insurance system. However, the private insurance companies apply a rigorous scale system for evaluating degrees of impairment. The Swedish Insurance Association [*Sveriges Försäkringsförbund*] has issued a handbook that assigns a degree of disability for each impairment that may confront the assessing doctor.[4] For instance, total dementia is

---

[3]   Cocchiarella *et al.*, 2001.

[4]   *Gradering*, 2004.

evaluated as 99% degree of impairment, total loss of sight as 68% degree of impairment, sterility as 30% degree of impairment for women and men below the age of 50, total loss of sensibility as 10%, and loss of a finger as 7%.

What help do we get from these tables? Can they be applied to the assessment of reduced work ability in the sense analysed in this book? No, quite obviously, a quantified measure of degree of impairment, related to separate diseases or injuries, cannot give an answer to the question that concerns the overall disability of the person in his or her life. Let me in the following list a number of reasons for rejecting not only the scale model of impairments but in general all kinds of uni-dimensional measures for the assessment of a person's work ability or reduced ability.

In general, a specific impairment can have an effect on one person which is so different from the effect of the same impairment on another person that the impairment itself cannot function as a reasonable crite-rion for decisions in the medical insurance system.

In addition, the effect of a type of impairment on one and the same person can vary from time to time and from situation to situation. These facts can have various explanations.

1. The impairment itself can *vary in degree*. With certain exceptions (like total dementia and total aphasia) the degree of the impairment itself is not determined. It is obvious that many kinds of impairment can vary in severity from extremely serious to very mild variants.

2. The scale does not contain any indication of *compensating bodily mechanisms*. A man who has lost one hand may have trained him-self so that he has become exceptionally skilled in using the other hand or even a foot for various tasks.

3. The man may have attained *competencies* (general, technical or personal) which may compensate for the loss of impairment. He may be applying for, or may have, a job, which is basically intellec-tual and for which he has been educated, and which does not require much use of his hand.

4. The man may have *other qualifications* which are such that he is crucially needed for a particular position. He may have an ethnic background that is required in an immigration agency. They may need a person with a particular cultural and linguistic background. For that they are prepared to accept any impairment.

5. The man may in general work in *a social milieu* which is helpful. The workplace may be carefully designed for a person with physical impairments. The atmosphere may be supportive so that the man is continuously helped by his mates to overcome the impairment.

My conclusions here are completely in line with the ones drawn by the WHO in their International Classification of Functioning, Disability and Health (ICF) and with the ones of Hans Magnus Solli. A person's impairment may but need not lead to an activity limitation. And an activity limitation may but need not lead to a participation restriction. Whether they do or do not have such consequences is dependent on external factors.

This means that the assessment of a person's work ability (which is in fact a species of ability to participate, viz. that of participating in work) in several pragmatic contexts – including not only the context of sickness insurance but also that of training for a vocation as well as job-seeking and employment – must be multidimensional and in the end holistic. By holistic I mean here that what ultimately counts is not whether the individual has one or two impairments of this or that kind, or whether the person has this or that education to a particular degree. The crucial matter is whether the person possesses the qualifications which are necessary or desirable for fulfilling the tasks involved in the vocation or profession as a whole in a proper way. The ability to perform a complex set of tasks can only to a very small extent be measured numerically. For certain menial jobs involving physical efforts of particular kinds this may be possible, for instance with regard to a builder who has to be able to lift objects of certain weights or to be able to affix objects of certain kinds to each other. But consider the job of a diplomat. How could one in any reasonable way numerically calculate the work ability of the diplomat? Shall we start counting the number of reports that he or she can write within a week, or the number of cocktail parties that he or she can attend within a similar period? An assessment of this person's work ability, as well as in practice the assessment of all professionals with regard to their work ability, can only be made qualitatively with due consideration of all qualifications, tasks, situations and work environments involved. It should also entail an investigation of possible alternative tasks within the job in question. The result of such an assessment will be a qualified statement. It will only marginally contain numbers and it will describe a person's situation given alternative scenarios.

CHAPTER 19

General Conclusions

I will now summarize my main conclusions in this book.

Taking my starting point in philosophical action theory I have shown how actions can be built up into complexes from more simple elements. One can construct hierarchies of actions starting with basic actions that only involve the agent's intentional bodily movements. Such basic actions can, with the help of causal and conventional mechanisms, generate more complex action-chains and action-sequences. In fact most of the actions that we perform daily are such complex actions. By scrutinizing such a hierarchy we can see in what different ways the subject can be disabled from performing actions. His or her bodily movements can be impeded – with regard to basic actions – or the generating mechanisms can fail – with regard to the complex action-chains or action-sequences. Some of these generating mechanisms depend on the subject's external situation. The external situation constitutes the opportunity for the person to perform the relevant action. In order for the person to perform the complex action of driving a car, for instance, there must be a functioning car available in the person's vicinity.

But an action can fail to materialize for many other reasons. One case is where the subject does not understand in what situation he or she is and therefore cannot take advantage of the opportunity. Another case is simply that the subject dislikes the activity in question.

A crucial element in the analysis of human ability is to get an understanding of and list all the various conditions for performing actions. That has been a main purpose in this study. In this context I have particularly noted that every assessment of ability must be made against a certain background, a set of circumstances. When these circumstances are not explicitly mentioned they must be presupposed implicitly. The presupposed circumstances are either considered to be *standard* in the culture in question or they are considered to be *reasonable* in the relevant context.

The section on work ability and its conditions has constituted the central analysis of this book. As a preparation for this I have introduced the notions of practical knowledge, skill and competence. I have presented a conceptual design where these three notions connote slightly different concepts. I suggest that competence is the overall concept covering practical knowledge and skill.

In my analysis I have proposed the term *standard basic competence* as denoting the platform for starting a job career that almost all people in a Western society have. This competence presupposes obligatory school training and the basic social training that is entailed in the ordinary upbringing in a family. It is from the standard basic competence that a person starts when he or she initiates a vocational or professional education. For certain menial jobs the standard basic competence is itself sufficient or almost sufficient for performing the tasks. Examples are jobs as cleaners, door-keepers or attendants. Here I am talking about performing the job in at least a minimally acceptable way. There is a crucial distinction between being able to do a job minimally and being able to do it well. This distinction is scrutinized in Chapter 13.

For most jobs, however, substantial education and training are indispensable conditions for attaining the competence required. Such occupational competence, I argue, has elements that are of saliently different kinds. In my analysis I have tried to distinguish between and characterize these more specific competencies. First, the occupational competence has two basic knowledge components: theoretical and practical knowledge. Theoretical knowledge implies knowledge not only in basic subjects such as mathematics, chemistry and biology but also in applied sciences such as ship technology, caring science or museum technology. *Know-how* (a combination of relevant theoretical and practical knowledge) is knowledge about *what to do*, what concrete actions to perform in certain crucial situations and how to perform these actions. I distinguish practical knowledge from *skill* (see the analysis in Chapter 7) in the following way. A person may have the practical knowledge to perform an action but still not the skill to do it. A pianist may have the practical knowledge to play a Beethoven sonata but at a particular moment not have the skill to do it, because he or she has not trained for the last couple of months. The pianist knows exactly "in the head" how the fingers should run and where to put an emphasis but will in practice not succeed in doing all this according to the formula. I will say that if a person has the theoretical knowledge, the practical knowledge and the skill required for a task then he or she has *competence* in the relevant respect.

According to a different ground for division I distinguish between the following competencies: *technical competence, general competence* and *personal competence*. Technical competence is probably the one mostly referred to in applied documents concerning work competence and skill. (See, in particular, the Norwegian, British and Dutch lists of capacities in Chapter 2 and Appendix 1.) Such competence includes the theoretical and practical knowledge and skill that are crucial for the most concrete or "technical" tasks of a certain occupation. It excludes, however, all social competence. Where communication and cooperation is necessary, technical competence is inadequate. Since no job only entails purely technical tasks, but also involves some communication and cooperation, this list is always an inadequate one.

By *general competence* I comprehend several abilities which are not specific to any particular vocation but which are nevertheless relevant for almost all vocations. This includes adaptability to new situations, ability to take responsibility as well as ability to communicate and cooperate.

Such items of general competence are certainly desirable for members of all occupations and professions. They are crucial for people who aspire to advanced positions in their professions. Caring professions and leadership positions require, however, a certain further set of abilities. These are the abilities I collect under the label *personal competence*. I argue that such professions and positions require that the person has empathy, entailing ability to establish deep contacts as well as ability to support and comfort other people. I also emphasize the importance of general ethical competence for these categories.

Competencies are not, however, enough for work to be performed. Among the further conditions for action the *will* plays a particularly crucial role. The worker must of course be willing to take the job in the first place, to fulfil the requirements of the job (including the codes of conduct) and retain such willingness over time. Much work also presupposes the existence of certain virtues and attitudes (presupposing the concept of will) on behalf of the subject. A person must be to some extent reliable and honest to fulfil his or her work tasks. Moreover he or she must have at least some minimal courage.

A want is a distinct condition for performing one's job, parallel to ability and opportunity. But can we completely uphold the distinction between want and ability, and is it preferable to uphold it in all instances? It may first be observed that a want or a series of wants is a *necessary condition for the acquisition* of most abilities. I have already noted that most abilities are acquired; some, the most basic ones, are the result of ordinary upbringing, others are the result of special training. But in most cases there are actions of an exercise type that the subject has to perform in order to acquire the ability. To perform these actions the subject must have – at least in a minimal sense – wanted to perform them. Hence all acquired abilities are the result of intentional, willed actions.

In relation to the notion of competence, with all its subspecies, I have added a notion of *qualification*. Among the conditions for doing a job we find not only what a person is able and willing to do but also a number of formal, for example legal, conditions of various kinds. Among these can be conditions pertaining to age, sex and place of residence. Such conditions I gather under the label of qualification. All such conditions must be taken into account, for instance when the person is recruited and acquires his or her position.

However competence, will and qualification do not add up to a *complete* set of conditions for action, given standard or otherwise reasonable circumstances. It is not always sufficient for a person to be completely competent, qualified and willing for an action to come about. The person must also be healthy; he or she must have the particular strength that is often lacking in the case of ill health.

The competent electrician who catches flu does not, in general, lose the competence to do the work of an electrician. The basic competence is there all the time. What has happened normally is that the person has lost the strength to execute the competence during a short period. He or she has an aching body and has become very tired. The e*xecutive ability* has temporarily disappeared.

I have also observed that ill health (in particular when it involves subjective suffering, such as pain, fatigue or anguish) may also strike against the person's *perception* of his or her work ability. In a study where two groups with comparable basic physical status were compared, the group who made a low assessment of their state abstained from work altogether whereas the group who made a favourable assessment of themselves normally worked at least part-time. The second group scored better than the first one in most relevant respects, including subjective quality of life.

The importance of *interaction*, in particular cooperation and support, has been highlighted in several analyses and illustrations throughout the book. Interaction is not only limited to occupations where one directly deals with human beings in their roles as customers, clients, patients or visitors. Interaction is crucial also in the relationship between the subject and his or her colleagues or other collaborators. Here conflicts may be even more frequent than in the case of subject and customer or client. There are cases of abuse of power by a manager in relation to a subordinate, or cases of unsound competition between colleagues on the same level in a hierarchy. To these we can add simple cases of genuine dislike between colleagues in an organization which can impede the involved people's achievement at work.

Thus, in order for a person to perform his or her job well many requirements must be fulfilled. The basic qualifications (in terms of authority and other qualifications) must be in order. He or she must have full technical, general, and personal competence. The capabilities for toleration and courage must be present. Moreover the motivational or volitional faculties must function perfectly. Certain virtues such as honesty, loyalty and courage must be present. The person must be willing to cooperate with and support his or her colleagues and must be empathic towards the clients. In short, the person must be enthusiastic about his or her work. These are the internal requirements. However, for the person to succeed the environment must be in order. The workplace must be excellent, not just tolerable, both physically and psychosocially. The person's colleagues must be cooperative and supportive in their turn and the bosses must be positive in their attitudes. Also other environmental conditions, both physical and psychosocial, have to be advantageous.

However, no situation is like this. We must in practice content ourselves with minimal requirements with regard to a person's competence, will and other qualifications. Thus when we attempt to formulate a formal definition of work ability (as in Chapter 15) the requirements have to be somewhat reduced:

A person *P* has complete (specific) work ability if, and only if, *P* has the work-specific manual and intellectual competence, strength, as well as toleration and courage, relevant virtues, other qualifications and has the physical, mental and social health that is required to fulfil the tasks (or alternatives within a set of tasks) and reach the goals (with some requirements of quality) which belong to the job in question, given that the physical, psychosocial and organizational work environment is acceptable to *P*, or can with adjustments easily be made acceptable to *P*.

(Since this definition is phrased in terms of ability and not in terms of a complete set of conditions, the will is not mentioned here.)

Part III and Part IV of this book have been devoted to the issue of work ability and its relation to medical conditions. I have discussed first some basic facts about the international and, in particular, the Norwegian and the Swedish legal arena. I have attempted to answer the question: What do the laws say about such work ability as can entitle to sickness or disability compensation from the state? Hereafter I turned to a substantial analysis of the notion of disease and attempted to answer the question whether there is a viable notion of disease that can answer the demands of objectivity often raised by the insurance offices.

In attempting to answer this question I arrived in a highly controversial arena, where different philosophical perspectives clash with each other. A main controversy concerns whether there is any place for values or subjectivity in the medical concepts of health, illness and disease. Some theorists indeed claim and argue that the medical concepts are value-free and descriptive in the same sense as the concepts of atom, metal and rain are value-free and descriptive. Others, however, claim that the concept of health, together with the other medical concepts, is essentially value-laden. To establish that a person is healthy does not just entail a certain amount of objective inspection and measurement. It presupposes also an evaluation of the general bodily and mental functioning of the person.

In this book I have compared two theories, the bio-statistical theory of medical concepts of Christopher Boorse that represents the objective standpoint and my own version of a holistic theory that represents the evaluative standpoint. Boorse takes as his starting-point the idea that a disease lowers the probability of the bearer's survival. Health in its turn is defined as the complete absence of diseases. I take, however, as my starting-point that health is identical with a person's basic ability to realize his or her vital goals. A disease, according to my reasoning, is a bodily or mental state of affairs that tends to reduce such ability. After a lengthy discussion of these theories I have concluded that Boorse's objective theory of health and disease is quite inadequate, since it cannot account for several obvious cases of human illness. Moreover, the procedure proposed by Boorse and others to ground a scientific concept is, even if it were in principle accepted, impracticable. We can with regard to many conditions not know for sure if they lower a person's probability of survival. We cannot either (as a universal rule) take the shortcut via accepted lists of diseases in the current disease classifications. These classifications contain contested items, some of which, such as obesity or unhappiness, cannot be directly applied to the social insurance context.

The basic purpose of my analysis has therefore been to show that we cannot in any easy way rely on a "scientific" concept of disease. This is not an original conclusion. It was in fact drawn by the Norwegian *Consensus Report* in 1995.

So what should be done? I propose that the theoretical background should be a holistic concept of health and disease. Diseases should be defined in terms of their propensity to cause suffering and disability. This is also more practicable. It is much easier to determine whether something causes suffering and disability than to determine whether it lowers the person's probability of survival. With disability and suffering as a starting point one could then in the manner sketched by me build up a list of diseases.

But then a further fundamental question crops up. Is it reasonable to say that only such disabilities as are dependent on established diseases or maladies can justify sickness compensation, as, for instance, the Swedish National Insurance Act requires? What about other obvious states of ill health which have inner causes (and we are now excluding factors such as laziness and lack of motivation)? Is it reasonable to exclude a person just because he or she suffers from something that is not (yet) part of the disease (or malady) classification? My own conclusion is that we must include also these kinds of sufferings and disabilities among the ones which justify sickness compensation.

In Chapters 17 and 18 I have outlined some guidelines for making the necessary distinctions in this area. I there discussed the distinctions between "legitimate" reasons for abstaining from work (such as external preventions, accidents, diseases) in relation to more contested conditions of illness (without disease), as well as cases of reactive depression and anguish.

Some Instruments for Assessing Work Ability Mainly in the Medico-Legal Context

In the following I will briefly present some further instruments proposed in the contemporary literature on occupational medicine and occupational therapy for the assessment of work ability in the medico-legal context. Two of them are designed for assessing work ability in the context of determining sickness benefits and one primarily for rehabilitative work.

1. Personal Capability Measurement (new version) Department for Work and Pensions, England, September 2006.

Recently the British Department for Work and Pensions' Health, Work and Wellbeing Directorate, was commissioned to develop proposals for transforming the previous instrument for assessing work ability, viz. the Personal Capability Assessment (PCA). The PCA lists fourteen physical and four mental areas of functional capability. It is a well-renowned instrument for assessment and has been used for more than ten years. The PCA has in fact greatly influenced the Dutch Functional Capacity List, described in Chapter 2. The shortcoming of this instrument was that it had been strictly based on the notion of incapacity, determining entitlement to Incapacity Benefit. Now there was a perceived need for a more positive type of assessment incorporating assessment of capability and of health-related interventions which would contribute to overcoming such health-related barriers as were preventing people from engaging in work. A special Technical Working Group was commissioned to undertake this reform. In particular the group proposed an extensively revised mental function assessment to address a lack in the assessment of cognitive and intellectual function, in conditions such as "learning disability, autistic spectrum disorder, and acquired brain injury".

Mental, cognitive and intellectual function assessment: learning tasks, understanding instructions, memory and concentration, forward planning, coping with change, execution of tasks, initiation of tasks, appropriate behaviour with other people (excluding for instance unpredictable outbursts), forming relationships with other people, ability to communicate appropriately with other people (excluding frequent misinterpretations), emotional resilience, maintaining appearance and hygiene, coping with social situations (excluding inability to visit new places and panic attacks), awareness of hazards.

Physical functional assessment: walking, standing in one place, bending and kneeling, reaching, picking up and moving, manual dexterity (for instance, turn knobs and undo buttons), speech, hearing, vision, continence, remaining conscious (excluding epilepsy and the like).

It can be noted that in spite of the expansion with regard to mental functions, the instrument remains quite conventional and focuses on technical abilities.

2. A Swedish Instrument: Assessment of Work Performance (AWP)

According to a conceptual framework presented by Sandqvist and Henriksson the following aspects must be considered when assessing a person's work functioning: the assessment dimension, the influence of personal and environmental factors, and the influence of temporal factors.[1] The three different dimensions of assessment are: work participation (society level), work performance (individual level) and individual capacity (body level). This is all in line with the conceptual framework of the International Classification of Functioning, Disability and Health (ICF). Personal factors are the physical and psychological aspects of the individual that affect the person's work functioning. Environmental factors contain two components that influence work functioning: 1) the physical, psychological and social circumstances under which the work activity is carried out, and 2) the socio-cultural consensus concerning how certain work activity should be carried out.[2]

Work functioning can be understood as the result of a dynamic interaction between an individual and the environment to enable the individual to function in the area of work. To sufficiently understand a person's functioning in the area of work, it is not enough to assess how efficient and appropriate a person's performance of work is from an assessor's perspective (an objective perspective). It is also necessary to discover why the person functions in a certain way. Therefore, it may be necessary to assess how the individual experiences the work situation and his or her work functioning (a subjective

---

[1]   Sandqvist and Henriksson, 2004.
[2]   Sandqvist *et al.*, 2006, p. 379.

perspective). The individual's total life-situation, including values and goals in relation to work, should also be analyzed.[3]

The development of the AWP started with the formulation of the purpose of the instrument and with the definition of its target group, i.e. people with work-related problems. After it had been decided to base the new instrument on the Model of Human Occupation a more profound analysis of the concepts and items that describe occupational performance skills was carried out.[4]

Here follow the items of the manual *Assessment of Work Performance*:

Motor skills:

- posture (stabilize, take position)
- mobility (walk. stretch, bend)
- coordination (coordinate, manipulate, be flexible)
- strength/handling of objects (grasp, shuttle, pull, lift, transport, adapt)
- physical energy (show endurance, keep up the pace).

Process skills:

- mental energy (show endurance, keep attention)
- knowledge (choose, use, ask for information, complete)
- temporal organisation of time (initiate, continue, accomplish in order, complete)
- organization of workplace (plan, put in order)
- adaptation (note, react, adapt behaviour, adapt environment).

Communication and interaction skills:

- physical communication and interaction (gesticulate, use eye contact, approach, take position, contact)
- language (adapt language, adapt speech, focus)
- social contacts (establish contact, keep contact, adapt behaviour, cooperate)
- information exchange (ask, inform).[5]

---

[3] Sandqvist *et al.*, 2006, p. 380.

[4] Kielhofner, 2002; Sandqvist *et al.*, 2006, p. 382.

[5] Sandqvist, 2007. My translation with regard to the most specific concepts.

The AWP is primarily to be used by the professional observer. It can however be supplemented by interviews with employers or colleagues. The explicit purpose of this manual is to classify observable skills. This means that hidden skills or background conditions such as tolerance, will or courage are not included. Some of these factors may be seen indirectly via endurance and adaptation. However, items such as responsibility ethics, care, critical stance and problem-solving, which can at least sometimes be apparent, are lacking.

3. DOA (Dialogue About Ability Related to Work): Irene Linddahl

This instrument has been developed within the Department of Occupational Therapy in the psychiatric clinic of Ryhov Regional Hospital in the town of Jönköping, Sweden, mainly for the purpose of rehabilitating people to enable a return to work.[6]

This instrument also uses the Model of Human Occupation as its theoretical basis. It emphasizes the motivation of behaviour, roles, modes of thinking and capacity in relation to work. It presupposes a humanistic, holistic and dynamic thinking. It focuses on inner capacities and excludes environmental factors. As a complement it recommends the Work Environment Impact Scale (WEIS-S, Version 2).

Work ability, according to DOA, can be defined as *the person's inner possibilities*, i.e. what the individual wants to do and the capacity that the individual has to perform work in relation to what the external environment allows. The use of DOA should involve the subject's own judgments about his or her inner possibilities.

The basic categories of the instrument are the following:

Voluntary motives for activity	Self-knowledge, interests and values
Roles and habits	{ Roles and habits Physical capacity
Capacity for performance	{ Capacity for organisation and problem solving Capacity for cooperation and communication

---

[6] For international presentations, see Norrby *et al.*, 2001, and Linddahl *et al.*, 2003.

The first section including *Self-knowledge, interests and values* is quite original to DOA since it involves categories outside pure work ability. It contains the following questions:

- Do you believe that you can do what you yourself want to do?
- Are you able to speak your mind when you do not want to do something?
- Do you think you have the ability to perform the tasks that you are assigned by your employer?
- Are you interested in learning new things?
- Do you usually take your own initiatives when you intend to perform a task?
- Can you accept the appreciation of other people when you have achieved something?
- Can you use the criticism of other people to improve your abilities?
- Can you work autonomously?
- Can you cooperate with other people?

This instrument is detailed and comprehensive. Its scope is broader than the category of ability and it covers various other kinds of inner possibilities for action.[7] The instrument includes items such as self-knowledge, motivation, responsibility and values. Other aspects included are hygiene, care and sensitive cooperation.

---

[7] See my analysis in Chapter 9 in this volume.

More about the Dictionary of Occupational Titles (DOT)

The Dictionary of Occupational Titles (DOT) is produced by the Division of Occupational Analysis of the US Employment Service in Washington. The DOT is a reference manual, intended mainly to assist Employment Service interviewers in placing workers in jobs. It also provides other users with a broad range of information on the content and characteristics of occupations.[1]

The DOT is a dictionary of occupational titles in common usage in US labour markets. The term "occupation" as used in the DOT refers to the ordinary description of individual jobs performed in many establishments. "Base" titles identify what the US Department of Labor's occupational analysts consider to be distinct occupations; they are intended to represent the job titles most frequently used by employers. Each base title is defined. "Master titles" refer to occupations found in a variety of work settings for which the work content may vary but the duties tend to be similar. Each master title is defined. "Term titles" refer to what is common to a number of jobs that may differ with respect to the knowledge required, the tasks performed, or the job location. Each term title is defined. For two other titles, definitions are not provided: "alternate titles", which are synonyms of base titles, and "undefined related titles", which are specialized offshoots of particular base titles. The fourth edition of DOT contains 28,801 titles of which 12,099 (42%) are base titles.

Titles are described in a nine-digit code. The first digit places occupations in one of nine broad categories: four are widely used groupings (professional, technical and managerial; clerical and sales; service; agricultural, fishery and forestry); four employ industrial trade terminology (processing; machine trades; benchwork; structural work); and one is a residual category, "miscellaneous".

The first three digits are intended to reflect with increasing specificity the kind of work performed. The fourth, fifth and sixth digits of the code are intended to reflect the levels of complexity at which a worker

---

[1]   Miller *et al.*, p. 18.

in a particular occupation functions in relation to *data, people and things*, respectively. The digits correspond to a structure of 24 worker functions, each of which is denoted by one or more verbs such as "compiling" or "handling". The structure of the worker functions is in the form of three listings that are arranged, in scale-like fashion, from relatively simple tasks (high numbers) to complex tasks (low numbers), such that "each successive relationship includes those that are simpler and excludes the more complex". Occupations are rated for level of functioning; an occupation's relationship to data, people and things is expressed in terms of the lowest-numbered (or most complex) function for each hierarchy.

The operations are of the following kinds:

Data: 0 synthesizing, 1 coordinating, 2 analysing, 3 compiling, 4 computing, 5 copying, 6 comparing.

People: 0 mentoring, 1 negotiating, 2 instructing, 3 supervising, 4 diverting, 5 persuading, 6 speaking/signalling, 7 serving, 8 taking instructions-helping.

Things: 0 setting up, 1 precision working, 2 operating-controlling, 3 driving-operating, 4 manipulating, 5 tending, 6 feeding, 7 handling.[2]

Data are intangible and include numbers, words, symbols, ideas, concepts, and oral verbalization. For example, by synthesizing data is meant integrating analyses of data to discover facts or develop knowledge, concepts or interpretations; coordinating is determining the time, place and sequence of operations or action to be taken on the basis of analysis of data; analysing is examining and evaluating data. Presenting alternative actions in relation to the evaluation is frequently involved.

People are not only human beings but also animals dealt with on an individual basis as if they were human. For example, by mentoring is meant dealing with individuals in terms of their total personality in order to advise, counsel or guide them with regard to problems that may be resolved by legal, scientific, clinical, spiritual and/or professional principles; negotiating is exchanging ideas, information, and opinions with others to formulate policies and programmes and/or arrive jointly at decisions, conclusions or solutions. Instructing is teaching subject matters to others, or training others (including animals) through explanation, demonstration and supervised practice; or making recommendations on the basis of technical disciplines. Supervising is determining or interpreting work procedures for a group of workers, assigning specific

---

[2]   Miller *et al.*, pp. 19-22.

duties to them and promoting efficiency. A variety of responsibilities are involved in this function. Diverting involves amusing others. This is the kind of work performed by authors and artists.[3]

Things are inanimate objects as distinguished from human beings, substances or materials, machines, tools, equipment and products. A thing is tangible and has shape, form, and other physical characteristics. For example, setting up is adjusting machines or equipment by replacing or altering tools, jigs, fixtures and attachments to prepare them to perform their functions, change their performance, or restore their proper functioning if they break down. Workers who set up one or a number of machines for other workers or who set up and personally operate a variety of machines are included here. Precision working is using body limbs and/or tools to work, move, guide or place objects or materials in situations where ultimate responsibility for the attainment of standards resides and selection of appropriate tools, objects or materials and the adjustment of the tool to the task requires the exercise of considerable judgment.[4]

The DOT titles are defined according to a highly structured format. Each definition begins with a statement that is intended to summarize the occupation in terms of (1) worker actions, (2) work fields, which are the purpose of worker actions (i.e. what gets done on the job), (3) machines, tools, equipment and/or work aids used by workers in performing their jobs, and (4) materials, products, subject matter and/or services that a worker produces on the job. The lead statement is followed by one or more task element statements, which describe the specific tasks a worker performs to accomplish the overall purpose of the job.[5]

In addition to the use of its definitions and titles to inform interviewers, counsellors and applicants about the nature of jobs, the DOT classification structure provides a mechanism for job-worker matching. Moreover, the DOT can be used for the determination of disability and eligibility for disability benefits. The determination of disability, and hence the eligibility for benefits according to the Social Security Act, depends on establishing that disabilities are debilitating in the sense that they prevent a person from being employed in the same or "similar" work as he or she has performed in the past.

In a later comprehensive document called the Revised Handbook for Analyzing Jobs the conceptual apparatus of DOT is presented, enabling

---

[3]   Miller *et al.*, p. 23.
[4]   *Ibid.*, p. 24.
[5]   *Ibid.*, p. 26.

various authorities and agencies to make detailed analyses of professions for their various purposes, including work assessment for determining disability benefits.[6] New job analysis data are continuously gathered according to the RHAJ methodology and are included in the Enhanced Dictionary of Occupational Titles (eDOT) which is distributed in a compact disc version.[7]

---

[6]   Revised Handbook for Analyzing Jobs, 1991.

[7]   PAQ Services, www.paq.com.

An Alternative Medical Paradigm:
Reznek's Theory of Disease

Introduction

Lawrie Reznek is a philosopher and psychiatrist who has written extensively on the philosophy of health and disease. His most important works are *The Nature of Disease* and *The Philosophical Defence of Psychiatry*.[1] In these works, he defends a medical view of the basic notion of disease. However, this view is quite distinct from the medical view advocated by Christopher Boorse, which I have analysed above. Reznek comes to the firm conclusion that the notion of disease is value-laden. It is not true, he says, that scientific methodology is sufficient for the identification of diseases. They are identified on the ground that they are processes with harmful consequences. And the notion of harm is an evaluative notion. On the other hand Reznek, as a practising psychiatrist, vigorously defends the idea that, once we have fixed the values and decided on what we consider to be harmful to people, a proper scientific project involves the characterization of diseases and the search for an adequate treatment of these diseases.

In one way, Reznek's theory is closer to Boorse's theory than to my own view. He has the viewpoint of the physician in that he focuses on the notion of disease and says virtually nothing about health. His starting-point is also what he defines as being the medical paradigm of disease.[2] Reznek wishes to remain as close as he can to traditional presuppositions in scientific medicine. He illustrates his argument with several examples from medical research. In spite of this focus, however, Reznek arrives at conclusions, as far as the characterization of disease and illness is concerned, which are far closer to my own conclusions than to those of Boorse.

---

[1]   Reznek, 1987 and 1991.
[2]   This is especially obvious in Reznek, 1991.

The Medical Paradigm

As I have indicated, Reznek's starting-point is a presentation of a medical paradigm of disease. Reznek's theses constituting his medical paradigm are central to his argument. I will here highlight four of them.[3]

T1: The Conceptual Thesis: A disease is a process causing a biological malfunctioning.

T2: The Demarcation Thesis: A mental illness is a process causing a malfunction predominantly of some higher mental function. All other diseases or illnesses are physical.

T3: The Universality Thesis: Diseases are not culture- or time-bound.

T4: The Identification Thesis: Scientific methodology enables us to identify diseases.

In the end, Reznek will not uphold the traditional medical paradigm and the malfunction criteria of diseasehood. He argues forcefully that the conceptual thesis and the identification thesis in the medical paradigm are untenable. What is crucial for Reznek in the determination of diseasehood is that the process has undesirable consequences. Some naturally selected processes have desirable consequences, while others have undesirable consequences. Thus, some naturally selected processes may emerge as diseases. This, for instance, is the case with the worm-infection Bilharzia, which is extremely common in Central Africa. But as a consequence, the medical paradigm is left without a resource to settle the issue of diseasehood in any "medically objective" way.

If diseasehood is not going to be connected with a notion of biological malfunction, then medicine will also face the problem of cultural relativism. Mental illness, in particular schizophrenia, is often identified through identifying delusions. These can hardly be identified independently of cultural norms, Reznek says:

> If a young man in our culture blames his abdominal pain on black magic inflicted by a former girlfriend, he is likely to be regarded as deluded. However, if the young man is living on a Caribbean island where the belief in black magic is commonplace, his belief would not be a delusion. Whether some belief or action is symptomatic of a mental illness depends not on norms that are universal, but on local and variable cultural norms. This leads to a disturbing relativity of our attributions of mental illness.[4]

---

[3]   Reznek, 1991.
[4]   *Ibid.*, p. 164.

Reznek's Definitions of Pathological Condition and Disease

In *The Nature of Disease* Reznek recognizes the highly generic concept of "pathological condition".[5] This is a concept which has "disease" as a subconcept. It also encompasses injuries, defects and handicaps. Reznek discusses possible distinctions among these subcategories but does not find any clear-cut boundaries between them. His conclusion is that they are concepts which have evolved for a long time and now have the character of family-concepts. Consider Reznek's definition of "pathological condition" including "disease/illness".

> A has a pathological condition C if and only if C is an abnormal bodily/mental condition which requires medical intervention and for which medical intervention is appropriate, and which harms standard members of A's species in standard circumstances.[6]

In this definition Reznek has taken care of the telling observation that not all diseases harm all their bearers. We can have instances of diseases which do not cause harm. What makes a condition a disease, or for that matter an injury or defect, is that standard bearers of it, under standard circumstances, will to some extent be harmed by it.

The notion of harm is a crucial criterion of diseasehood for Reznek. Diseases normally do harm – that is, they diminish our well-being by causing such things as suffering and disability. "This ensures that the concept of disease is value-laden – what counts as suffering and disability depends on our values".[7] Reznek says that blindness is a disability because being able to see is desirable, while the inability to curl one's tongue is not because such a trait is not desirable. The notion of harm itself is thoroughly analysed in *The Nature of Disease* but it is left completely unanalysed in his later work.[8] This will be discussed below.

The notion of abnormality which is referred to here is not statistical abnormality (cf. above). It is a notion of "constructed" abnormality.[9] Reznek also builds into his definition of disease a relation to appropriate medical interventions. A reason for introducing this clause is given in the following example:

> It might be further objected that being extremely cold is both unpleasant and mildly disabling (one's limbs are stiff), but it is not a pathological condition. I suspect that this condition is not regarded as pathological because its cor-

---

5   Reznek, 1987.

6   *Ibid.*, p. 167.

7   Reznek, 1991, p. 164.

8   Reznek, 1987, pp. 134-153; Reznek, 1991.

9   Reznek, 1991, p. 163.

rection does not require medical intervention. On the other hand, conditions like hypothermia are pathological because they do require such intervention.[10]

So something is a disease or a pathological condition in general only if it is best treated by medical means. The medical treatment should not only be efficient; it should also be appropriate. Drug addiction, for instance, is an abnormal condition that produces harm, and we might be able to do something about it by medical means. However, we might not wish to classify it as a mental illness because we feel that the problem ought to be handled by the law.[11]

An Examination of Reznek's Theory of Disease

In turning to an examination of Reznek's doctrines, I concentrate on his ideas of normality and harm. The clause on treatability will be briefly commented on within this discussion.

(1) *Reznek's idea of normality.* A disease, says Reznek, is an abnormal condition. But the abnormality here has nothing to do with statistics. An unusual bodily or mental process is not necessarily pathological. Nor is a process which subnormally contributes to the survival of the individual necessarily a disease.[12] So what kind of normality are we talking about?

To be abnormal in the constructed sense (the term chosen by Reznek) is to fall short of a norm that has been selected by people, presumably in a culture.[13] This norm has been selected because of its practical consequences. If the practical consequences of the norm are bad, then we will not select the norm. If they are good, then we might select the norm. Does Reznek say anything more?

In fact Reznek also appeals to political norms, as in his discussion about homosexuality.

Though he finds that heterosexuals are for various reasons better off than homosexuals, he says that we cannot conclude that homosexuality is a disease:

> But judging heterosexuals are better off does not mean that homosexuality is a disease. This is because in judging that a condition is a disease, we have to make a political judgment. We have to ask not only what sort of people it is

---

10 Reznek, 1987, p. 163.
11 Reznek, 1991, pp. 164-165.
12 Cf. Boorse, 1997.
13 Reznek, 1987, p. 97.

218

worthwhile being, but also what sort of society we ought to create. A society where we stigmatize homosexuals is cruel and divisive.[14]

What is going on here? It seems as if the norm of health is (and should be) the result of a political decision. Not all harmful bodily or mental processes should qualify as diseases. They must also pass a political test. For political reasons it would not be suitable to call every harmful bodily or mental process a disease. According to Reznek, it would be a great mistake to classify homosexuals as ill. And it would not be proper to say that a grieving person is ill, since we wish to be the sort of people who feel grief when good reasons occur for it.

If this is what Reznek intends, as the quotations indicate, it has considerable consequences for his theory of disease. It undermines all the sharp theoretical analysis that Reznek performs at other places. What is the point in making a close theoretical characterization of the notion of disease, if the whole thing in the end is to be determined by a political decision? Or does he mean that the political decision can only come in as an extreme exception? First, a condition must fulfil all other criteria for diseasehood (for instance, being an involuntary and harmful process), and then a question arises as to whether it passes the political test: would it be harmful to society to accept this condition as a disease?

Before further analysing this position, I will comment on Reznek's programme for analysis. One interpretation of his reasoning is that he wishes to be as empirical as possible. He attempts to describe a conceptual reality. In the end, political decisions are behind the official classifications of diseases and causes of death (cf. the ICD and the DSM). Authorities make decisions to include some conditions and exclude others from these classifications. An illustrative example of this is the 1973 conference of the American Psychiatric Association where a vote occurred concerning the status of homosexuality. As a result, homosexuality was excluded from the list of mental illnesses in the DSM.[15] These authorities simply decided what should be counted as a disease.

Reznek does not, however, recognize that medical authorities try to rely on some theoretical characterization of diseasehood in their classification. Such reliance was most evident in the case of homosexuality. Here the leading theoreticians, in particular R.M. Spitzer, presented a theoretical analysis of the notion of mental illness. The majority of the psychiatrists who were present at the time of the crucial voting procedure accepted this theoretical characterization, according to which

---

[14] Reznek, 1991, p. 169.
[15] See Bayer, 1981.

homosexuality could not be a disease, and they voted for the exclusion of homosexuality from the classification. They considered the previous inclusion of the condition to have been a mistake. In their self-understanding they would parallel this mistake with the following. Assume that a group of mathematics teachers at a conference found that a frequently used textbook contained an arithmetic error. For several reasons this error had not been recognized by their predecessors. As a result of their discovery, the teachers decided to remove it. In a superficial sense, they would be making a decision, namely to remove the error from the textbook. But in doing so, they would not construct a new norm for arithmetic, nor would they believe that they were doing so. Nor did the 1973 psychiatrists, presumably, believe that they had constructed a new norm for psychiatry. They had instead, as they believed, become much clearer about what are the criteria of diseasehood.

Admittedly, the story behind the abolition of homosexuality as a mental illness is complex. For some people, and not just the members of the gay community but also psychiatrists, the issue was predominantly political. However, Spitzer, the leading theoretician at the time, saw himself as making a "scientific" analysis of the concept of mental illness and an unbiased scrutiny of whether homosexuality falls under the heading of illness.

Consider now Reznek's idea that diseases or illnesses, by definition, warrant medical treatment. A person may for various reasons not want to be medically treated for a condition. That person, for instance, may not find this condition as harmful as those around him do. Or the person may be afraid of the treatment available. Assume now that a condition about which many people have this feeling exists. To insist that it is a condition which ought to be treated might then cause general unrest. Thus society may decide not to do so. Since the notion of disease/illness in Reznek's theory already contains a prescription about treatment, society might decide not to classify this condition as a disease/illness. So the argument may go.

This strikes me as an argument to the effect that the prescriptive content should be removed altogether from the definition of disease. I think in many instances we have good reasons for abstaining from treating diseases in a medical way. I am now talking about conditions which without question are diseases. Mild diseases exist; cases occur where the treatment of a disease might cause more harm than good; in other cases people for religious or other external reasons do not wish to have treatment; and then terminal diseases occur. In such instances people have good reasons for abstaining from treatment. At the same time, according to ordinary language, there can be no question but that the underlying conditions are diseases/illnesses.

By including the possibility of a political decision in the very definition of disease, Reznek has made the concept much less useful for many of its principal objectives. Medical or social authorities can no longer use diseasehood as an argument for a political decision. But that this should be a possibility is part of the common understanding of diseases. The authorities can no longer say the following: modern medical science has shown that alcoholism is a disease; thus alcoholics should have the right to medical treatment if they want it, and, as a consequence, we must establish clinics for alcoholics. This is impossible, because medical science can do nothing of the sort, according to Reznek. Ultimately, as he sees it, a condition C is a disease because we (the medical authorities) find it appropriate to so classify it.

This conclusion does not deprive the authorities of the possibility of using the other parts of the definition of disease in their argument. The medical scientists and practitioners can observe that a condition is an involuntary bodily or mental process which is harmful to its bearer, and this can be used as an argument for reforming a section of health care. We may then say that they can use a "reduced" conception of – or a theoretically purified conception of – disease for their purposes. The question is whether this theoretically purified conception is a better alternative as a reconstruction of the notion of disease than Reznek's proposal. By calling it a theoretically purified conception, I am not saying that it has been rid of all its evaluative content. I agree with Reznek that this is not possible. It need not, however, be evaluative or normative in all the dimensions that Reznek proposes.

My solution to the dilemma is different from Reznek's. I would look much closer into the notion of harmful consequences, in particular into the bearer of the harmful consequences. I would ask the question: Is the condition of, say, homosexuality harmful to most bearers, given the bearers' own long-term assessment of the condition? If the answer is yes, then this condition is a candidate for being a disease. The answer, however, as we know, is the opposite.

Concluding Remarks on Reznek's Theory of Disease

Reznek finds that the medical paradigm has many virtues. If this were true, then the epistemology of medicine would be clear and questions about diseasehood could be easily resolved by the science of medicine itself. During the course of his analysis, Reznek discovers, however, several flaws in the medical paradigm. Some of its cornerstones must be mistaken, he says. Diseases do not in general cause biological malfunctions. They cause harm. Harm is not something that scientific methodology can discover. Harm is an evaluative notion, and a person's judgment as to what counts as harm may be quite dependent on that person's ethical platform. Thus the medical paradigm, given Reznek's analysis, is far from true.

In spite of this, Reznek claims that the concept of disease is a necessary concept for the practice and science of medicine. And he defends the concept vigorously and effectively against several attacks which have come mainly from theorists of mental health and illness. These attacks have entailed saying either that no such thing as mental illness exists, or that many so-called mental illnesses do not fulfil reasonable criteria of illness. Most protagonists of these attacks have committed what Reznek calls the essentialist fallacy. They have for different reasons believed that a disease must have a special ontology, for instance, be caused by a microbe, be constituted by a bodily change, such as a tumour, or be a statistically abnormal process. No such essence is common to all diseases, says Reznek. The only thing that diseases have in common is that they are involuntary processes which cause harm.

Boorse and Reznek, who have both been taught within the Western medical tradition, arrive at quite divergent conclusions with regard to the notions of disease and illness. Boorse concludes that diseases are dysfunctional processes in relation to the bearer's survival or to the survival of the species to which the bearer belongs. Reznek concludes that diseases are involuntary processes which cause harm. They arrive at these diverging conclusions in spite of the fact that they use examples from the same medical tradition. And they both consult works from roughly the same analytical philosophical tradition.

Bibliography

Abiala, K., 2000, *Säljande samspel: En sociologisk studie av privat service-arbete*, Uppsala: Almqvist & Wiksell International.

Ainley, P., 1990, *Vocational Education and Training*, London: Cassell Educational Limited.

Ainley, P., 1994, *Degrees of Difference: Higher Education in the 1990s*, London: Lawrence & Wishart.

Ainley, P. and Corney, M., 1990, *Training for the Future: The Rise and Fall of the Manpower Services Commission*, London: Cassell Educational Limited.

Andersson, E.R. and Harriman, A., 1999, *Rätt lön på rätt sätt – metod för bedömning av kvalifikationer vid individuell lönesättning*, Stockholm: The National Institute for Working Life.

Applebaum, H.A., 1992, *The Concept of Work: Ancient, Medieval and Modern*, New York: State University of New York Press.

Aristotle, 1908, *The Works of Aristotle*, translated into English under the editorship of Sir David Ross, Volume VIII Metaphysica, Oxford: The Clarendon Press.

Audi, R., 1993, *Action, Intention and Reason*, Ithaca: Cornell University Press.

Bang, J., 2002, *Arbejdsevne metode: En teoretisk og praktisk indföring*, Copenhagen: Nyt juridisk forlag.

Bauhn, P., 2003, *The Value of Courage*, Lund: Nordic Academic Press.

Bayer, R., 1981, *Homosexuality and American Psychiatry: The Politics of Diagnosis*, New York: Basic Books Inc.

Benner, P., 1984, *From Novice to Expert: Excellence and Power in Clinical Nursing Practice*, London: Addison Wesley Publishing Company.

Berner, B., 1985, *Den komplicerade kvalifikationen. Tankar och resultat från fransk arbetslivsforskning*, Lund: Sociologiska institutionen.

Berner, B., 1989, *Kunskapens vägar: Teknik och lärande i skola och arbetsliv*, Lund: Arkiv förlag.

Bickenbach, J.E., Chatterji, S., Badley, E.M. and Üstün, T.B., 1999, "Models of disablement, universalism and the international classification of impairments, disabilities and handicaps", *Social Science and Medicine*, 48, pp. 1173-1187.

Blomqvist, M., 1990, *Hundra år av undantag. Handikappades förhållande till lönearbete*, Uppsala: Dept of Sociology, Uppsala University.

Blomqvist, M., 2001, "The Outer Boundaries of Wage Work", in A. Thörnquist (ed.) *Work Life, Work Environment and Work Safety Transition: Historical and Sociological Perspectives on the Development in Sweden during the 20th Century*, Stockholm: The National Institute for Working Life, 2001:9, pp. 193-213.

Boorse, C., 1977, "Health as a Theoretical Concept", *Philosophy of Science*, 44, pp. 542-573.

Boorse, C., 1997, "A Rebuttal on Health", in J.1: Humber and R. Almeder (eds.) *What is Disease?*, Totowa NJ, Humana Press, pp. 1-134.

Brage, S., Fleten, N., Knudsröd, O.G., Reiso, H. and Ryen, A., 2004, "Norsk Funksjonsskjema – et nytt instrument ved sykmelding og uførhetsvurdering", *Tidsskrift for Norsk Laegeforening*, 124, pp. 2472-2474.

Brenneman, Baron K. and Littleton, M. J., 1999, "The model of human occupation: a return to work case study", *Work*, 18, pp. 3-12.

Brülde, B., 2008, "Arbetsförmåga: Begrepp och etik", in L. Westerhäll (ed.) *Arbets(o)förmåga ur ett mångdisciplinärt perspektiv*, Stockholm: Santérus Academic Press, pp. 195-224.

Brülde, B. and Tengland P.-A., 2003, *Hälsa och Sjukdom: En begreppslig utredning* Lund: Studentlitteratur.

Canadian Labour Force Development Board, 1994, *Putting the Pieces Together: Toward a Coherent Transition System for Canada's Labour Force*, Ottawa: Canada Employment and Immigration Commission.

Canguilhem, G., 1978, *The Normal and the Pathological*, Dordrecht: D. Reidel Publishing Company.

Castel, R., 2003, *From Manual Workers to Wage Labourers: Transformation of the Social Question*, New Brunswick, US.: Transaction Publishers.

Cocchiarella, L. and Andersson, G.B.J. (eds.), 2001, *Guides to the Evaluation of Permanent Impairment*, 5th ed., Chicago: American Medical Association Press.

Consensus Report (Norway), 1995, *Sykdomsbegrepet i folketrygdloven: Konsensusrapport til Trygderetten*, Report 95:2, Oslo: Dept of Social Medicine, University of Oslo.

Copp, D., 1979, "Collective actions and secondary actions", *American Philosophical Quarterly*, 16, pp. 177-186.

Department for Work and Pensions, 2006, *A New Deal for Welfare: Empowering People to Work*, Presented to the parliament by the secretary of state for work and pensions by command of her majesty, January 2006.

De Boer, W.E.L., Brenninkmeijer, W. and Zuidam, W., 2004, *Long-term disability arrangement. A comparative study of assessments and quality control*, Hoofddrop, The Netherlands: TNO Work and Employment.

De Boer, W.E.L. and Houwaart, E.S., 2006, *Geschiktheid gewogen* [Ability Assessed], Amsterdam: The Dutch Association for Insurance Medicine (NVVG).

Dewey, J., 1998 [1938], *Experience and Education*, West Lafayette, Indiana: Kappa Delta Pi.

De Zwart, B.C.H., Frings-Dresen, M.H.W. and Duivenbooden, J.C. 2002, "Test-retest reliability of the Work Ability Index Questionnaire", *Occupational Medicine*, 52, pp. 177-181.

Diagnostic and Statistical Manual of Mental Disorders (DSM IV), 1994, Washington: The American Psychiatric Association.

Dictionary of Occupational Titles (DOT), 2006, http://www.wave.net/upg/immigration/dot_index.htm

Dreyfus, S.E. and Dreyfus, H.L., 1980, *A five-stage model of the mental activities involved in directed skill-acquisition*. Unpublished report supported by the Air Force Office of Scientific Research (AFSC), Berkeley: University of California.

Ellström, P-E., 1992, *Kompetens, utbildning och lärande i arbetslivet*, Stockholm: Publica.

Ellström, P-E., 1997, "The Many Meanings of Occupational Competence and Qualification", in A. Brown (ed.) *Promoting Vocational Education and Training: European Perspectives*, Hämeenlinna: Tampereen yliopiston opettajankoulutuslaitos, pp. 47-58.

Engelstad, F., 1984, *Hva mener vi med arbeid? Noen begrepsmessige refleksioner*, Oslo: Institutt for samfunnsforskning.

Engeström, Y., 1993, "Work as a Testbench for Activity Theory", in S. Chaiklin and J. Lave (eds.) *Understanding Practice: Perspectives on Activity and Context*, Cambridge: Cambridge University Press, pp. 64-103.

Estes, J., 1974, "Welfare Client Employability: A Model Assessment System", *Public Welfare*, Autumn, pp. 46-55.

FEU, 1982, *Basic Skills*, London: Further Education Curriculum Review and Development Unit.

Fleishman, E.A. and Quaintance, M.K., 1984, *Taxonomies of Human Performance: The Description of Human Tasks*, New York: Academic Press.

Fleishman, E.A. and Reilly, M.E., 1995, *Handbook of Human Abilities: Definitions, Measurements, and Job Task Requirements*, Bethesda MD: Management Research Institute, Inc.

Försäkringskassan [Swedish Social Insurance Agency], 2004, *Sjukpenning och samordnad rehabilitering*, Vägledning 2004:2, Stockholm: Försäkringskassan.

Freire, P., 2005, *Education for Critical Consciousness*, London: Continuum.

Fulford, K.W.M., 1989, *Moral Theory and Medical Practice*, Cambridge: Cambridge University Press.

Galen, 1997, *Selected Works*, translated with an Introduction and Notes by P.N. Singer, Oxford: Oxford University Press.

Gazier, B., 1999, "Executive summary", in B. Gazier (ed.) *Employability: Concepts and Policies, Report 1998*, Berlin: Employment Observatory Research Network, Institute for Applied Socio-Economics, pp. 11-28.

Gert, B., Culver, C.M. and Clouser, K.D., 2006, *Bioethics: A Systemic Approach*, Oxford: Oxford University Press.

Giddens, A., 1979, *Central Problems in Social Theory: Action, Structure and Contradiction in Social Analysis*, London: The MacMillan Press.

Goldman, A.I., 1969, *A Theory of Human Action*, Englewood Cliffs NJ: Prentice-Hall Inc.

Gradering, 2004, *Gradering av Medicinsk Invaliditet 2004*, edited by Sveriges Försäkringsförbund [The Swedish Insurance Association], Stockholm: Sveriges Försäkringsförbund.

Gräsbeck, R. and Alström, T., (eds.)1981, *Reference Values in Laboratory Medicine*, Chichester: John Wiley & Sons.

Guidelines, 1998, *From Guidelines to Action: The National Action Plans for Employment*, Brussels: Commission Communication, D/98/6, 13 May 1998.

Guile, D. and Griffiths, T., 2001, "Learning through work experience", *Journal of Education and Work*, 14, pp. 113-131.

Guile, D., 2002, "Skill and Work Experience in the European Knowledge Economy", *Journal of Education and Work*, 15, pp. 251-276.

Gustafsson, R.Å. and Lundberg, I., 2005, *Worklife and Health in Sweden*, Stockholm: The National Institute for Working Life.

Harrison's Principles of Internal Medicine 1998, A. S. Fauci *et al.* (eds.), 14th ed., New York: McGraw Hill.

Hogstedt, C., Bjurvald, M., Marklund, S., Palmer, E. and Theorell T. (eds.), 2004, *Den höga sjukfrånvaron – sanning och konsekvens*, Stockholm: Statens folkhälsoinstitut 2004:15.

Holt, M. 1987, "Introduction", in M. Holt (ed.) *Skills and Vocationalism: The Easy Answer*, Milton Keynes: Open University Press, pp. 1-11.

Hultgren, P., 2000, *Vem är arbetsför? Gränsdragningar inom den sociala arbetsmarknaden*, FOU-rapport 2000:1, Växjö: FOU Kronoberg.

Ilmarinen, J.E., 2001a, "Aging Workers", *Occupational and Environmental Health*, 58, pp. 546-552.

Ilmarinen, J.E., 2001b, "Functional capacities and work ability as predictors of good 3rd age", in S. Keizo, S. Sueko and K.Y. Mohamed (eds.) *Physical Fitness and Health Promotion in Active Ageing*, Leiden, The Netherlands: Backhuys Publishers, pp. 61-80.

International Classification of Impairments, Disabilities and Handicaps (ICIDH), 1980, Geneva: World Health Organization.

International Classification of Diseases and Related Health Conditions (ICD 10), 1992, Geneva: World Health Organization.

International Classification of Functioning, Disability and Health (ICF), (2001), Geneva: World Health Organization.

Järvholm, B. and Olofsson, C., 2002, "Sjukdom – ett försäkringsmedicinskt perspektiv", in B. Järvholm and C. Olofsson (eds.) *Försäkringsmedicin*, Lund: Studentlitteratur, pp. 28-33.

Järvholm, B. and Olofsson, C., 2005, *Sjukskrivningsboken*, Lund: Studentlitteratur.

Johansson, G. and Lundberg, I., 2004, "Adjustment latitude and attendance requirements as determinants of sickness absence of attendance. Empirical tests of the illness flexibility model", *Social Science and Medicine*, 58, pp. 1857-1868.

Johansson, G., Lundberg, O. and Lundberg, I., 2006, "Return to Work and Adjustment Latitude among Employees on Long-term Sickness Absence", *Journal of Occupational Rehabilitation*, 16, pp. 185-195.

Johansson, G., 2007, *The Illness Flexibility Model and Sickness Absence*, PhD dissertation, Stockholm: Karolinska Institute.

Karasek, R. and Theorell, T., 1990, *Healthy Work: Stress, Productivity, and the Reconstruction of Working Life*, New York: Basic Books.

Karlsson, J.C., 1986, *Begreppet arbete: definitioner, ideologier och sociala former*, Göteborg: Arkiv avhandlingsserie.

Kielhofner, G., 2002, *Models of Human Occupation*, 3rd ed., Baltimore, Md: Lippincott Williams and Wilkins.

Kjönstad, A. & Syse, A., 2005, *Velferdsrett I. Grunnleggende rettigheter. Rettssikkerhet. Tvang 3*, Oslo: Gyldendal Akademisk.

Kristensson, M., Eriksen, H.R., Sluiter, J.K., Starke, D. and Ursin, H., 2004, "Psychobiological mechanisms of socioeconomic differences in health", *Social Science and Medicine*, 58, pp. 1511-1522.

Kutchins, H. and Kirk, S. A., 1997, *Making Us Crazy: DSM: The Psychiatric Bible and the Creation of Mental Disorders*, New York: The Free Press.

Lave, J. and Wenger, E., 1991, *Situated Learning: Legitimate Peripheral Participation*, Cambridge: Cambridge University Press.

Linddahl, I., Norrby, E. and Bellner, A-B., 2003, "Construct Validity of the Instrument DOA – A Dialogue About Ability Related to Work", *Work*, 24, 215-224.

Lov om uføretrygd av 19 januar 1960 [Norwegian National Insurance Act], Oslo: Norges Lovtidend.

Ludvigsson, M., Svensson, T. and Alexandersson, K., 2006, *Begreppet arbetsförmåga vid sjukfrånvaro – en litteraturgenomgång*, Stockholm: Swedish Institute for Working Life, 2006:8.

Marx, K., 1890/1991, *Das Kapital: Kritik der Politischen Ökonomie*, Erster Band. Berlin: Dietz Verlag.

Masuch, M., 1974, *Uddannelsesektorens politiske økonomi – laerearbejdet og lönearbejdet i kapitalismen*, Copenhagen: Rhodos.

McQuaid, R.W. and Lindsay, C., 2005, "The Concept of Employability", *Urban Studies*, 42, pp. 197-219.

Miller, A., Treiman, D., Cain, P., & Roos, P., 1980, *Work, Jobs and Occupations: A Critical Review of the Dictionary of Occupational Titles*, Washington D.C.: National Academy Press.

Myrdal, A. and Myrdal, G., 1935, *Kris i befolkningsfrågan*, Stockholm: Bonniers.

National Insurance Act, Sweden, 1962 [*Lag om Allmän Försäkring* 1962:381], Stockholm: Ministry of Social Affairs.

National Insurance Act, Norway, 1997 [*Ny Folketrygdlov av 28 februar 1997*], Oslo: Norges Lovtidend.

Nordenfelt, L., 1995, *On the Nature of Health*, Second, revised, edition, Dordrecht: Kluwer.

Nordenfelt, L., 1997, *On Disabilities and Their Classification*, Linköping: Linköping University, Studies on Health and Society 1.

Nordenfelt, L., 2000, *Action, Ability and Health: Essays in the Philosophy of Action and Welfare*, Dordrecht: Kluwer.

Nordenfelt, L., 2001, *Health, Science, and Ordinary Language*, Amsterdam: Rodopi Publishers.

Nordenfelt, L., 2006, *Animal and Human Health and Welfare: A Comparative Philosophical Analysis*, Wallingford: CABI publishers.

Norrby, E. and Linddahl, I., (2001) "Reliability of the Instrument DOA – A Dialogue About Ability Related to Work", *Work*, 20, pp. 131-139.

Payne, J. 1999, *All things to all people: Changing perceptions of 'skill' among Britain's policy makers since the 1950s and their implications.* SKOPE Research Paper No. 1, Coventry: University of Warwick, Skope.

Philpott, J., 1998, "Improving employability and welfare to work policies: a UK perspective", in B. Gazier (ed.) *Employability: Concepts and Policies*, Berlin: European Employment Observatory, pp. 97-120

Pörn, I., 1993, "Health and Adaptedness", *Theoretical Medicine*, 14, pp. 295-303.

Revised Handbook for Analyzing Jobs, 1991, published by the US Department of Labor Employment and Training Administration, Indianapolis: Jist Works Inc.

Reznek, L., 1987, *The Nature of Disease*, London: Routledge & Kegan Paul.

Reznek, L., 1991, *The Philosophical Defence of Psychiatry*, London: Routledge & Kegan Paul.

Rogoff, B. and Lave, J.,1984, *Everyday Cognition: Its Development in Social Context*, Cambridge Mass.: Harvard University Press.

Rolf, B., 1998, *Militär kompetens: Traditioners förnyelse 1500-1940* [The Growth of Knowledge in Military Institutions 1500-1940] Nora, Sweden: Nya Doxa.

Rosenberg, K., 2004, *Värdet av arbete: Arbetsvärdering som ett lönepolitiskt instrument*, Göteborg: Bokförlaget BAS.

Ryle, G., 1971, "Knowing How and Knowing That", in G. Ryle (ed.) *Collected Papers 2*, London: Hutchinson & CO, pp. 212-225.

Sandqvist, J. L.and Henriksson, C. M., 2004. "Work functioning: A conceptual framework", *Work*, 23, pp. 147-157.

Sandqvist, J. L., Törnquist, K. B, and Henriksson, C. M., 2006, "Assessment of Work Performance (AWP) – development of an instrument", *Work*, 26, pp. 379-387.

Sandqvist, J. L., 2007, *Development and Evaluation of Validity and Utility of the Instrument Assessment of Work Performance (AWP)*, PhD Dissertation, Linköping, Sweden: Linköping University Medical Dissertations, No 1009.

Schult, M.-L., Söderback, I. and Jacobs, K., 2000, "Multidimensional aspects of work capability: A comparison between individuals who are working or not working because of chronic pain", *Work*, 19, pp. 41-53.

Searle, J. R., 1969, *Speech Acts*, Cambridge: Cambridge University Press.

Seedhouse, D., 2001, *Health: Foundations of Achievement*, Second edition, Chichester: John Wiley & Sons.

Smith, R., 1987, "Teaching on Stilts: A Critique of Classroom Skills", in M. Holt (ed.) *Skills and Vocationalism: The Easy Answer*, Milton Keynes: Open University Press, pp. 43-55.

SNOMED, 2007, *Clinical Terms, User Guide*, College of American Pathologists, www.cap.org/apps/docs/snomed/documents.

Socialstyrelsen, 2005, http://www.sos.se/sosfs/1992_16/1992_16.htm, 21/10 2005

Solli, H. M., 2007, *Rettferdighet og objektivitet i trygdemedisinske uførhetsvurderinger: En etisk og vitenskapsfilosofisk analyse av tre uførhetsmodeller i et historisk perspektiv*, Oslo: Institutt for allmenn- og samfunnsmedisin.

Strauss, A.L., Fagerhaugh, S., Suczek, B. and Wiener, C., 1985, *Social Organization of Medical Work*, Chicago: Chicago University Press.

Svensson, L.G., 2002, "Arbete och kompetens", in L. Hansen & P. Orban (eds.) *Arbetsliv*, Lund: Studentlitteratur.

Swedish Government Bill, 1962:381, *Lagen om allmän försäkring* [The National Insurance Act], Stockholm: Ministry of Social Affairs.

Swedish Government Bill, 1994/95:147, *Rätten till förtidspension och sjukpenning samt folkpension för gifta* [The Right to Early Pension and Sickness Benefit and Old Age Pension for Married People], Stockholm: Ministry of Social Affairs.

Swedish Government Bill, 1996/97:28, *Kriterier för rätt till ersättning i form av sjukpenning och förtidspension* [Criteria for the Entitlement to Compensation in Terms of Sickness Benefit and Early Pension] Stockholm: Ministry of Social Affairs.

Swedish Government Ministry Communication 2008:3, *Introduction of a rehabilitation chain*, Stockholm: Ministry of Social Affairs

Swedish Government Official Report of the Commission of Social Care, SOU 1944:15, *Socialvårdskommitténs betänkande VII*, Utredning och förslag angående lag om allmän försäkring, Stockholm: Ministry of Social Affairs.

Swedish Government Official Report, SOU 1988:37, *Den framtida arbetsskadeförsäkringen*, Stockholm: Ministry of Social Affairs.

Swedish Government Official Report, SOU 1988: 41, *Tidig och samordnad rehabilitering: Samverkansmetoder och rehabiliteringsinriktad ersättning mm.* Betänkande av rehabiliteringsutredningen, Stockholm: Ministry of Social Affairs.

Swedish Government Official Report, SOU 1995:149, *Försäkringsskydd vid sjukdom – Ett delbetänkande om rätten till ersättning och beräkning av inkomstunderlag under sjukpenningtid*, Stockholm: Ministry of Social Affairs.

Swedish Government Official Report, SOU 1996:133, *En allmän och aktiv försäkring vid sjukdom och rehabilitering. Del 1 Slutbetänkande.* Slutbetänkande av Sjuk- och arbetsskadekommittén, Stockholm: Ministry of Social Affairs.

Swedish Government Official Report, SOU 1997:166, *Ohälsoförsäkringen: Trygghet och aktivitet*, Betänkande av Förtidspensionsutredningen, Stockholm: Ministry of Social Affairs.

Temkin, O., 1963, "The Scientific Approach to Disease: Specific Entity or Individual Sickness", in A.C. Crombie (ed.) *Scientific Change: Historical Studies in the Intellectual, Social and Technical Conditions for Scientific Discovery and Technical Invention from Antiquity to the Present*, New York: Basic Books Inc., pp. 629-647.

Tengland, P.-A., 2006. *Begreppet arbetsförmåga*, IHS Report 2006:1, Linköping, Sweden: Linköping University.

Tilly, C. and Moss P. 1996. "'Soft' skills and race: An investigation of Black men's employment problems", *Work and Occupation*, 10, pp. 252-276.

Torgén, M., 2006, *Experiences of WAI (Work Ability Index) in a random sample of the Swedish working population*, Stockholm: National Institute for Working Life.

Tuomela, R., 1995, The *Importance of Us: A Philosophical Study of Basic Social Notions*, Stanford Ca: Stanford University Press.

Tuomi, K., Ilmarinen, J.E., Jahkola, A., Katajarinne L. and Tulkki, A., 1994, *Work Ability Index*, Helsinki: Helsinki Institute of Occupational Health.

Tuomi, K., Ilmarinen, J.E., Jahkola, A., Katajarinne, L. and Tulkki, A., 1998, *AFM-indexet*, Helsinki: Institutet för Arbetshygien.

Tuomisto, J., 1986, "The ideological and sociohistorical bases of industrial training", *Adult Education in Finland*, 4, pp. 14-26.

Twaddle, A. and Nordenfelt, L., 1993, *Disease, Illness and Sickness: Three Central Concepts in the Theory of Health*, Linköping, Sweden: Linköping University Studies on Health and Society, SHS 18.

Vreede, C.F.,1993, *A Guide to ADL: The Activities of Daily Living*, Delft: Eburon Publisher.

Wadel, C., 1979, "The hidden work of every-day life", in S. Wallman (ed.) *Social Anthropology of Work*, London: Academic Press, pp. 365-384.

Waerness, K., 1979, "Omsorgsarbeid i den private og offentlige sfaere", in I. N. Gornitzka (ed.), *Lönnet og ulönnet omsorg*, Oslo: NAVF.

Westerhäll, L., 1983, *Sjukdom och arbetsoförmåga: Om rätten till sjukpenning*, Stockholm: Norstedts.

Westerhäll, L., 1997, "Rättsliga aspekter på arbetsoförmåga på grund av sjukdom", *Socialmedicinsk tidskrift*, 8-9, pp. 356-365.

Westerhäll, L., 2006, "Sjukdom och arbetsoförmåga i ett försäkringsrättsligt perspektiv", in L. Westerhäll, A. Bergroth and J. Ekholm (eds.) 2006, *Rehabiliteringsvetenskap: Rehabilitering till arbetslivet i ett flerdisciplinärt perspektiv*, Lund: Studentlitteratur.

Westerholm, P. and Bostedt G., 2004, "Kan företagshälsovården lösa sjukskrivningskrisen?" in C. Hogstedt, M. Bjurvald, S. Marklund, E. Palmer and T. Theorell (eds.) *Den höga sjukfrånvaron: Sanning och konsekvens*, Stockholm: Statens folkhälsoinstitut, pp. 303-344.

Westerholm, P. and Lindenger G., 2008, "Arbetsförmåga: Det humana kapitalets värde", in L. Westerhäll (ed.) *Arbets(o)förmåga ur ett mångdisciplinärt perspektiv*, Stockholm: Santérus Academic Press, pp. 304-339.

Index

Printed by
CPI books GmbH, Leck

Zeitfracht Medien GmbH
Ferdinand-Jühlke-Straße 7
99095 Erfurt, Deutschland
produktsicherheit@kolibri360.de